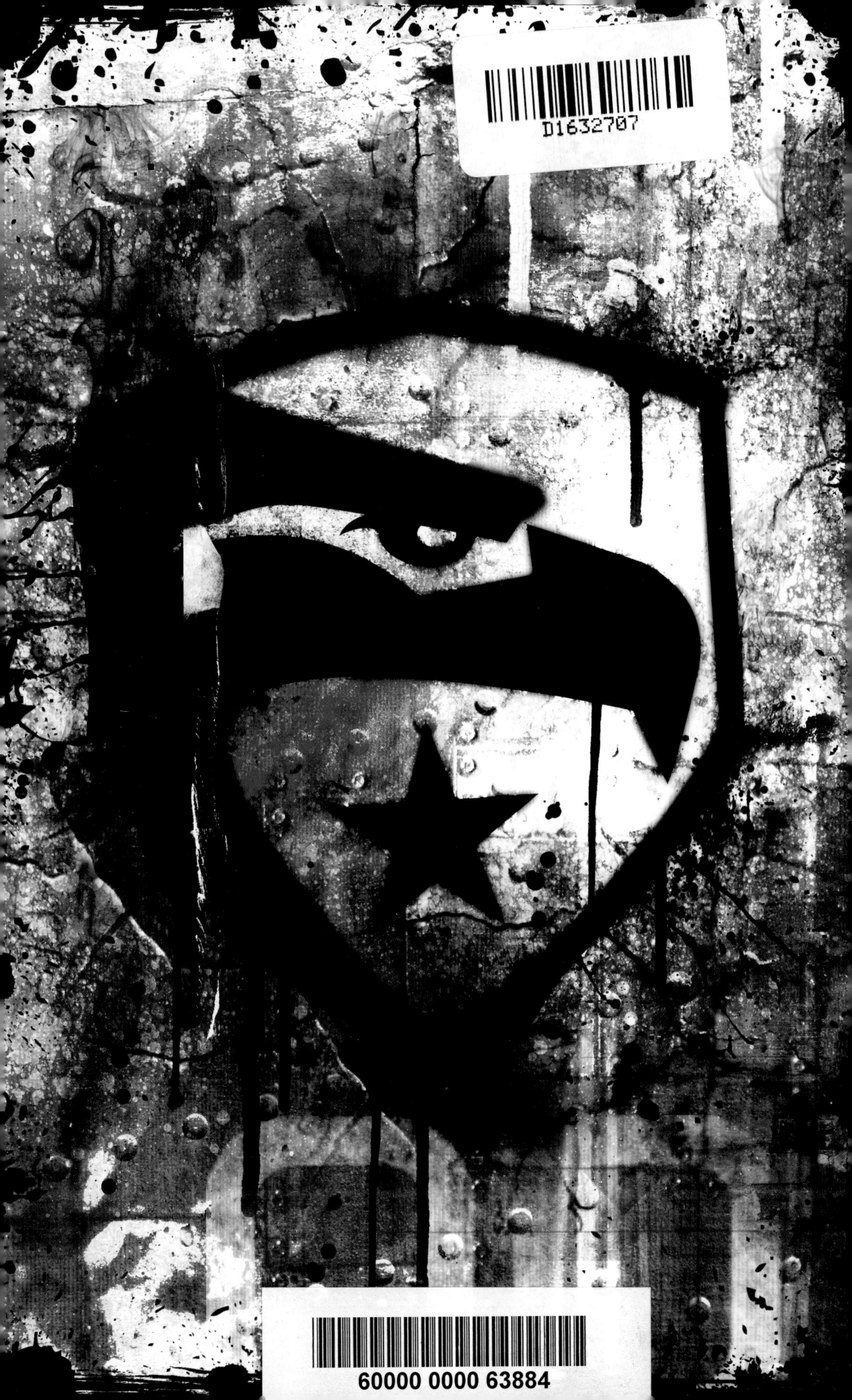

OFFICIAL MOVIE PREQUEL

G.I. JOE
RETALIATION

WRITER: JOHN BARBER

ARTISTS: SALVADOR NAVARRO
AND ATILIO ROJO

COLORIST: ESTHER SANZ

LETTERERS: CHRIS MOWRY, SHAWN LEE,
AND ROBBIE ROBBINS

SERIES EDITOR: CARLOS GUZMAN

COVER ARTIST: SALVADOR NAVARRO!

COVER COLORIST: ESTHER SANZ

COLLECTION EDITORS: JUSTIN EISINGER AND ALONZO SIMON

COLLECTION DESIGN: CHRIS MOWRY

Peterborough City Council	
60000 0000 63884	
Askews & Holts	May-2012
GRA	£13.50

Special thanks to Hasbro's Aaron Archer, Andy Schmidt, Derryl DePriest, Joe Del Regno, Ed Lane, Joe Furfaro, Jos Huxley and Michael Kelly for their invaluable assistance.

IDW founded by Ted Adams, Alex Garner, Kris Oprisko, and Robbie Robbins | International Rights Representative, Christine Meyer: christine@gfloystudio.com

ISBN: 978-1-61377-203-4   15 14 13 12   1 2 3 4

IDW®

Licensed By:
Hasbro

Ted Adams, CEO & Publisher
Greg Goldstein, President & COO
Robbie Robbins, EVP/Sr. Graphic Artist
Chris Ryall, Chief Creative Officer/Editor-in-Chief
Matthew Ruzicka, CPA, Chief Financial Officer
Alan Payne, VP of Sales

Become our fan on Facebook **facebook.com/idwpublishing**
Follow us on Twitter **@idwpublishing**
Check us out on YouTube **youtube.com/idwpublishing**
www.IDWPUBLISHING.com

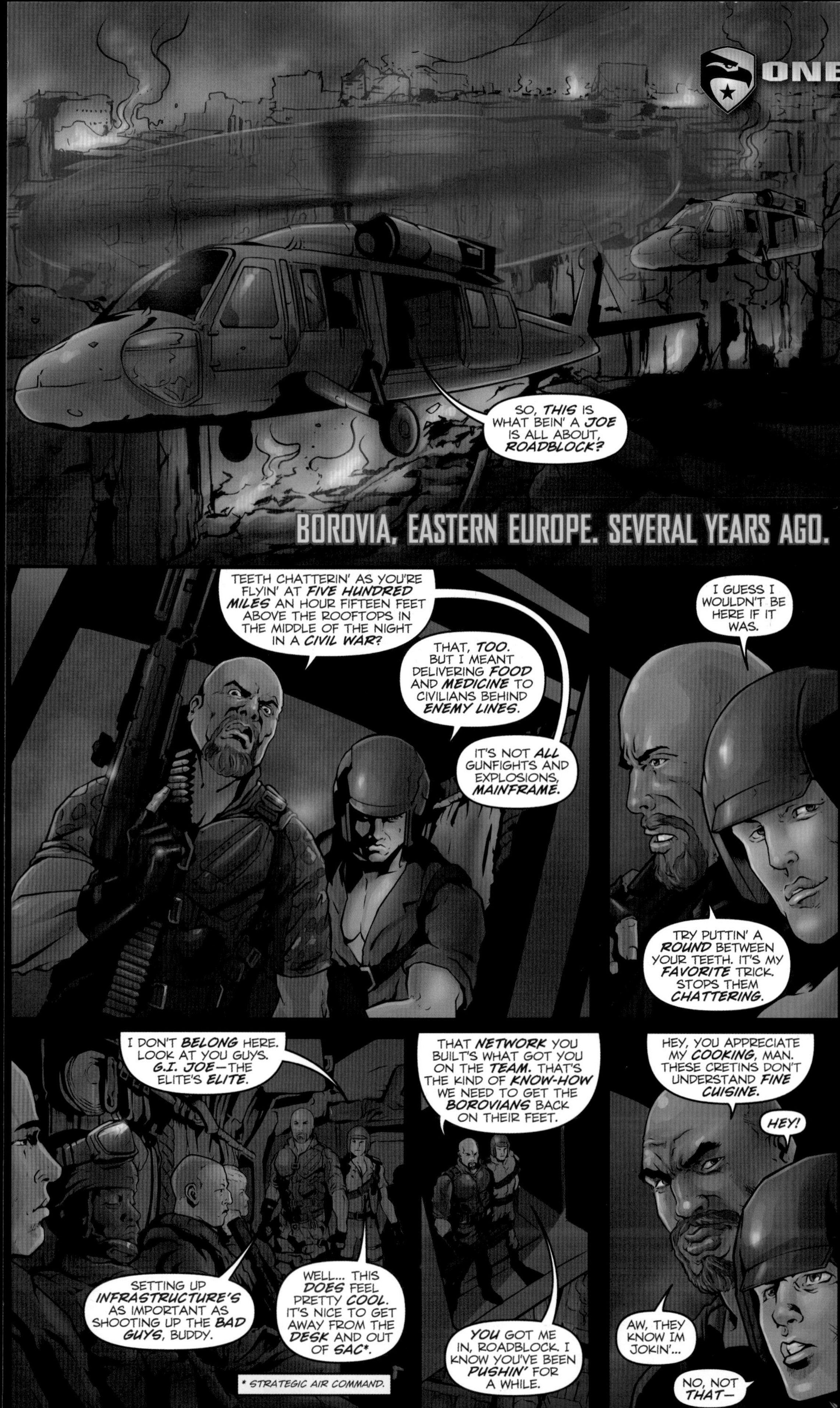
ONE
SO, THIS IS WHAT BEIN' A JOE IS ALL ABOUT, ROADBLOCK?
BOROVIA, EASTERN EUROPE. SEVERAL YEARS AGO.
TEETH CHATTERIN' AS YOU'RE FLYIN' AT FIVE HUNDRED MILES AN HOUR FIFTEEN FEET ABOVE THE ROOFTOPS IN THE MIDDLE OF THE NIGHT IN A CIVIL WAR?
THAT, TOO. BUT I MEANT DELIVERING FOOD AND MEDICINE TO CIVILIANS BEHIND ENEMY LINES.
IT'S NOT ALL GUNFIGHTS AND EXPLOSIONS, MAINFRAME.
I GUESS I WOULDN'T BE HERE IF IT WAS.
TRY PUTTIN' A ROUND BETWEEN YOUR TEETH. IT'S MY FAVORITE TRICK. STOPS THEM CHATTERING.
I DON'T BELONG HERE. LOOK AT YOU GUYS. G.I. JOE—THE ELITE'S ELITE.
SETTING UP INFRASTRUCTURE'S AS IMPORTANT AS SHOOTING UP THE BAD GUYS, BUDDY.
WELL... THIS DOES FEEL PRETTY COOL. IT'S NICE TO GET AWAY FROM THE DESK AND OUT OF SAC*.
* STRATEGIC AIR COMMAND.
THAT NETWORK YOU BUILT'S WHAT GOT YOU ON THE TEAM. THAT'S THE KIND OF KNOW-HOW WE NEED TO GET THE BOROVIANS BACK ON THEIR FEET.
YOU GOT ME IN, ROADBLOCK. I KNOW YOU'VE BEEN PUSHIN' FOR A WHILE.
HEY, YOU APPRECIATE MY COOKING, MAN. THESE CRETINS DON'T UNDERSTAND FINE CUISINE.
HEY!
AW, THEY KNOW IM JOKIN'...
NO, NOT THAT—

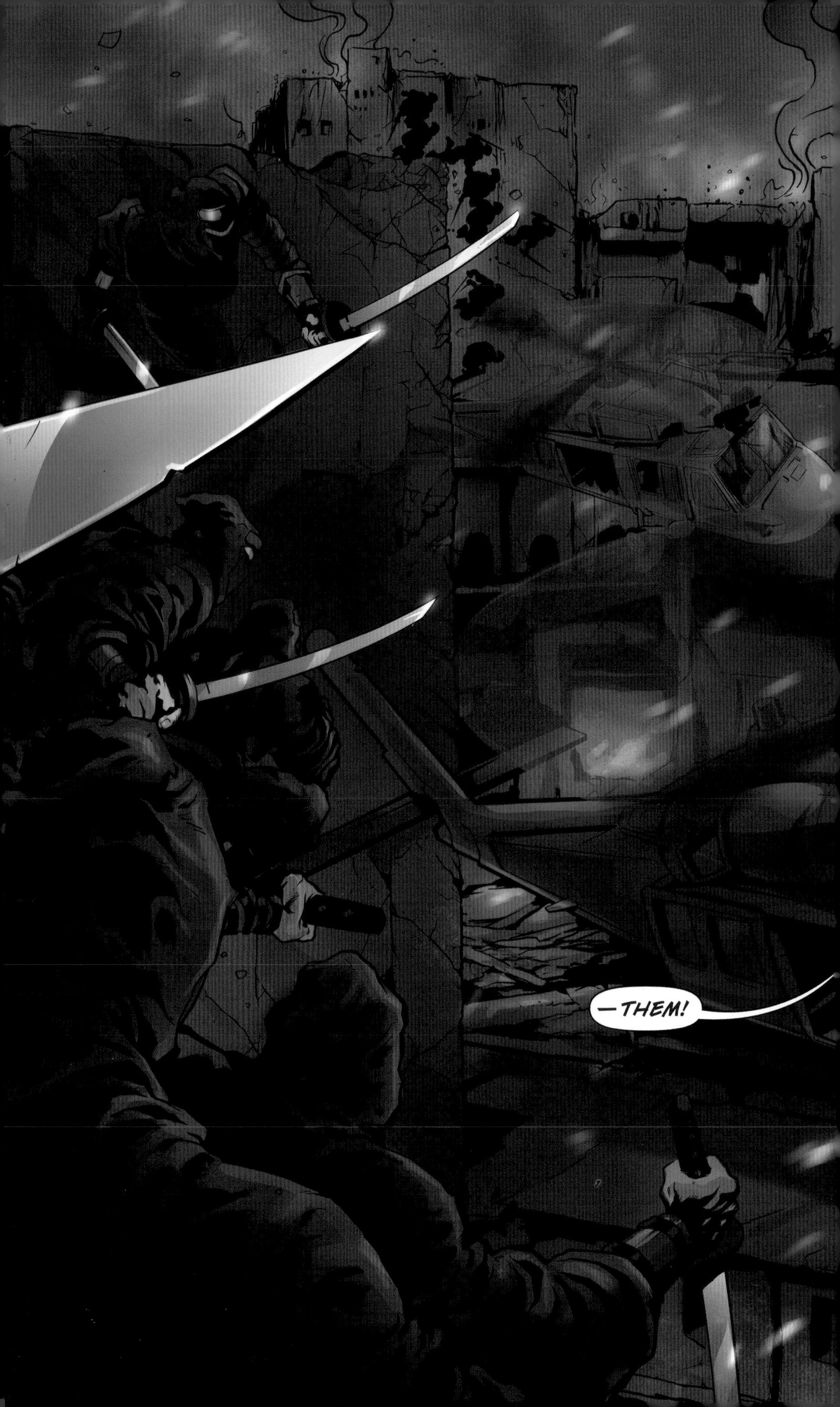
—THEM!

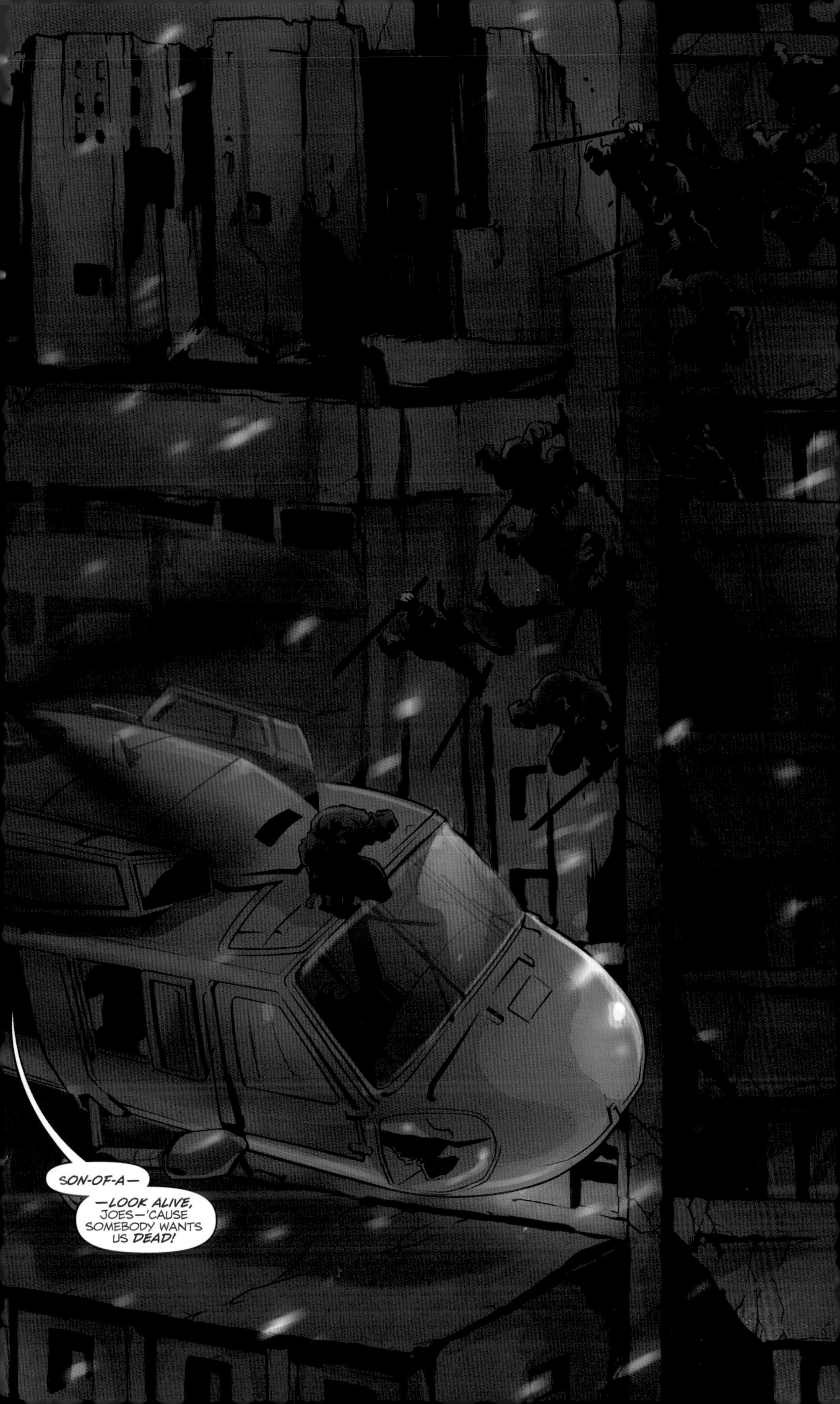
SON-OF-A—
—LOOK ALIVE, JOES—'CAUSE SOMEBODY WANTS US DEAD!

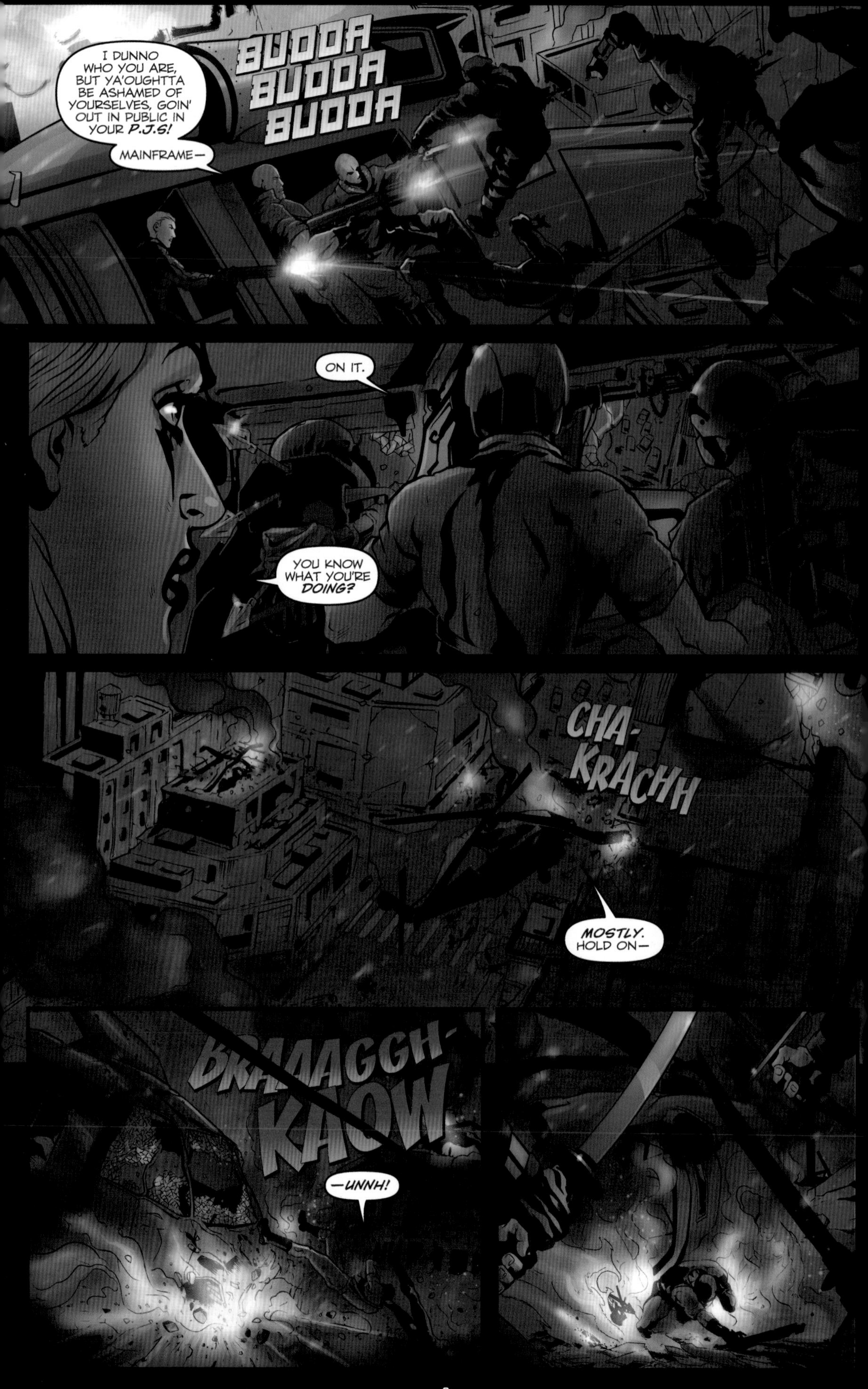
I DUNNO WHO YOU ARE, BUT YA'OUGHTTA BE ASHAMED OF YOURSELVES, GOIN' OUT IN PUBLIC IN YOUR P.J.S!
BUDDA BUDDA BUDDA
MAINFRAME—
ON IT.
YOU KNOW WHAT YOU'RE DOING?
CHA-KRACHH
MOSTLY. HOLD ON—
BRAAAGGH-KAOW
—UNNH!

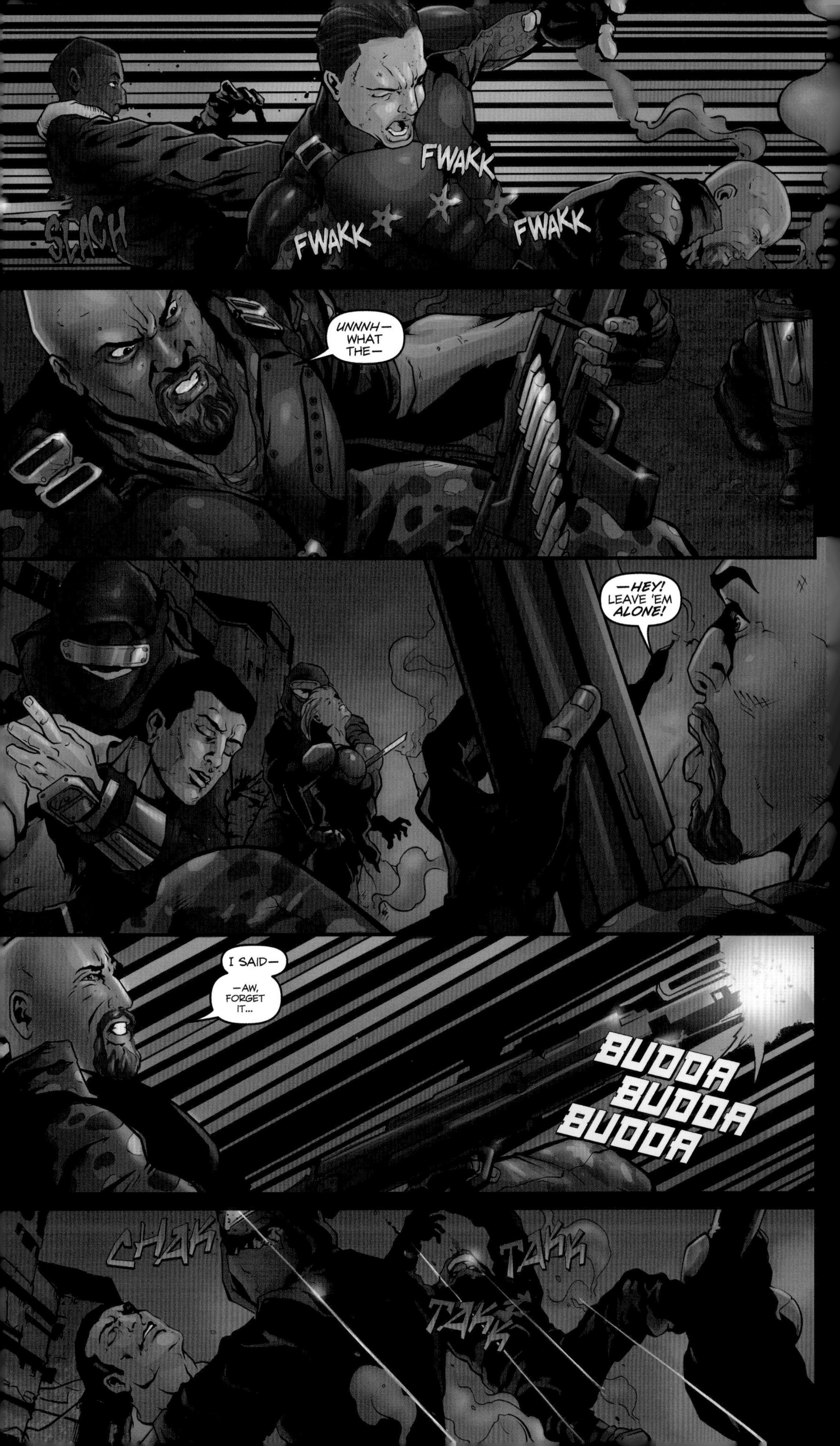
FWAKK
SLACH
FWAKK
FWAKK
UNNNH— WHAT THE—
—HEY! LEAVE 'EM ALONE!
I SAID—
—AW, FORGET IT...
BUDDA BUDDA BUDDA
CHAK
TAKK
TAKK

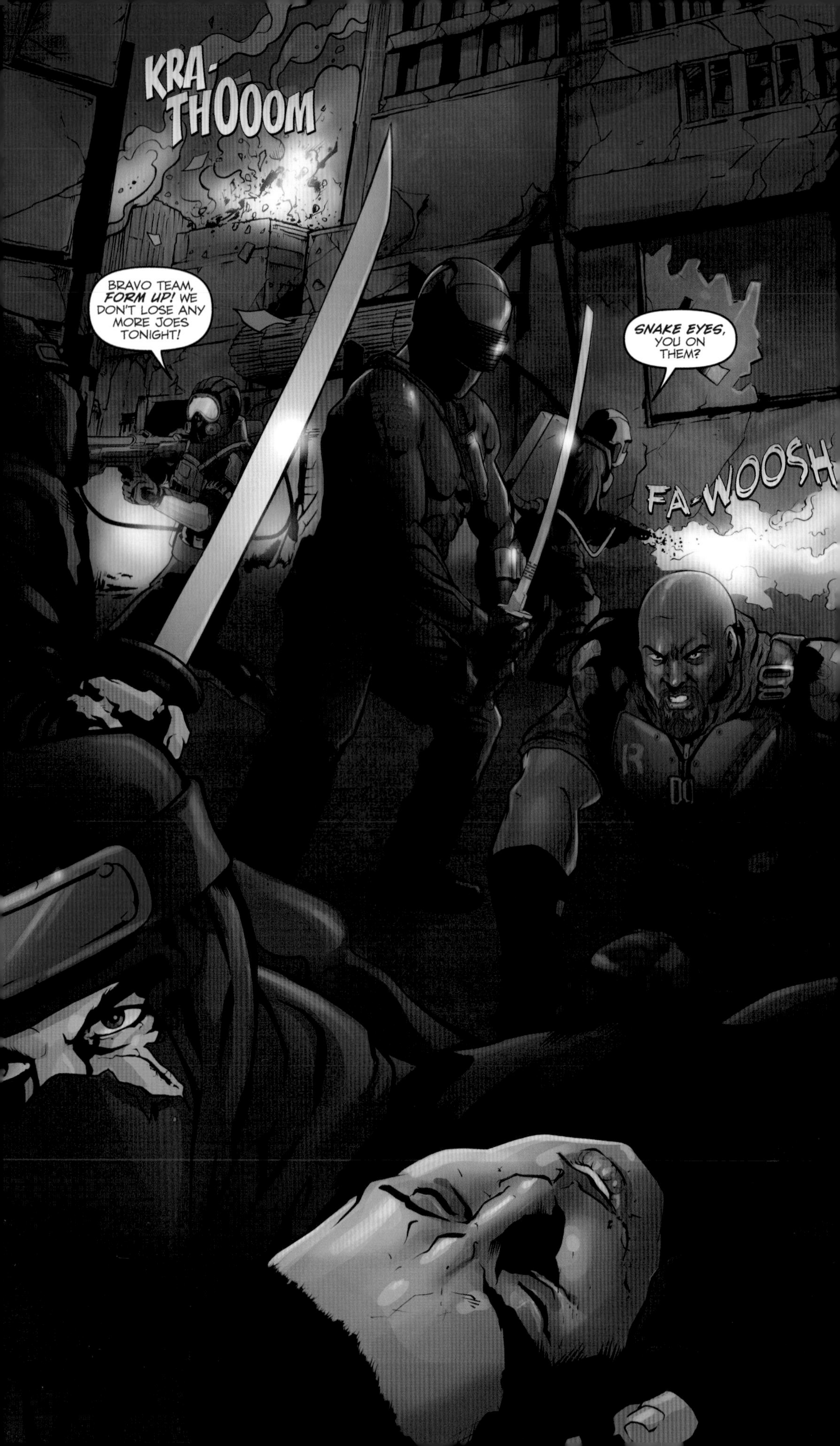
KRA-THOOOM
BRAVO TEAM, FORM UP! WE DON'T LOSE ANY MORE JOES TONIGHT!
SNAKE EYES, YOU ON THEM?
FA-WOOSH

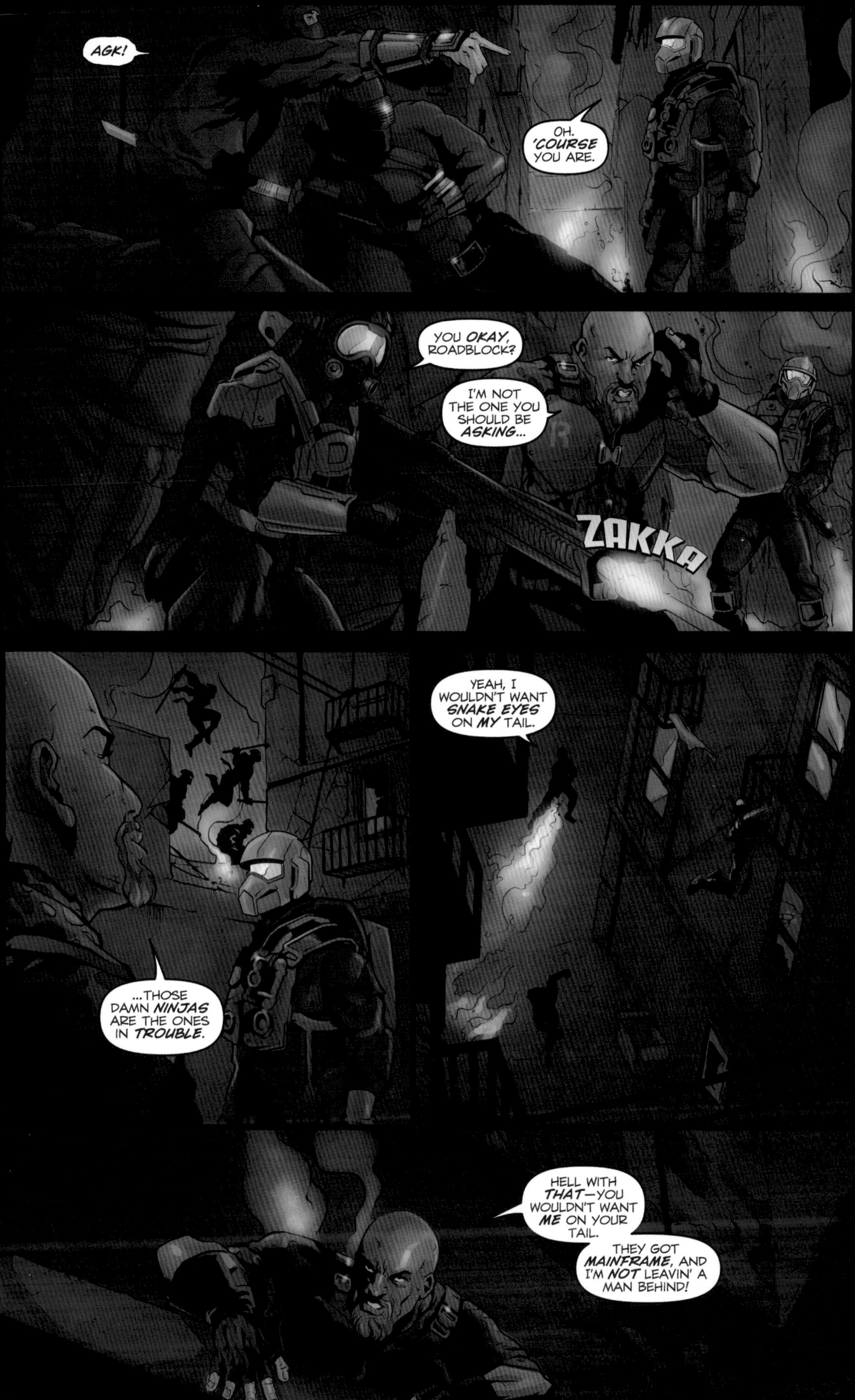
AGK!
OH. 'COURSE YOU ARE.
YOU OKAY, ROADBLOCK?
I'M NOT THE ONE YOU SHOULD BE ASKING...
ZAKKA
...THOSE DAMN NINJAS ARE THE ONES IN TROUBLE.
YEAH, I WOULDN'T WANT SNAKE EYES ON MY TAIL.
HELL WITH THAT—YOU WOULDN'T WANT ME ON YOUR TAIL.
THEY GOT MAINFRAME, AND I'M NOT LEAVIN' A MAN BEHIND!

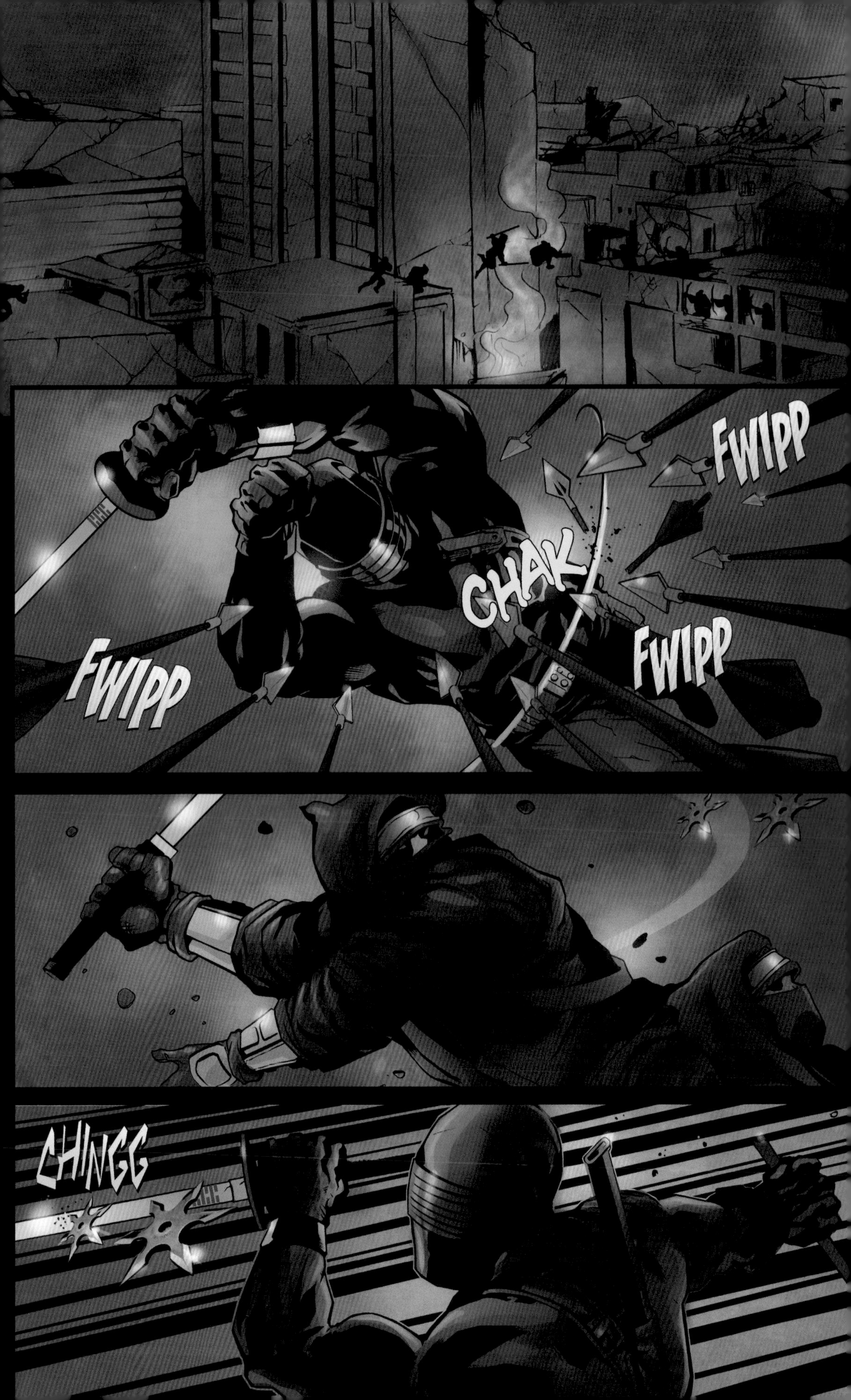
FWIPP
CHAK
FWIPP
FWIPP
CHINGG

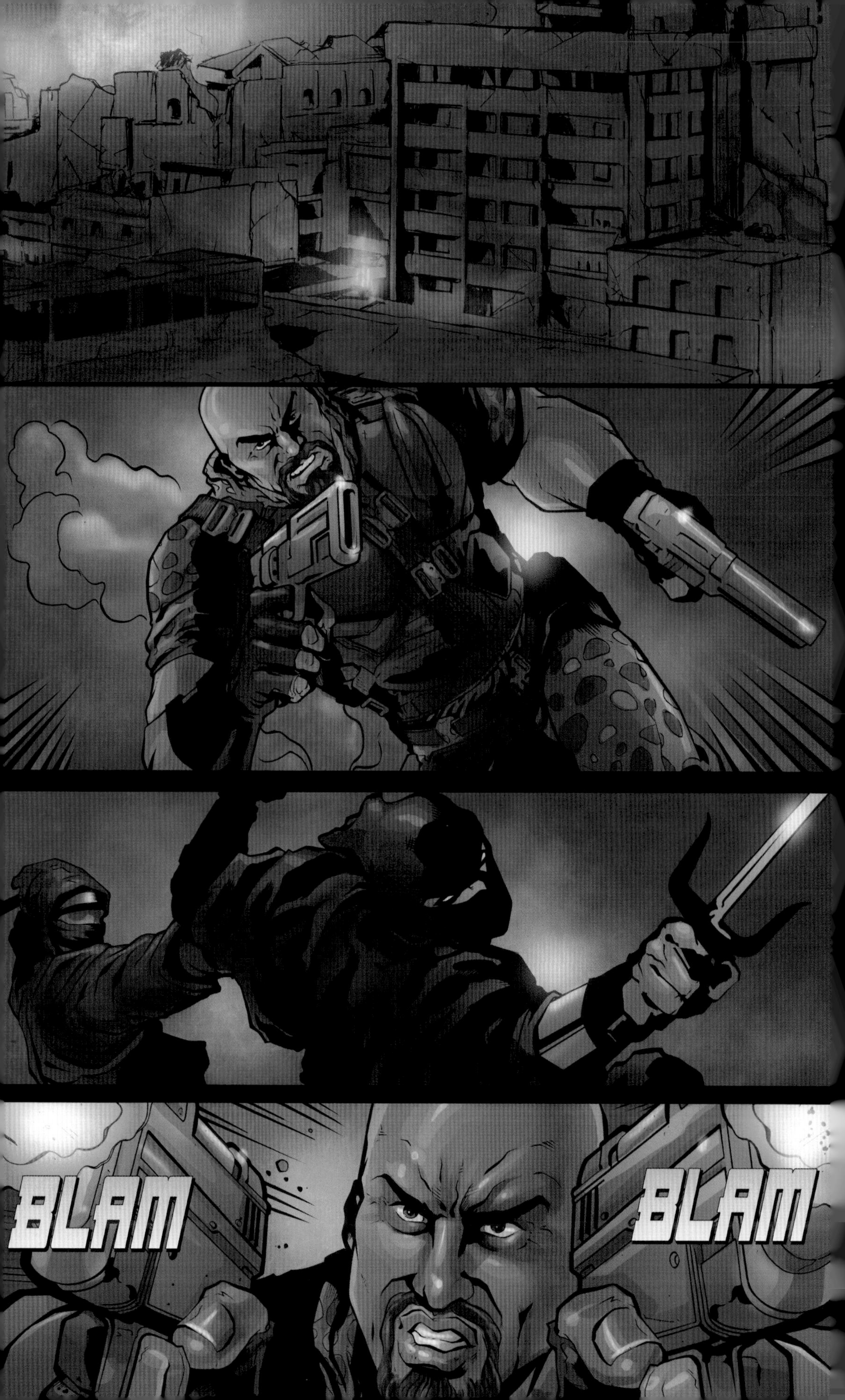
BLAM
BLAM

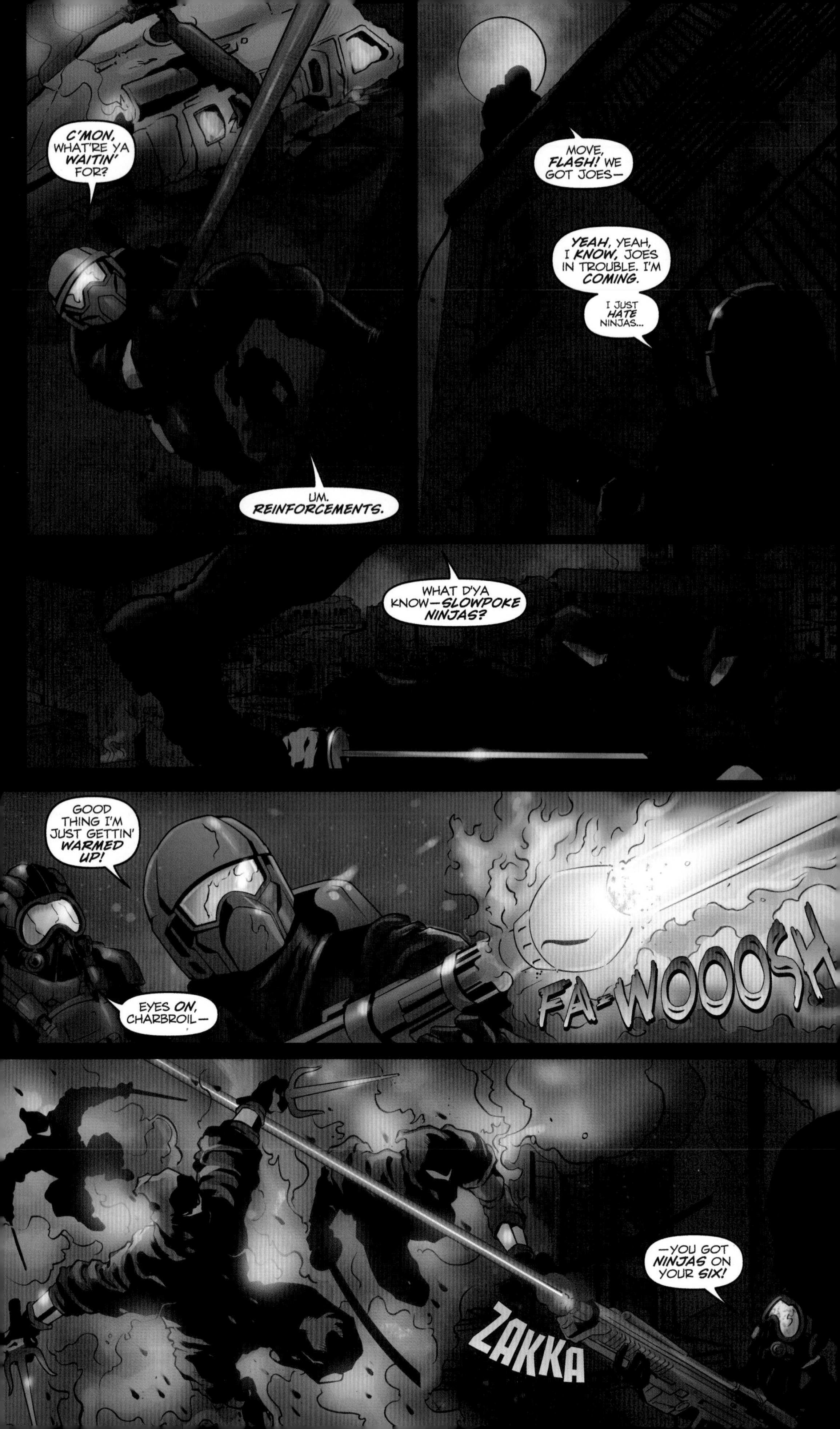
C'MON, WHAT'RE YA WAITIN' FOR?
UM. REINFORCEMENTS.
MOVE, FLASH! WE GOT JOES—
YEAH, YEAH, I KNOW, JOES IN TROUBLE. I'M COMING.
I JUST HATE NINJAS...
WHAT D'YA KNOW—SLOWPOKE NINJAS?
GOOD THING I'M JUST GETTIN' WARMED UP!
EYES ON, CHARBROIL—
FA-WOOOSH
—YOU GOT NINJAS ON YOUR SIX!
ZAKKA

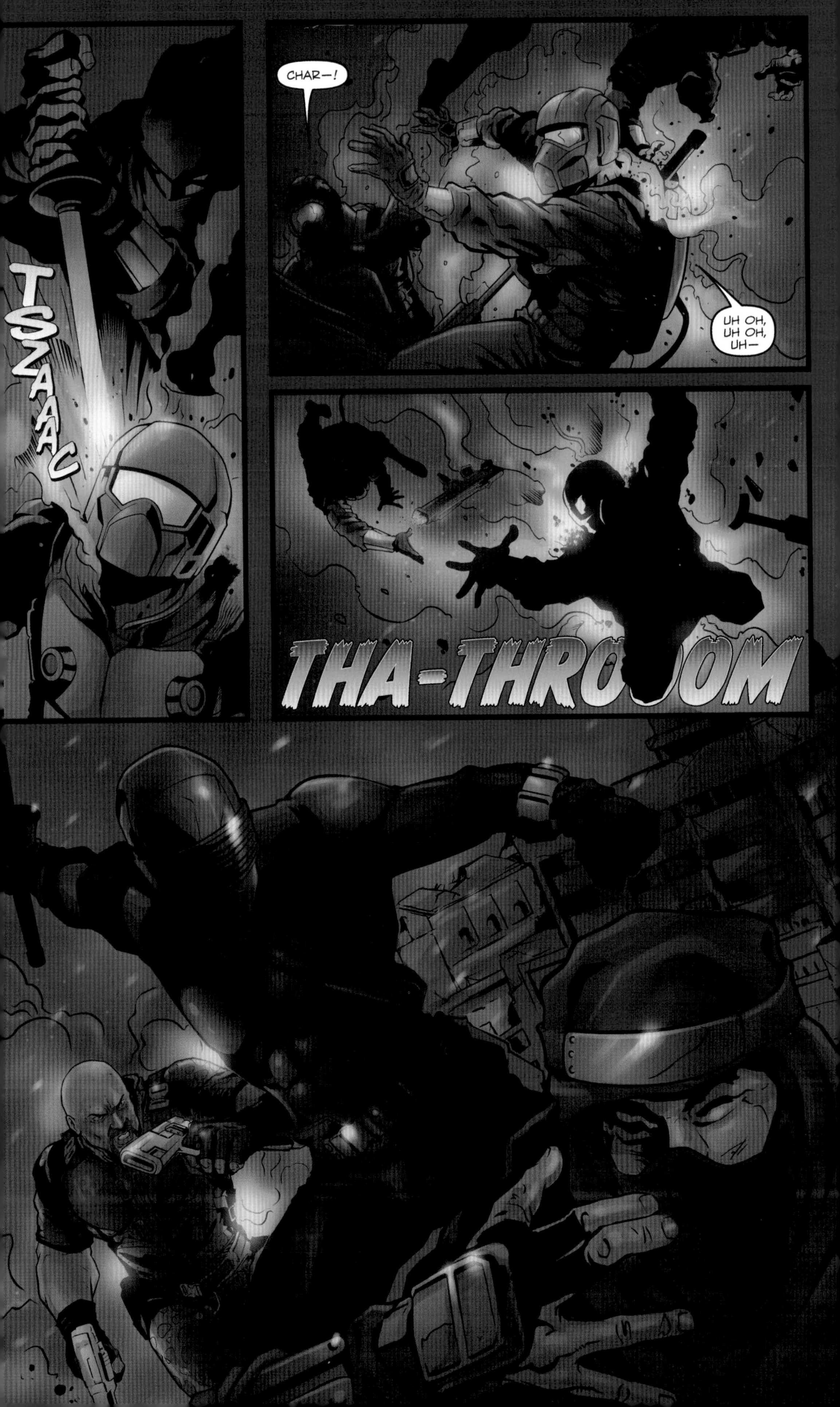
TSZAAAC
CHAR—!
UH OH, UH OH, UH—
THA-THROOOM

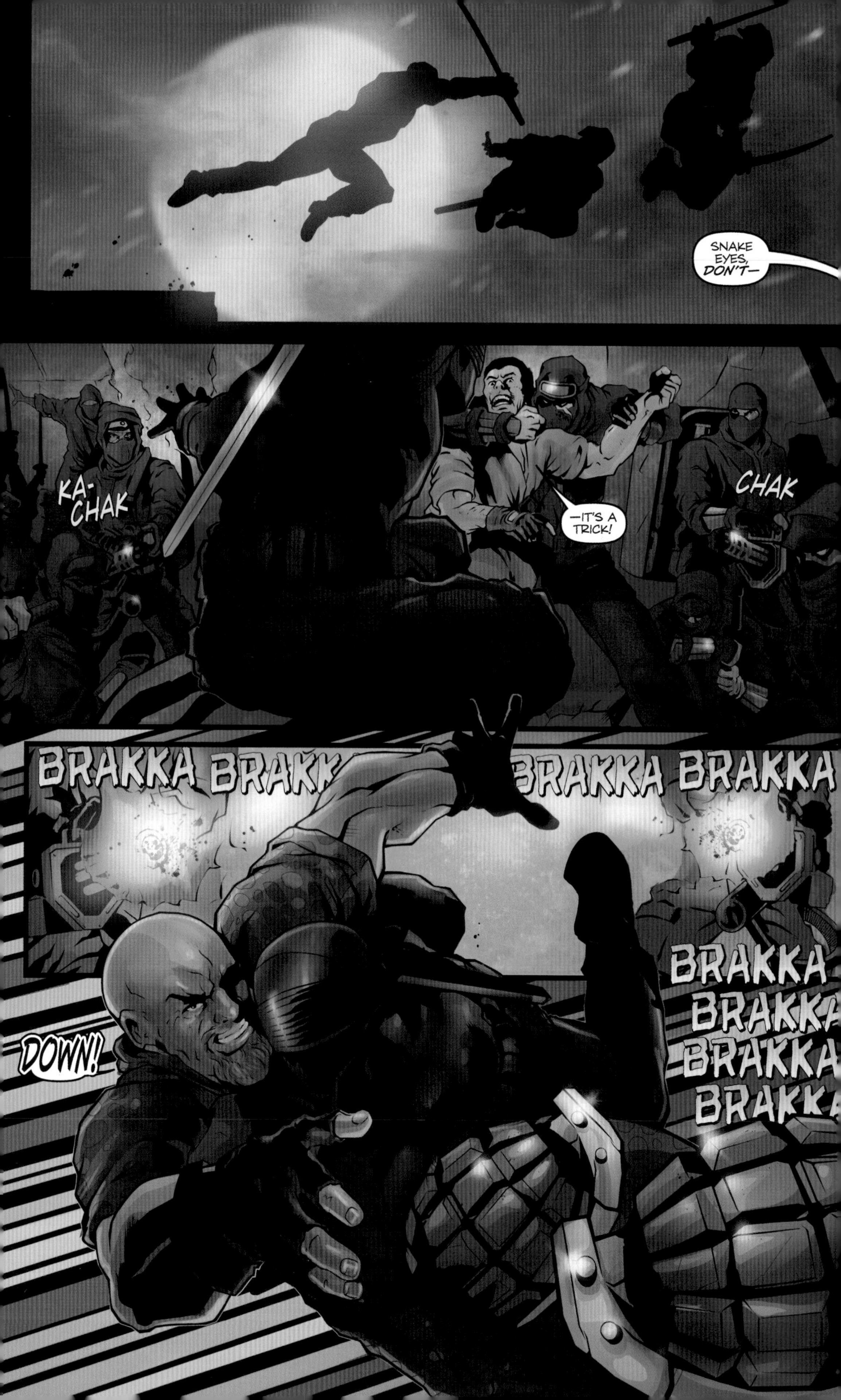

SNAKE EYES, DON'T—
KA-CHAK
—IT'S A TRICK!
CHAK
BRAKKA BRAKK
BRAKKA BRAKKA
DOWN!
BRAKKA
BRAKKA
BRAKKA
BRAKKA

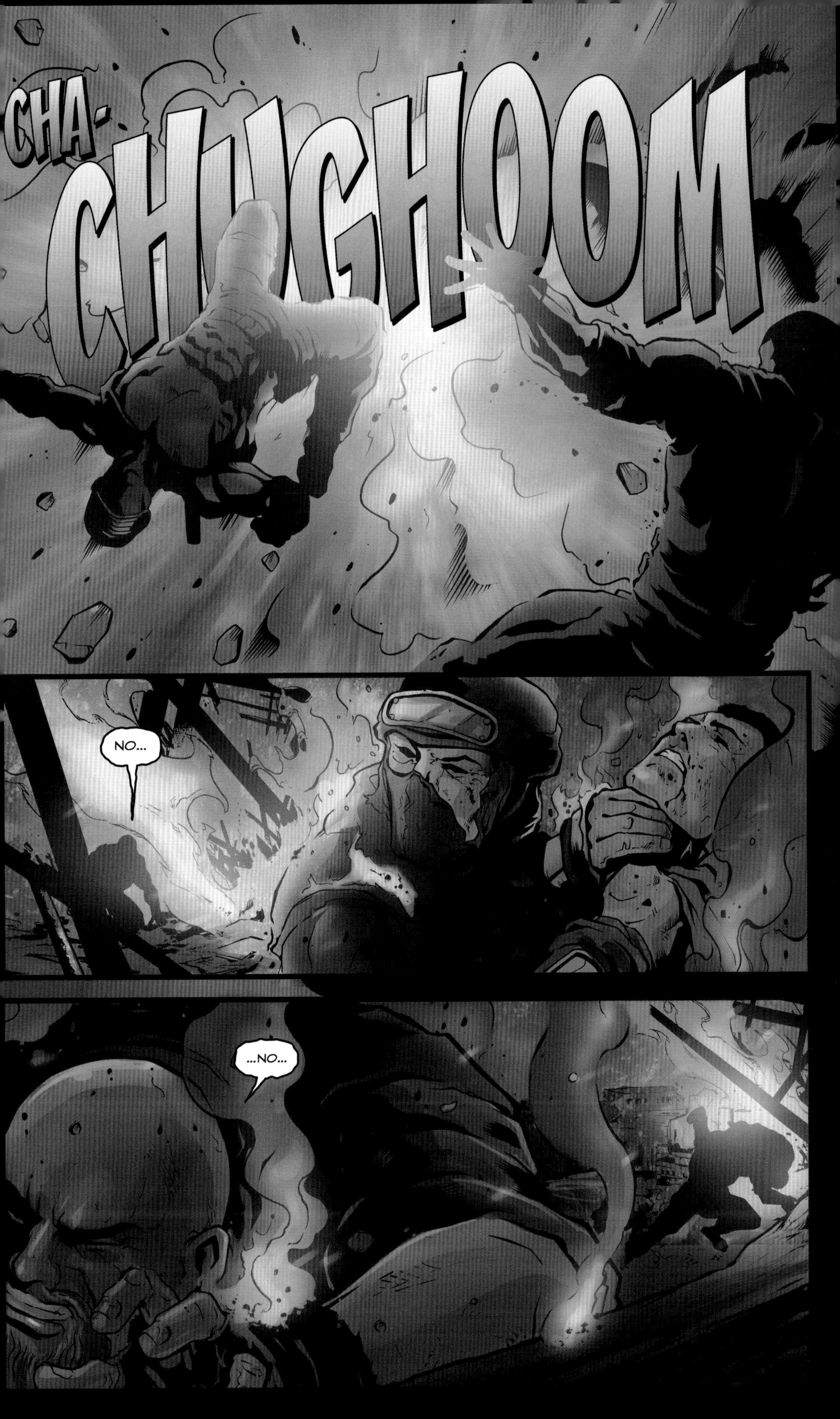
CHA-
CHUGHOOM
NO...
...NO...

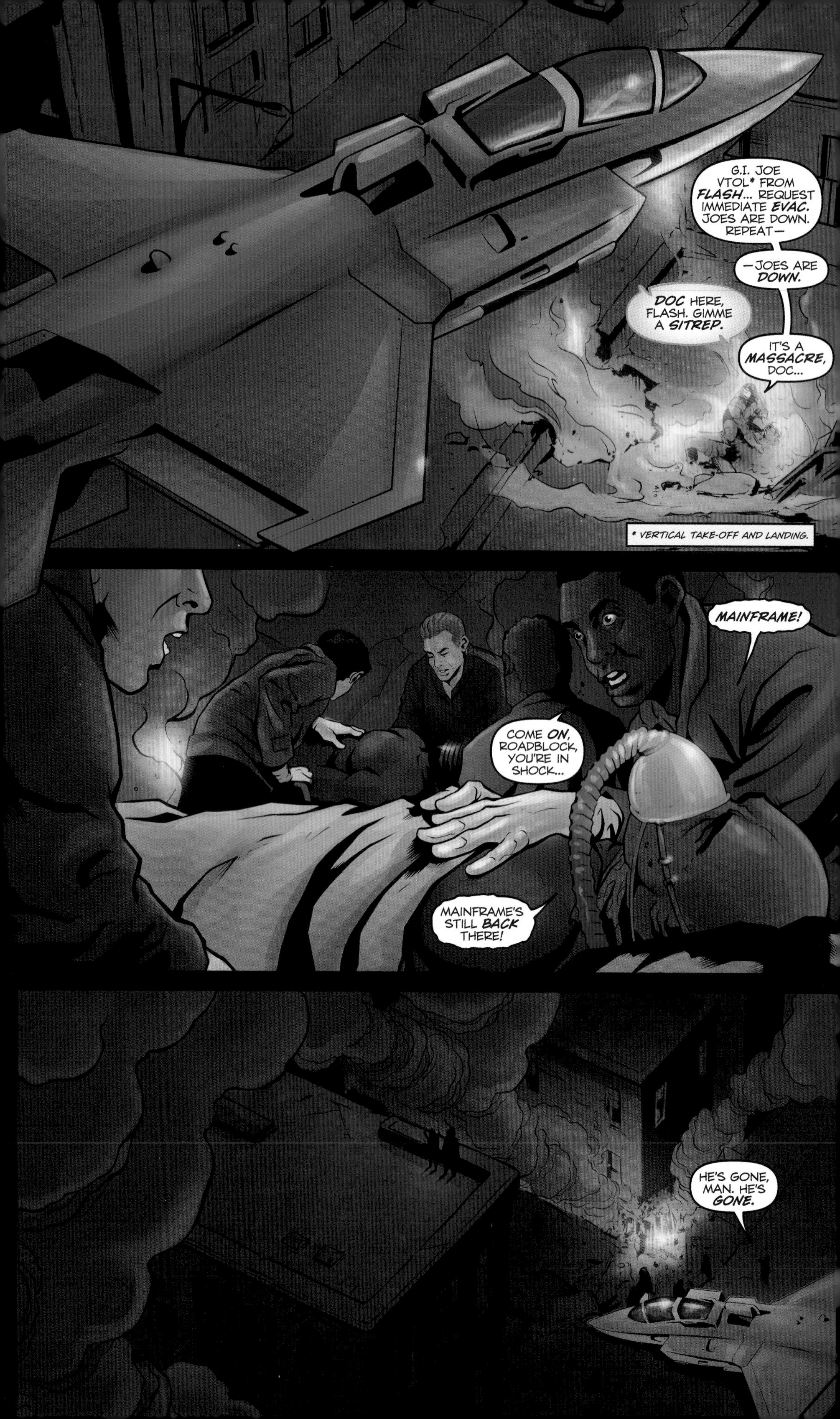
G.I. JOE VTOL* FROM FLASH... REQUEST IMMEDIATE EVAC. JOES ARE DOWN. REPEAT—
—JOES ARE DOWN.
DOC HERE, FLASH. GIMME A SITREP.
IT'S A MASSACRE, DOC...
* VERTICAL TAKE-OFF AND LANDING.
MAINFRAME!
COME ON, ROADBLOCK, YOU'RE IN SHOCK...
MAINFRAME'S STILL BACK THERE!
HE'S GONE, MAN. HE'S GONE.

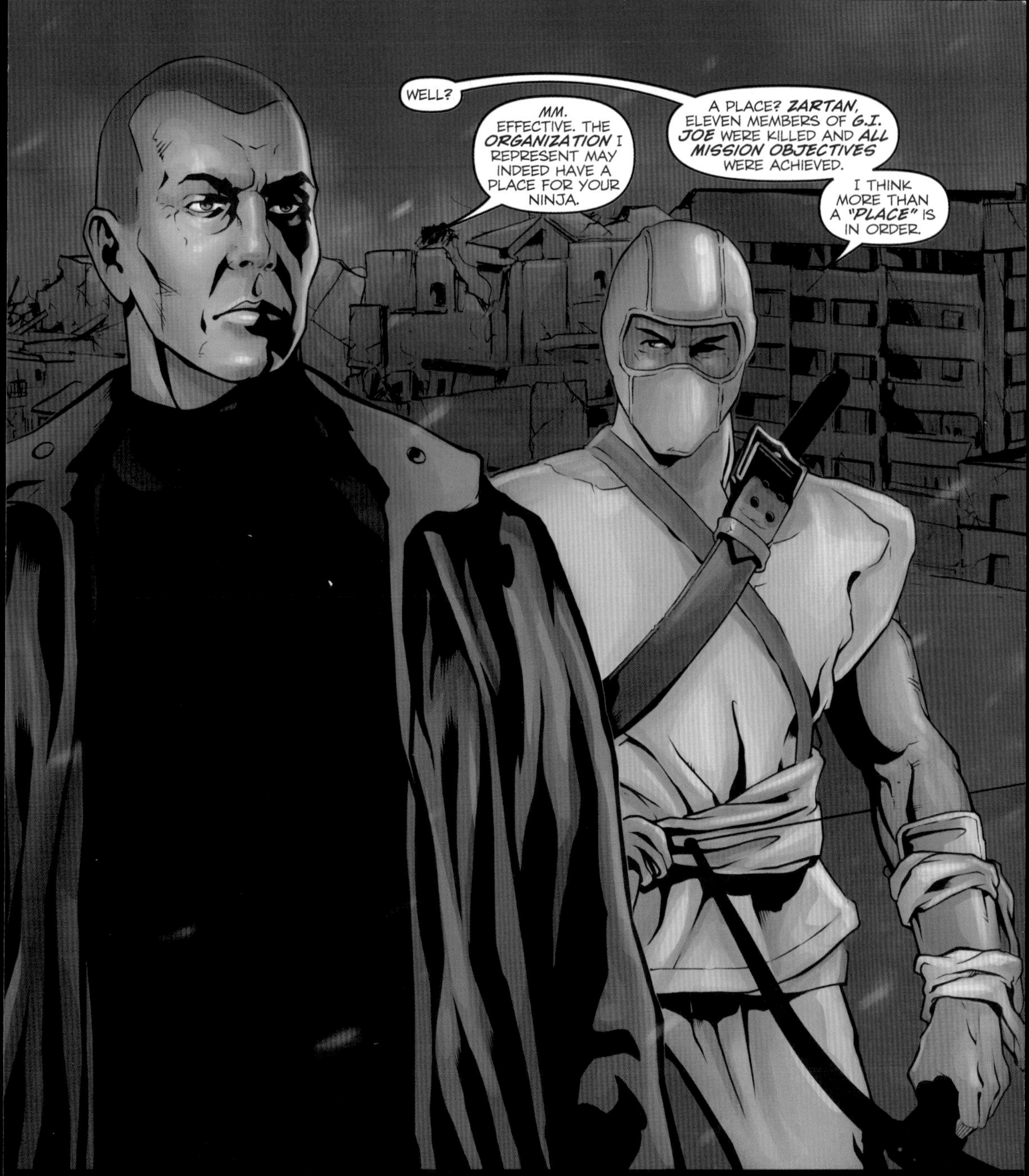
WELL?
MM. EFFECTIVE. THE ORGANIZATION I REPRESENT MAY INDEED HAVE A PLACE FOR YOUR NINJA.
A PLACE? ZARTAN, ELEVEN MEMBERS OF G.I. JOE WERE KILLED AND ALL MISSION OBJECTIVES WERE ACHIEVED.
I THINK MORE THAN A "PLACE" IS IN ORDER.

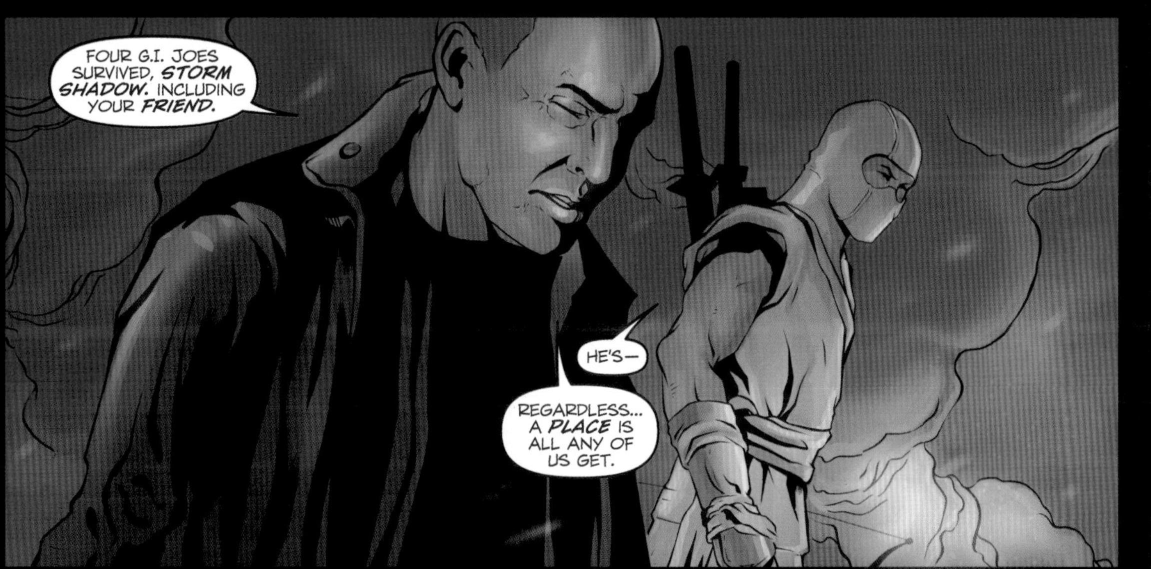
FOUR G.I. JOES SURVIVED, STORM SHADOW. INCLUDING YOUR FRIEND.
HE'S—
REGARDLESS... A PLACE IS ALL ANY OF US GET.

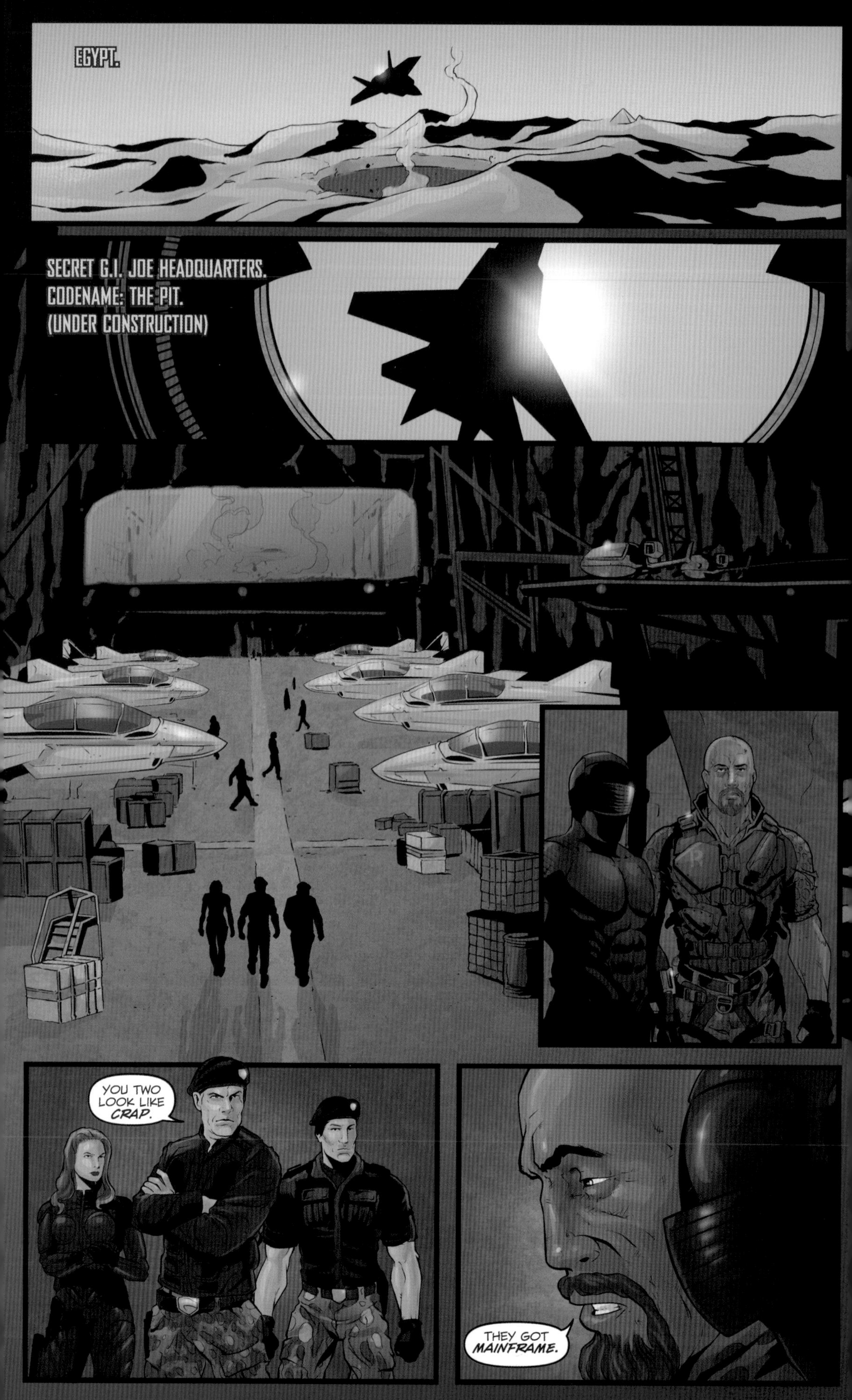
EGYPT.
SECRET G.I. JOE HEADQUARTERS.
CODENAME: THE PIT.
(UNDER CONSTRUCTION)
YOU TWO LOOK LIKE *CRAP*.
THEY GOT *MAINFRAME*.

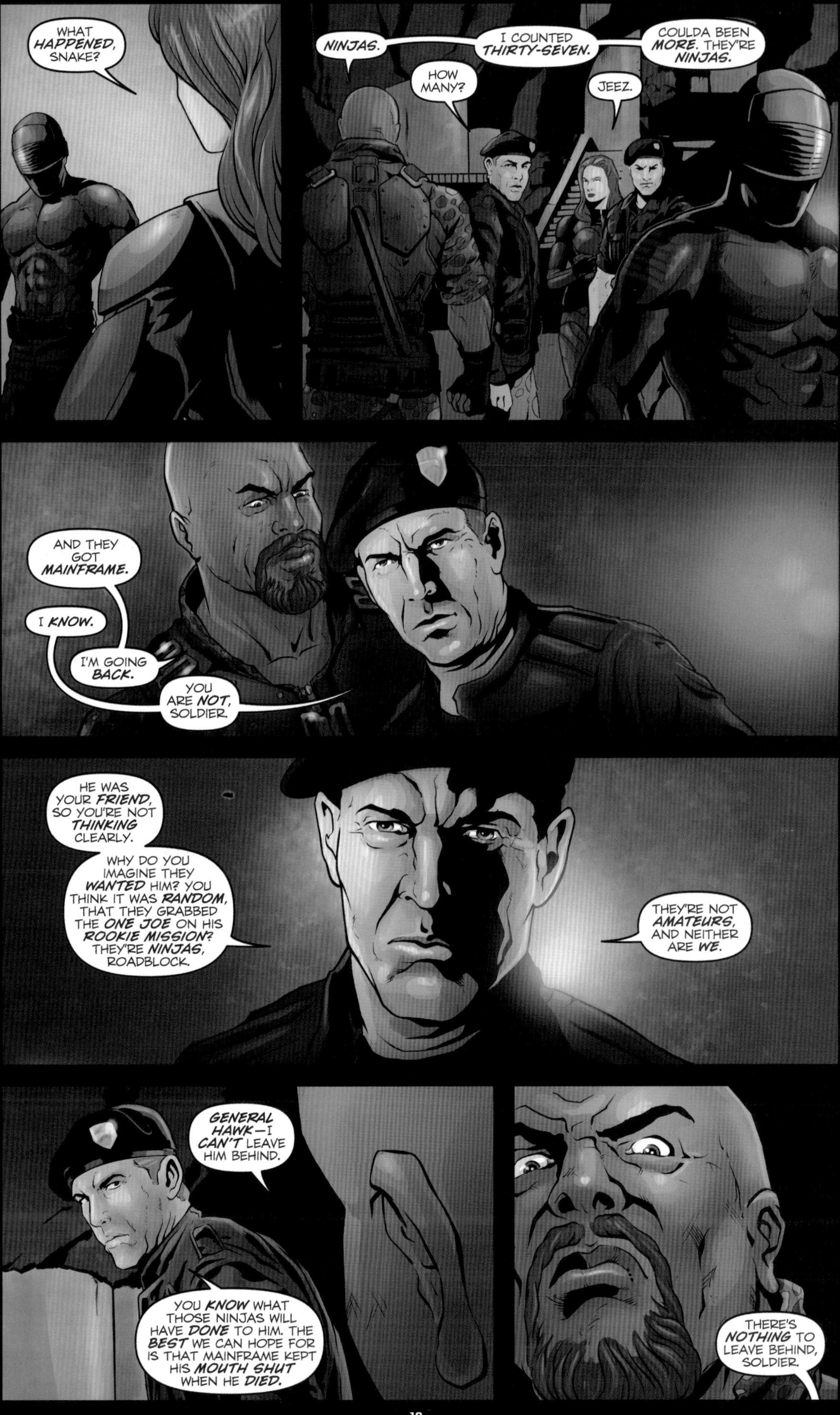
WHAT HAPPENED, SNAKE?
NINJAS.
HOW MANY?
I COUNTED THIRTY-SEVEN.
COULDA BEEN MORE. THEY'RE NINJAS.
JEEZ.
AND THEY GOT MAINFRAME.
I KNOW.
I'M GOING BACK.
YOU ARE NOT, SOLDIER.
HE WAS YOUR FRIEND, SO YOU'RE NOT THINKING CLEARLY.
WHY DO YOU IMAGINE THEY WANTED HIM? YOU THINK IT WAS RANDOM, THAT THEY GRABBED THE ONE JOE ON HIS ROOKIE MISSION? THEY'RE NINJAS, ROADBLOCK.
THEY'RE NOT AMATEURS, AND NEITHER ARE WE.
GENERAL HAWK—I CAN'T LEAVE HIM BEHIND.
YOU KNOW WHAT THOSE NINJAS WILL HAVE DONE TO HIM. THE BEST WE CAN HOPE FOR IS THAT MAINFRAME KEPT HIS MOUTH SHUT WHEN HE DIED.
THERE'S NOTHING TO LEAVE BEHIND, SOLDIER.

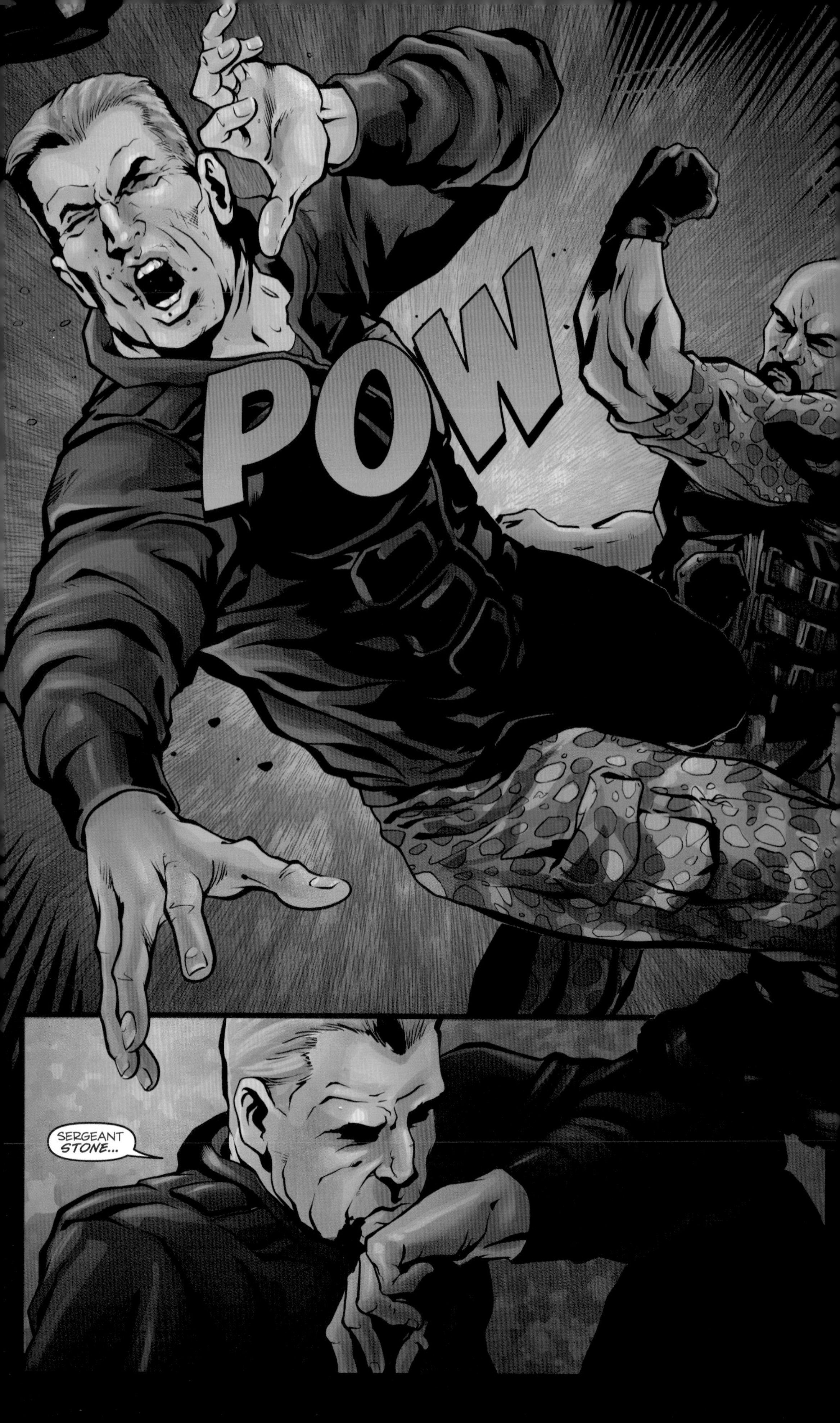
POW
SERGEANT STONE...

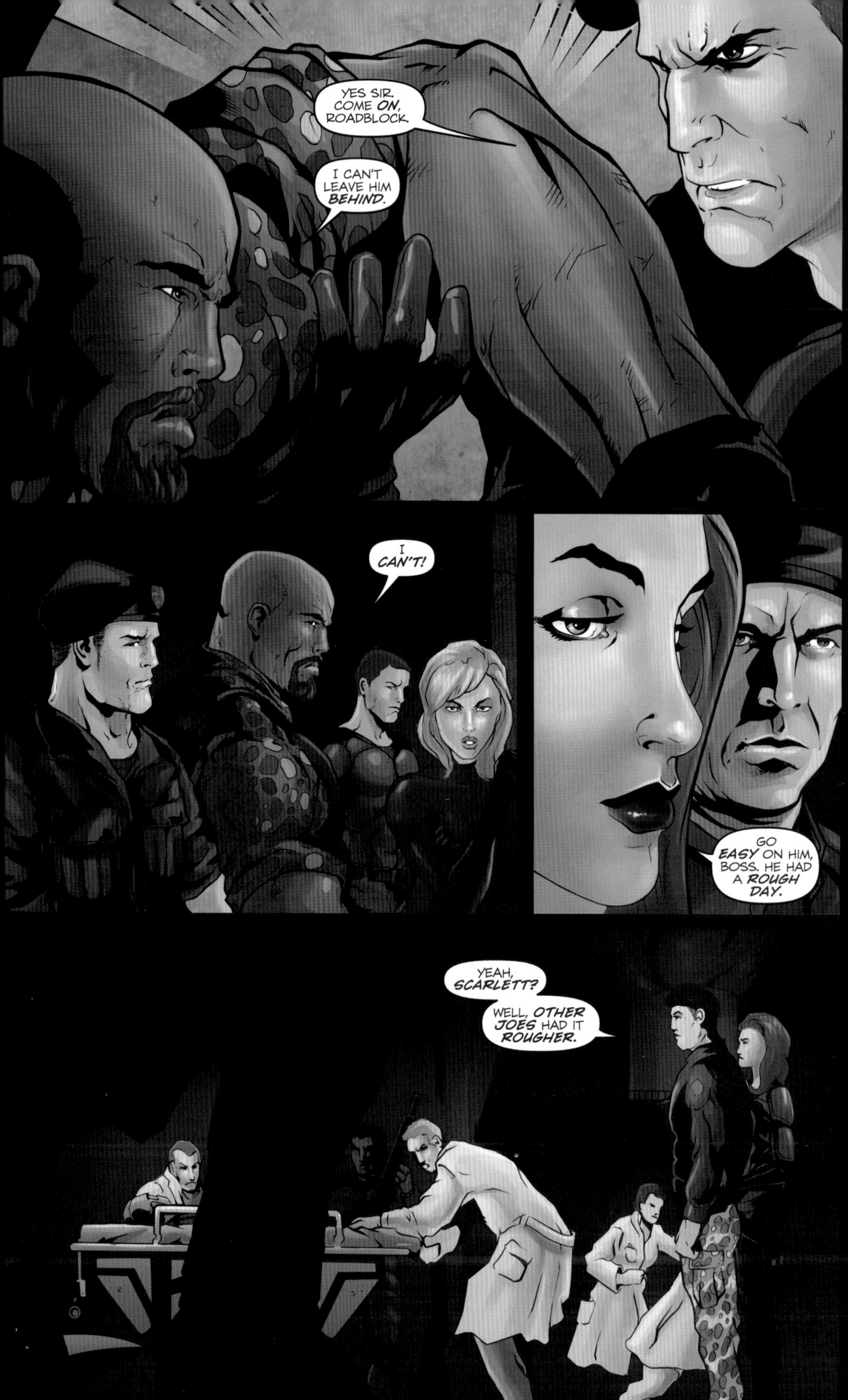
YES SIR. COME ON, ROADBLOCK.
I CAN'T LEAVE HIM BEHIND.
I CAN'T!
GO EASY ON HIM, BOSS. HE HAD A ROUGH DAY.
YEAH, SCARLETT?
WELL, OTHER JOES HAD IT ROUGHER.

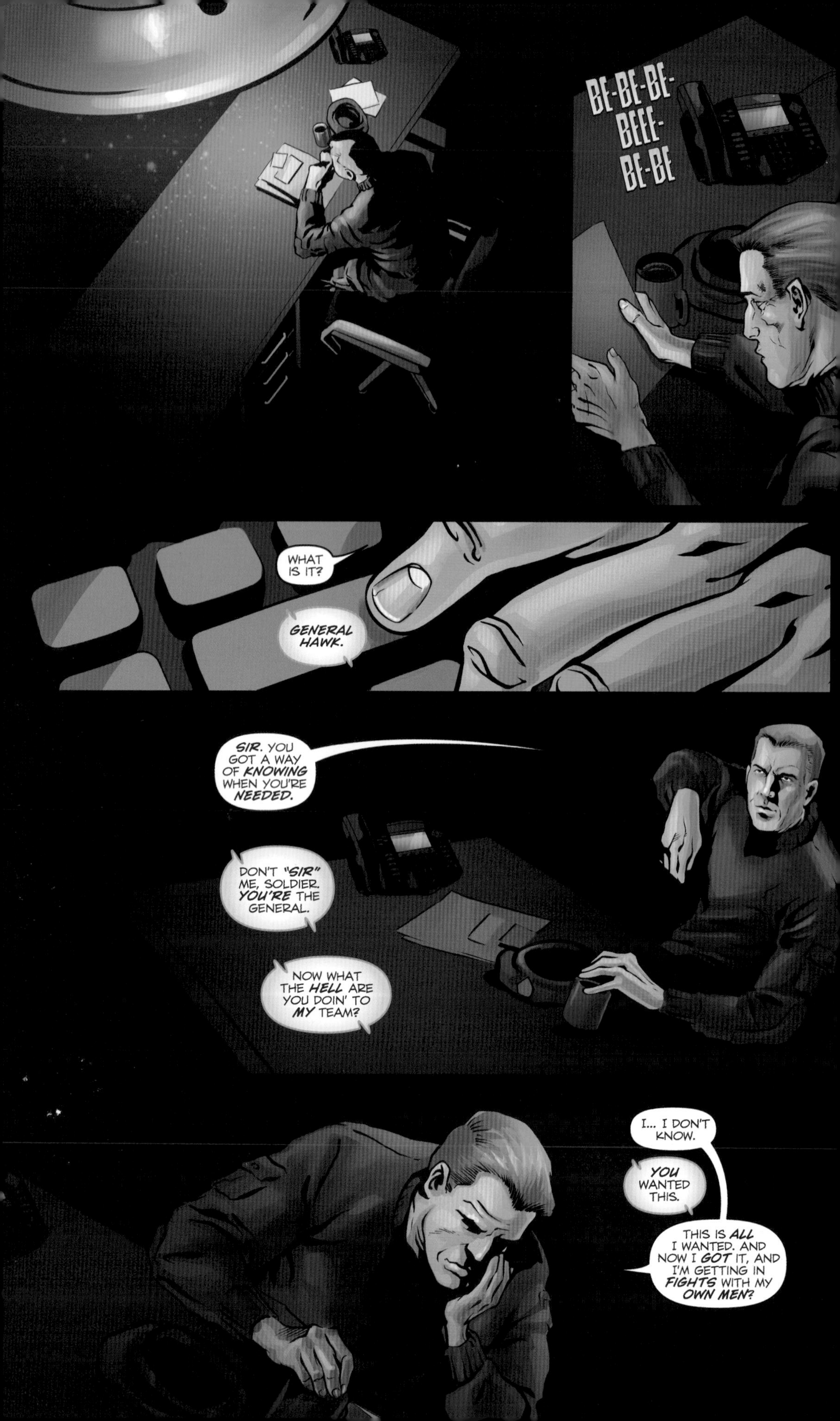
BE-BE-BE-BEEE-BE-BE
WHAT IS IT?
GENERAL HAWK.
SIR. YOU GOT A WAY OF KNOWING WHEN YOU'RE NEEDED.
DON'T "SIR" ME, SOLDIER. YOU'RE THE GENERAL.
NOW WHAT THE HELL ARE YOU DOIN' TO MY TEAM?
I... I DON'T KNOW.
YOU WANTED THIS.
THIS IS ALL I WANTED. AND NOW I GOT IT, AND I'M GETTING IN FIGHTS WITH MY OWN MEN?

CODE NAME: ROADBLOCK
FILE NAME: HINTON, MARVIN F.
SERIAL NUMBER: 825-38-MF48
...THPLACE: BILOXI, MI
...TED: WASHINGTON, D.C.

MEN WHO STARED DOWN A *SWARM* OF *NINJAS* DOING *GOD-KNOWS-WHAT* IN THE MIDDLE OF A *CIVIL WAR.*

THE PLURAL OF *NINJA* IS *NINJA,* BUT THAT'S NEITHER HERE NOR THERE. *LOOK,* ABERNATHY...

YOU WERE THE ONE WHO WANTED TO STOP RECRUITING GUYS STRAIGHT OUT OF *WEST POINT* AND *ANNAPOLIS.*

INCOMING CALL... ENCRYPTION INITIATED

AND YOU WERE *RIGHT.* YOU *NEED* SOMEBODY LIKE ROADBLOCK, WITH THOSE KIND OF *SMARTS*—BUT WHO'S GOT THE EXPERIENCE AFFORDED BY A *HARD LIFE.*

HE'S CLEVER AND HE'S *TOUGH*—HE'S JUST HARD TO *WRANGLE.*

SO, WHAT DO I *DO* WITH HIM? WHAT DO I DO ABOUT THE *NINJA?*

YOU BE A *GENERAL,* GENERAL. *CLICK*

"BE A GENERAL."

WELL?

DON'T JUST *STAND* THERE, SNAKE EYES. *SAY* WHAT YOU CAME HERE TO *SAY.*

IS *THAT* RIGHT? WELL, SOLDIER...

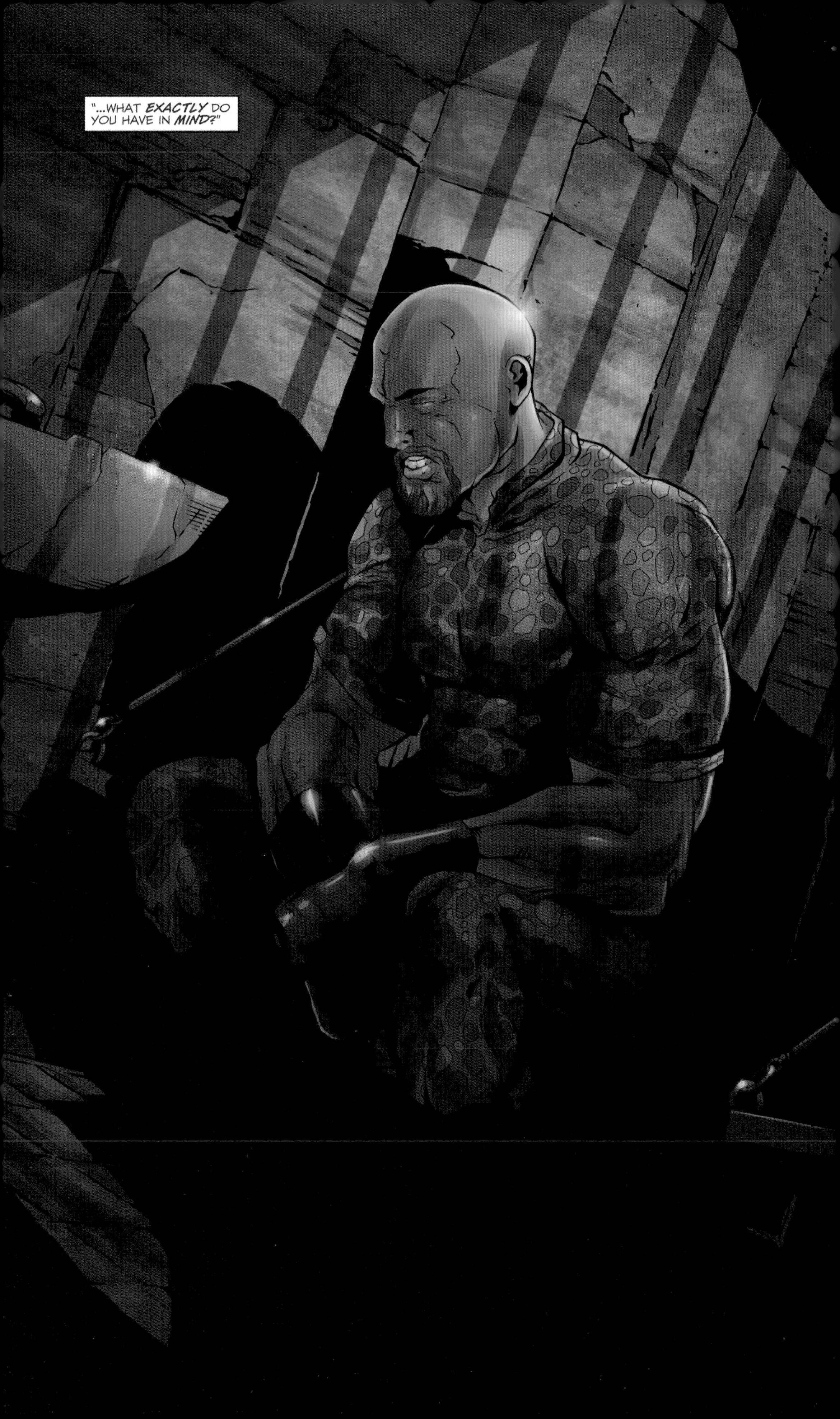
"...WHAT EXACTLY DO YOU HAVE IN MIND?"

TWO

BUZZARD POINT, WASHINGTON, D.C. SOME TIME AGO.

HEY, NEW KID!

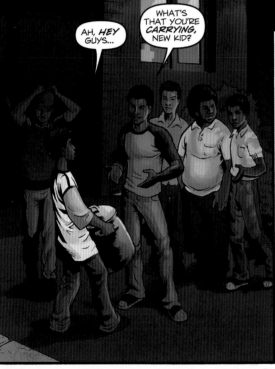

AH, HEY GUYS...

WHAT'S THAT YOU'RE CARRYING, NEW KID?

SOUS-VIDE CHICKEN WITH MUSHROOM RAGOUT AND TRUFFLE SAUCE.

'WELL, IT'S REALLY A GARLIC-BUTTER SAUCE, BUT IT'S SUPPOSED TO BE—

SOUNDS FANCY. THIS AIN'T A FANCY NEIGHBORHOOD.

MAYBE YOUR FOSTER MOM DIDN'T TELL YOU, SO OL' STOOP'LL HAVE TO FILL YOU IN, SON.

AN' ANYWAY, LOOKS TO ME LIKE YOU'RE CARRYIN' NOTHIN'.

WAP

SCHLIK

SO, TELL ME—WHATDYA THINK OF THAT, NEW KID?

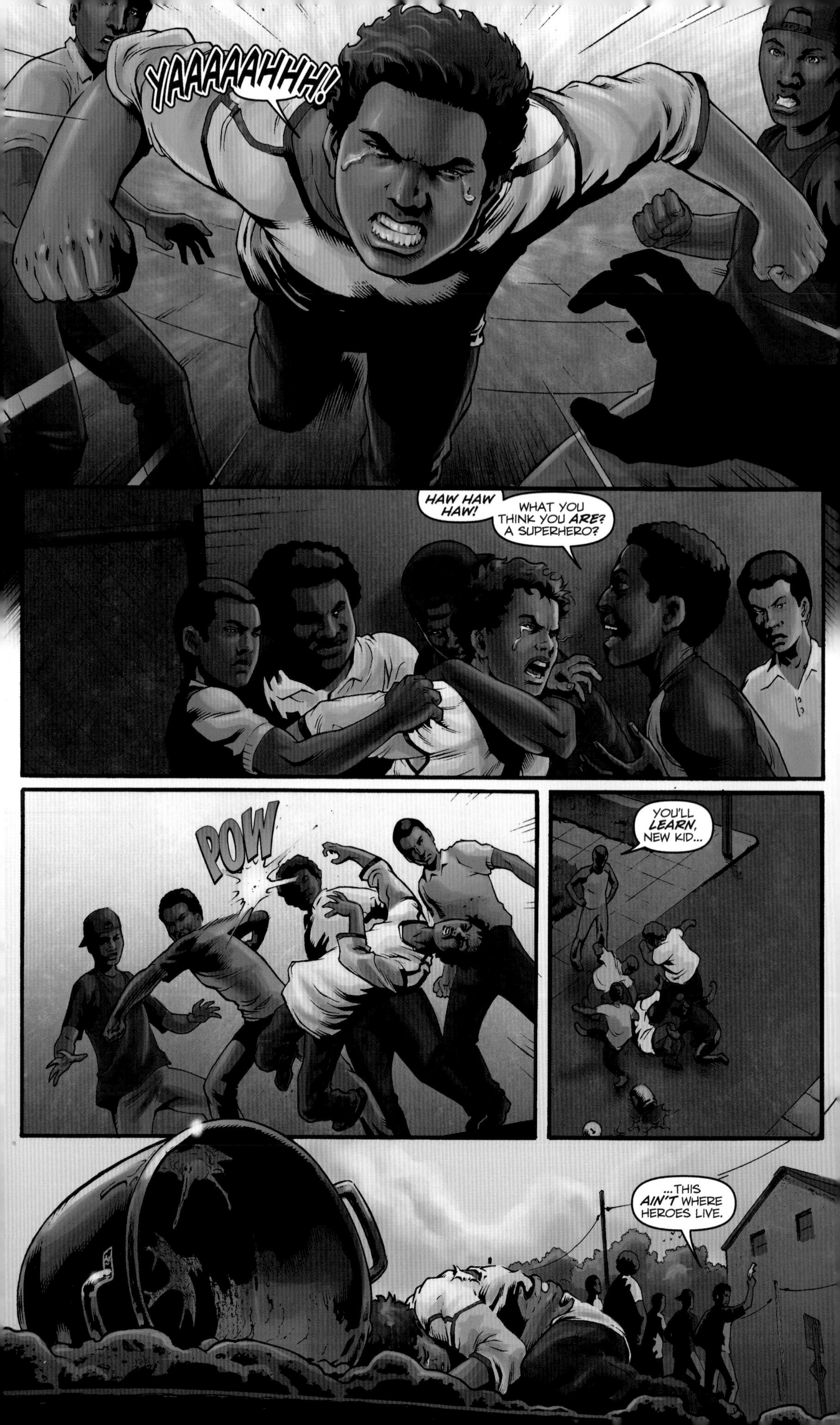
YAAAAAHHH!
HAW HAW HAW!
WHAT YOU THINK YOU ARE? A SUPERHERO?
POW
YOU'LL LEARN, NEW KID...
...THIS AIN'T WHERE HEROES LIVE.

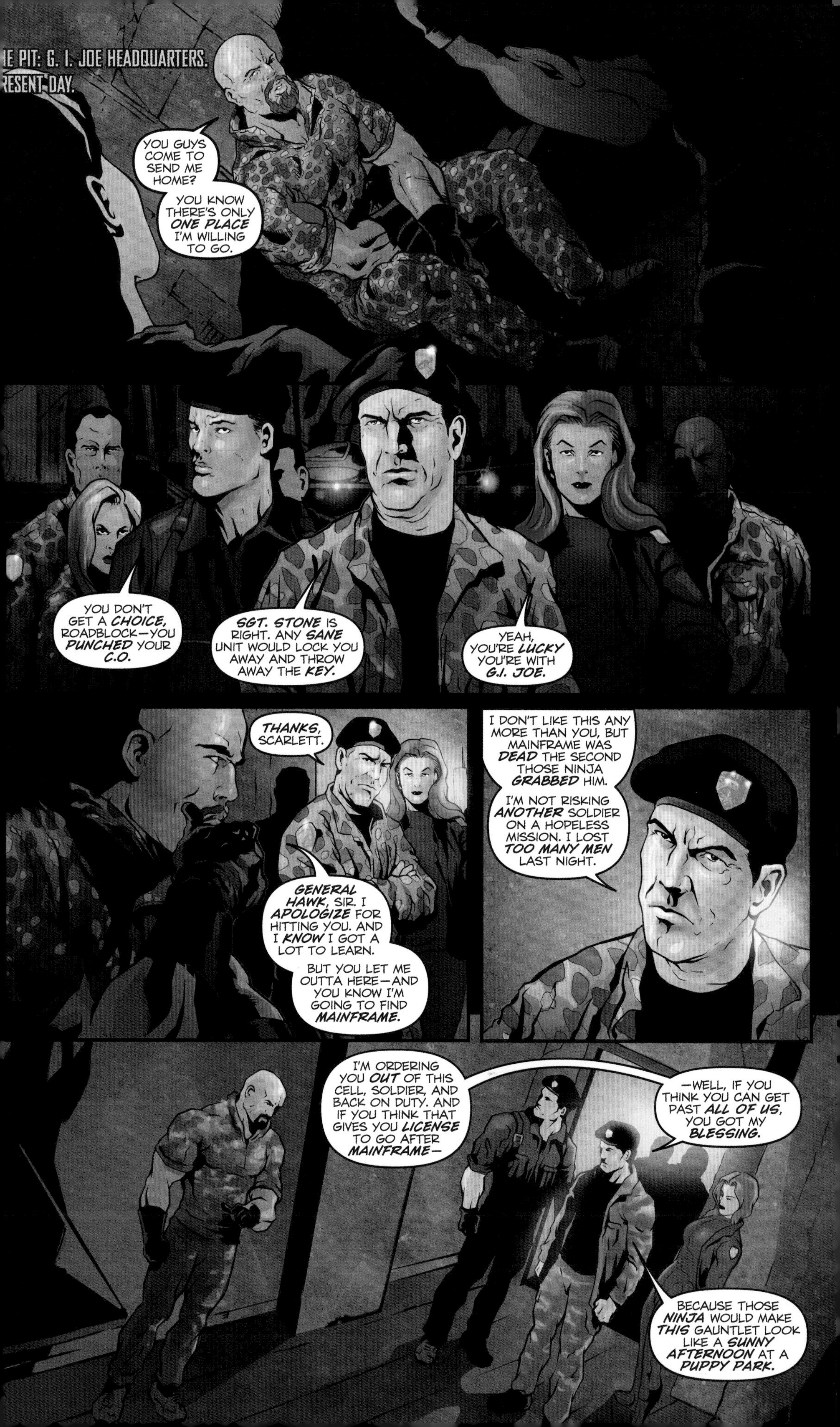

E PIT: G. I. JOE HEADQUARTERS.
RESENT DAY.
YOU GUYS COME TO SEND ME HOME?
YOU KNOW THERE'S ONLY ONE PLACE I'M WILLING TO GO.
YOU DON'T GET A CHOICE, ROADBLOCK—YOU PUNCHED YOUR C.O.
SGT. STONE IS RIGHT. ANY SANE UNIT WOULD LOCK YOU AWAY AND THROW AWAY THE KEY.
YEAH, YOU'RE LUCKY YOU'RE WITH G.I. JOE.
THANKS, SCARLETT.
GENERAL HAWK, SIR. I APOLOGIZE FOR HITTING YOU. AND I KNOW I GOT A LOT TO LEARN.
BUT YOU LET ME OUTTA HERE—AND YOU KNOW I'M GOING TO FIND MAINFRAME.
I DON'T LIKE THIS ANY MORE THAN YOU, BUT MAINFRAME WAS DEAD THE SECOND THOSE NINJA GRABBED HIM.
I'M NOT RISKING ANOTHER SOLDIER ON A HOPELESS MISSION. I LOST TOO MANY MEN LAST NIGHT.
I'M ORDERING YOU OUT OF THIS CELL, SOLDIER, AND BACK ON DUTY. AND IF YOU THINK THAT GIVES YOU LICENSE TO GO AFTER MAINFRAME—
—WELL, IF YOU THINK YOU CAN GET PAST ALL OF US, YOU GOT MY BLESSING.
BECAUSE THOSE NINJA WOULD MAKE THIS GAUNTLET LOOK LIKE A SUNNY AFTERNOON AT A PUPPY PARK.

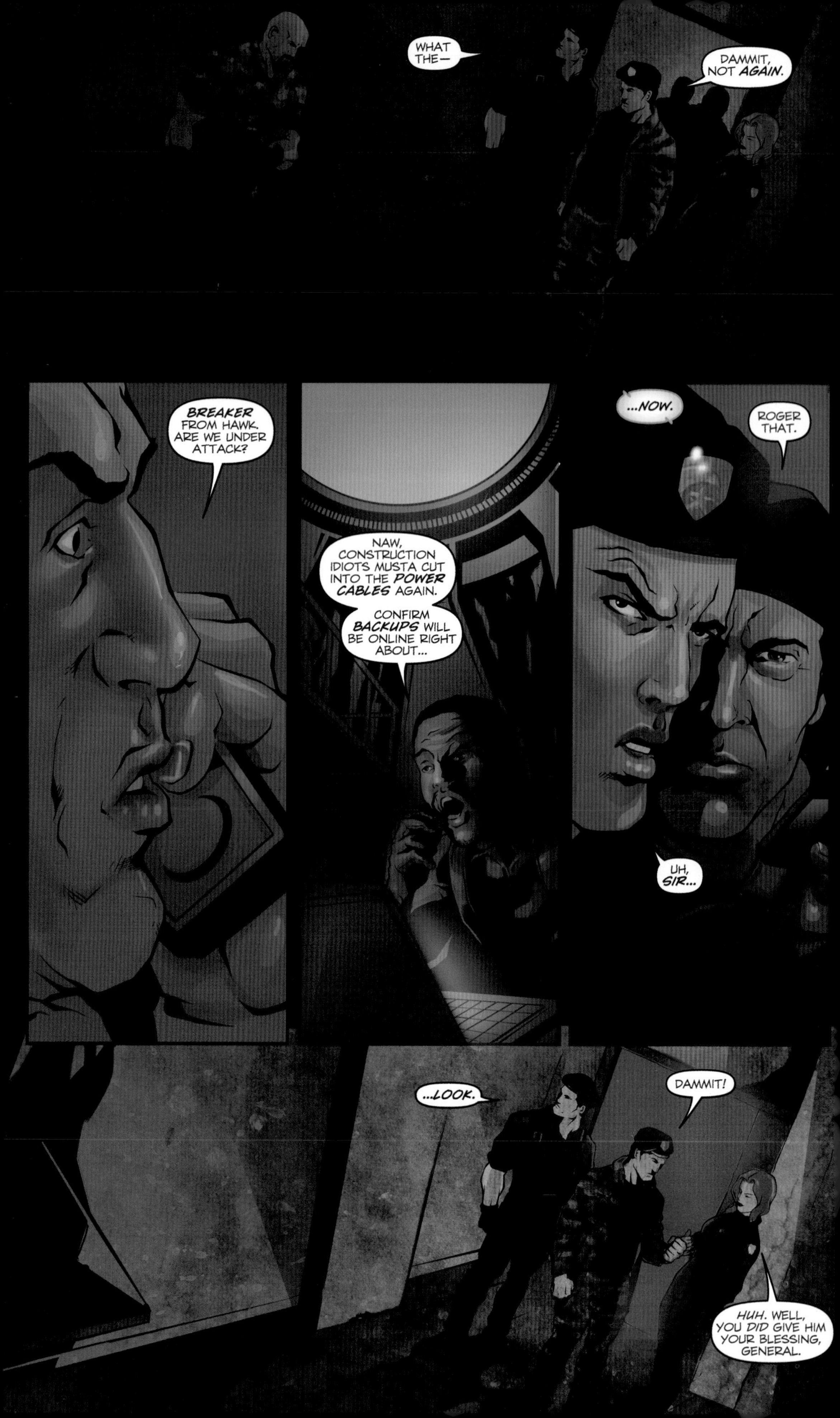

WHAT THE—
DAMMIT, NOT AGAIN.
BREAKER FROM HAWK. ARE WE UNDER ATTACK?
NAW, CONSTRUCTION IDIOTS MUSTA CUT INTO THE POWER CABLES AGAIN.
CONFIRM BACKUPS WILL BE ONLINE RIGHT ABOUT...
...NOW.
ROGER THAT.
UH, SIR...
...LOOK.
DAMMIT!
HUH. WELL, YOU DID GIVE HIM YOUR BLESSING, GENERAL.

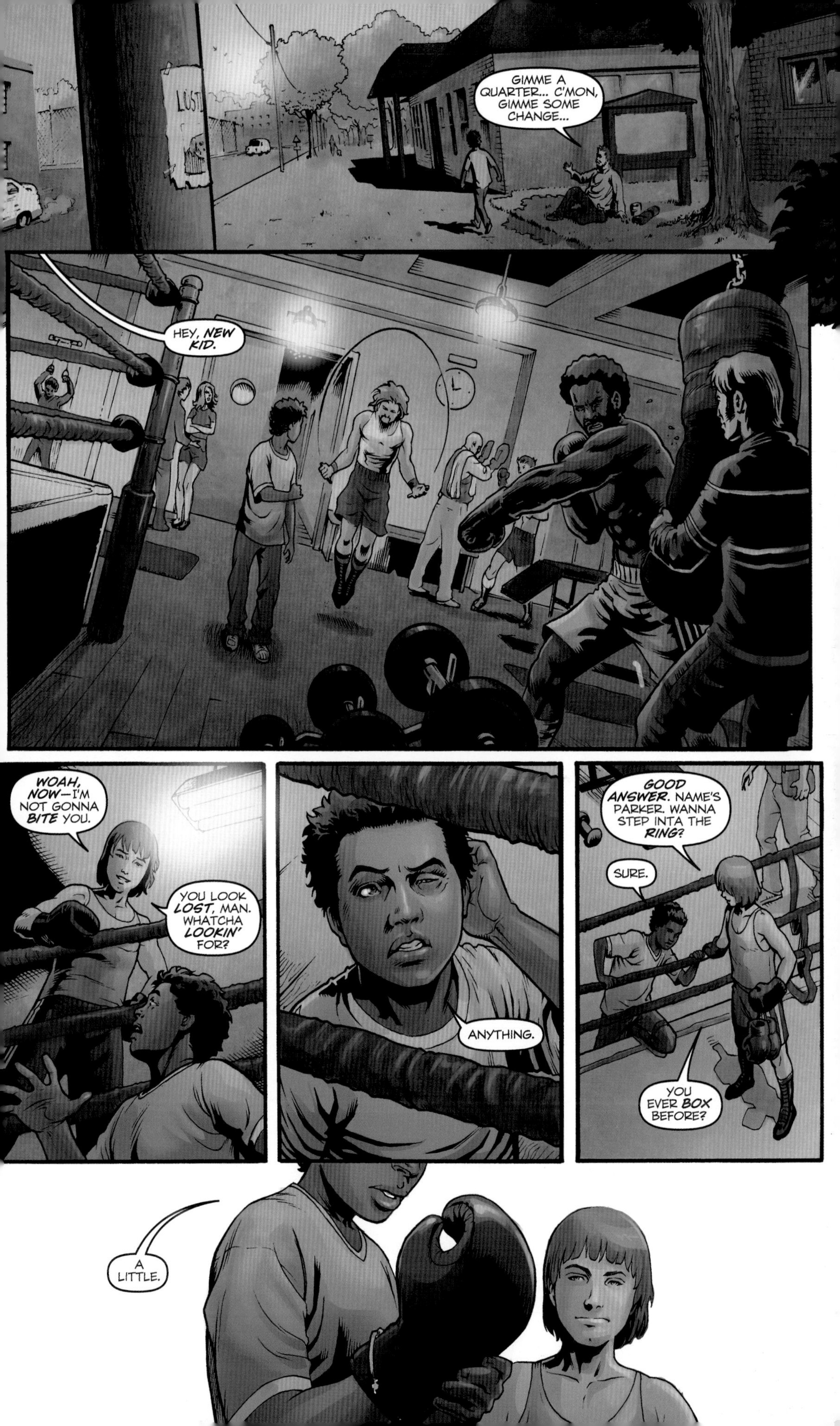
LOST
GIMME A QUARTER... C'MON, GIMME SOME CHANGE...
HEY, NEW KID.
WOAH, NOW—I'M NOT GONNA BITE YOU.
YOU LOOK LOST, MAN. WHATCHA LOOKIN' FOR?
ANYTHING.
GOOD ANSWER. NAME'S PARKER. WANNA STEP INTA THE RING?
SURE.
YOU EVER BOX BEFORE?
A LITTLE.

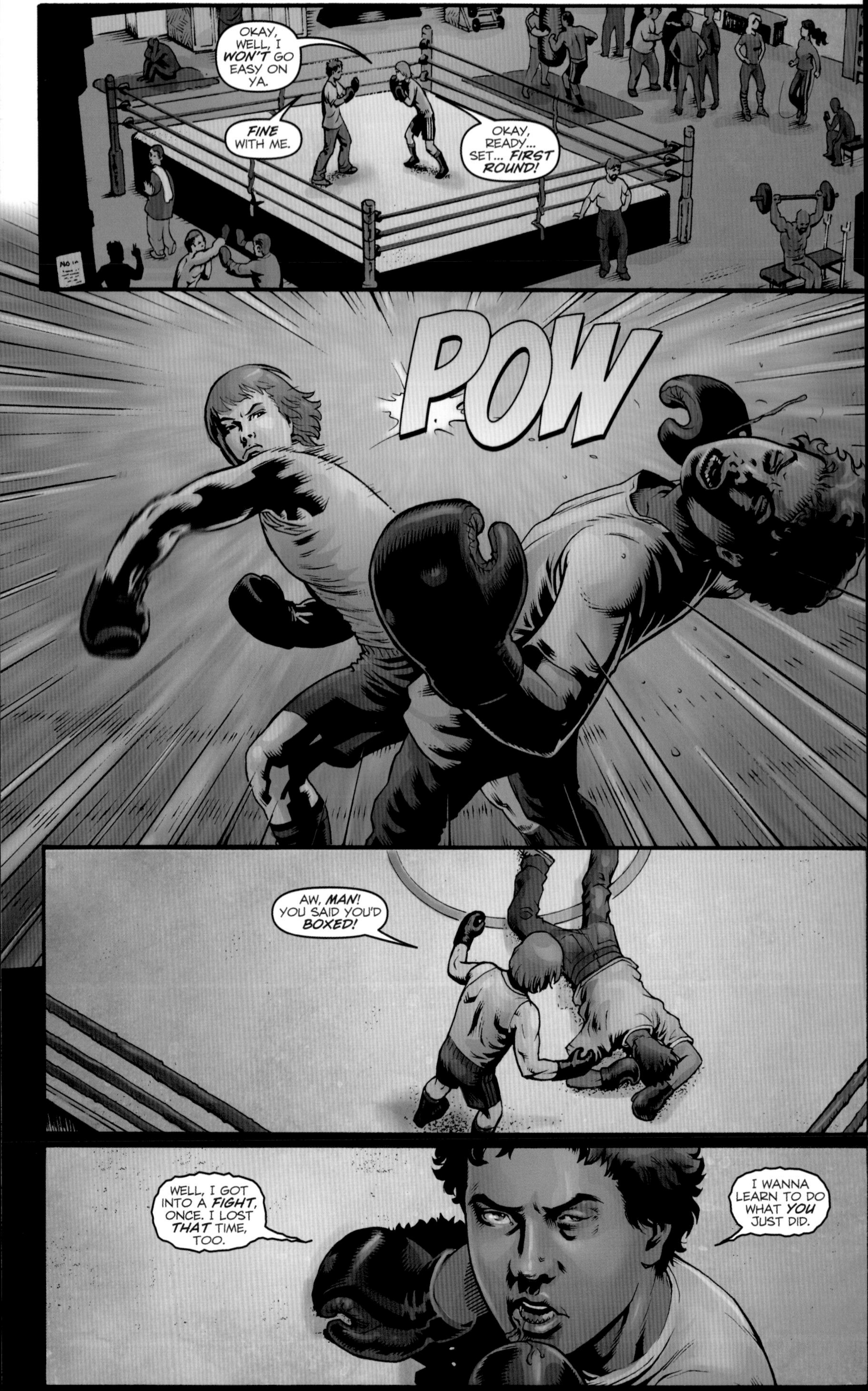

OKAY, WELL, I WON'T GO EASY ON YA.
FINE WITH ME.
OKAY, READY... SET... FIRST ROUND!
POW
AW, MAN! YOU SAID YOU'D BOXED!
WELL, I GOT INTO A FIGHT, ONCE. I LOST THAT TIME, TOO.
I WANNA LEARN TO DO WHAT YOU JUST DID.

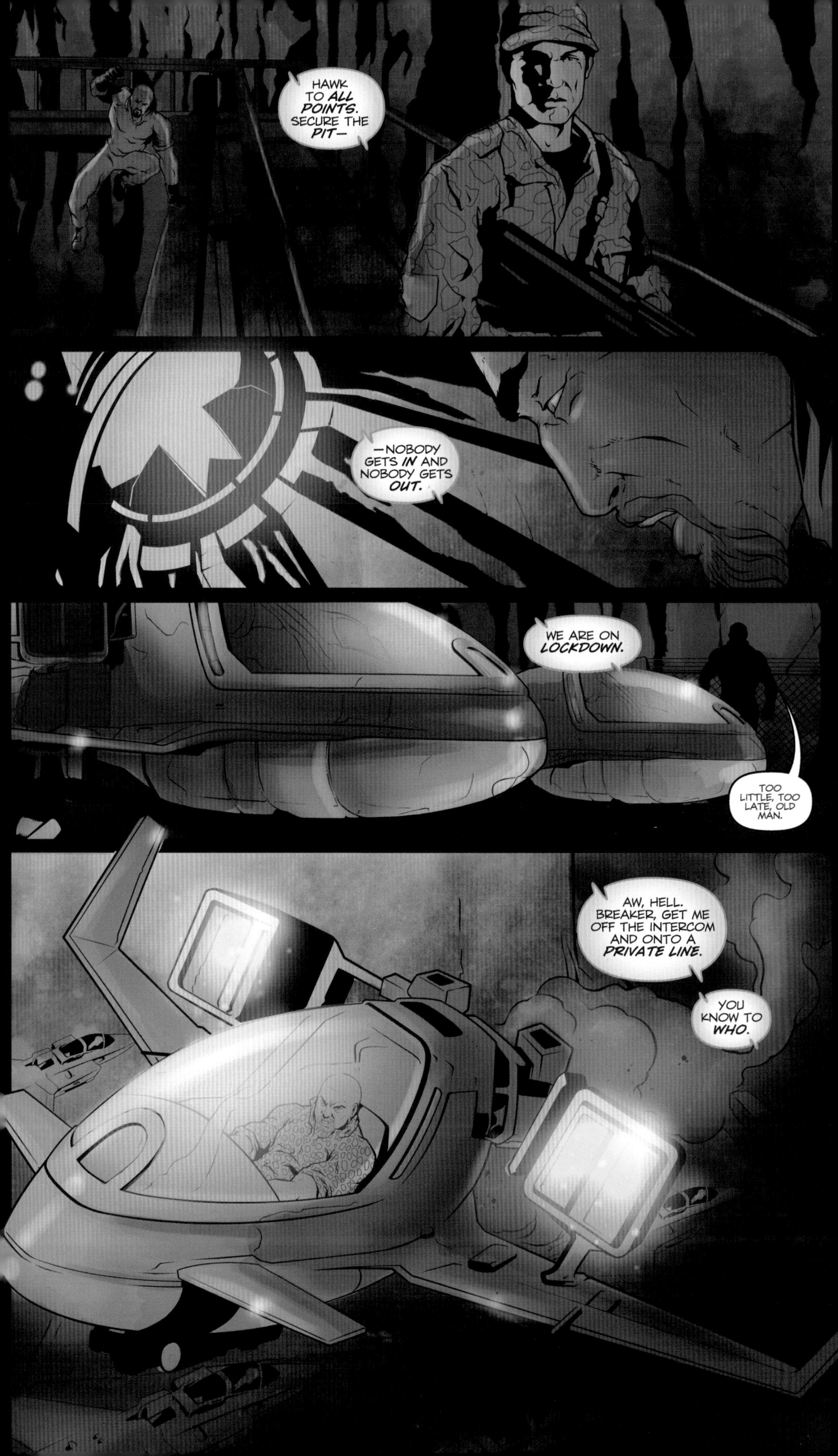
HAWK TO ALL POINTS. SECURE THE PIT—
—NOBODY GETS IN AND NOBODY GETS OUT.
WE ARE ON LOCKDOWN.
TOO LITTLE, TOO LATE, OLD MAN.
AW, HELL. BREAKER, GET ME OFF THE INTERCOM AND ONTO A PRIVATE LINE.
YOU KNOW TO WHO.

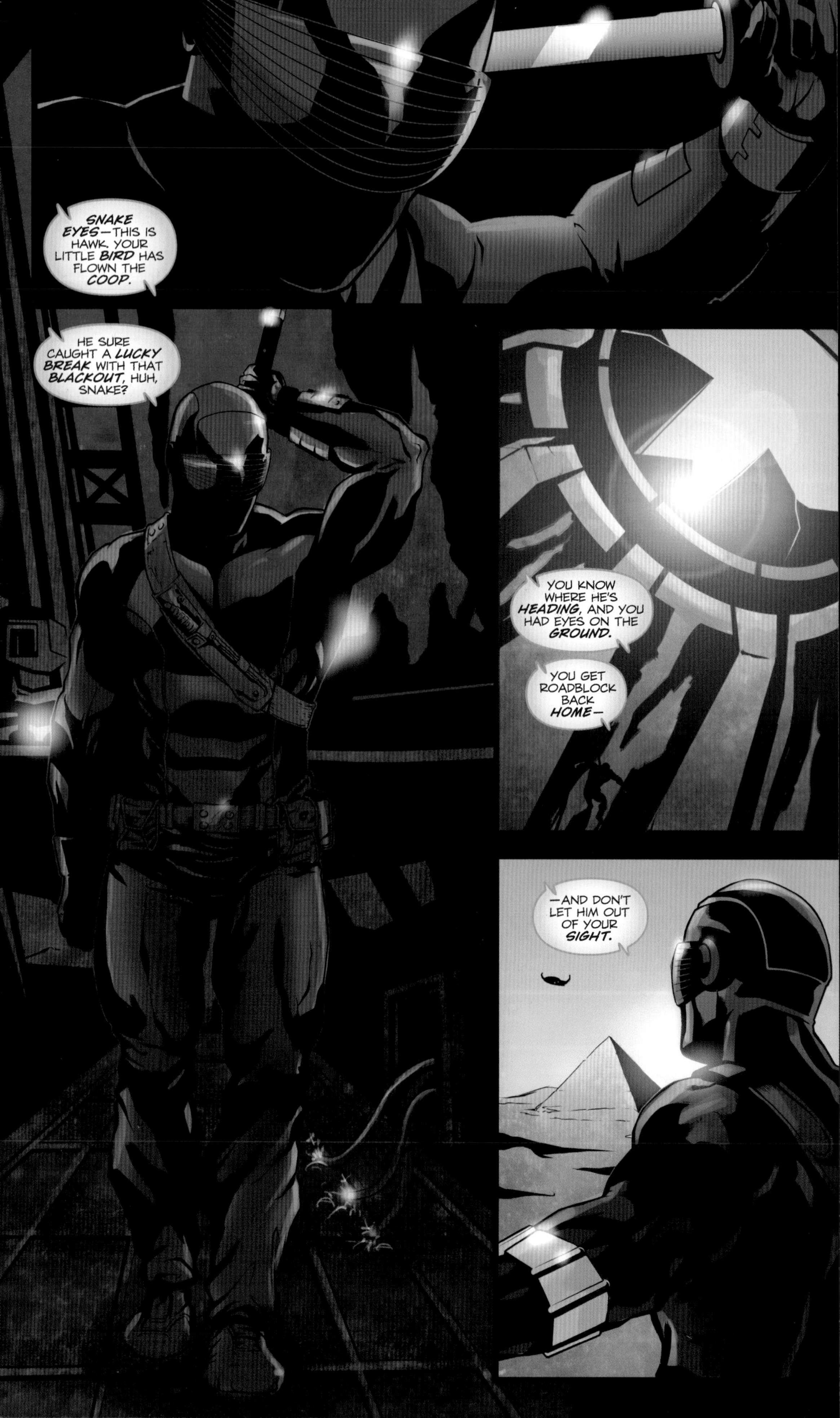
SNAKE EYES—THIS IS HAWK. YOUR LITTLE BIRD HAS FLOWN THE COOP.
HE SURE CAUGHT A LUCKY BREAK WITH THAT BLACKOUT, HUH, SNAKE?
YOU KNOW WHERE HE'S HEADING, AND YOU HAD EYES ON THE GROUND.
YOU GET ROADBLOCK BACK HOME—
—AND DON'T LET HIM OUT OF YOUR SIGHT.

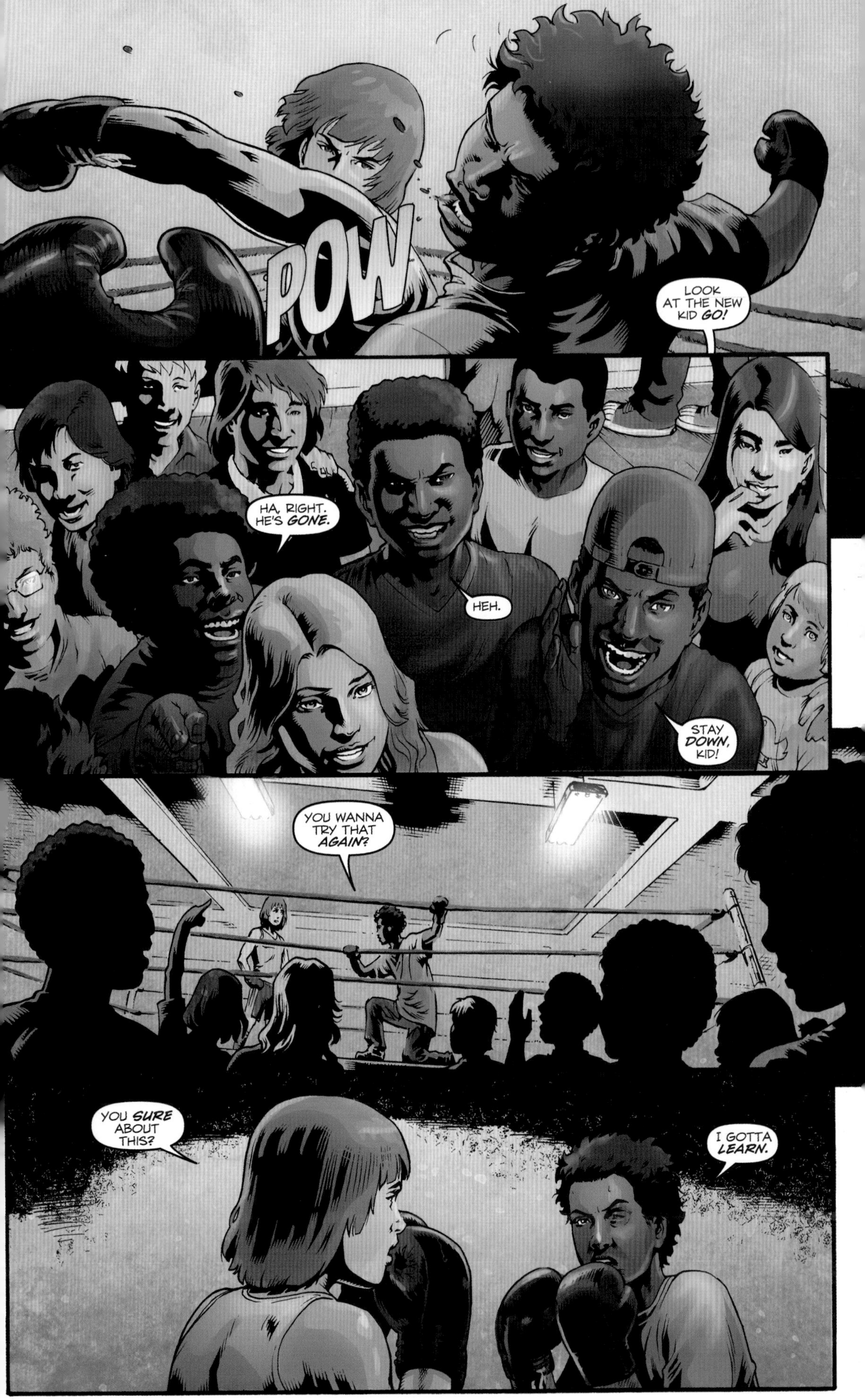
POW
LOOK AT THE NEW KID GO!
HA, RIGHT. HE'S GONE.
HEH.
STAY DOWN, KID!
YOU WANNA TRY THAT AGAIN?
YOU SURE ABOUT THIS?
I GOTTA LEARN.

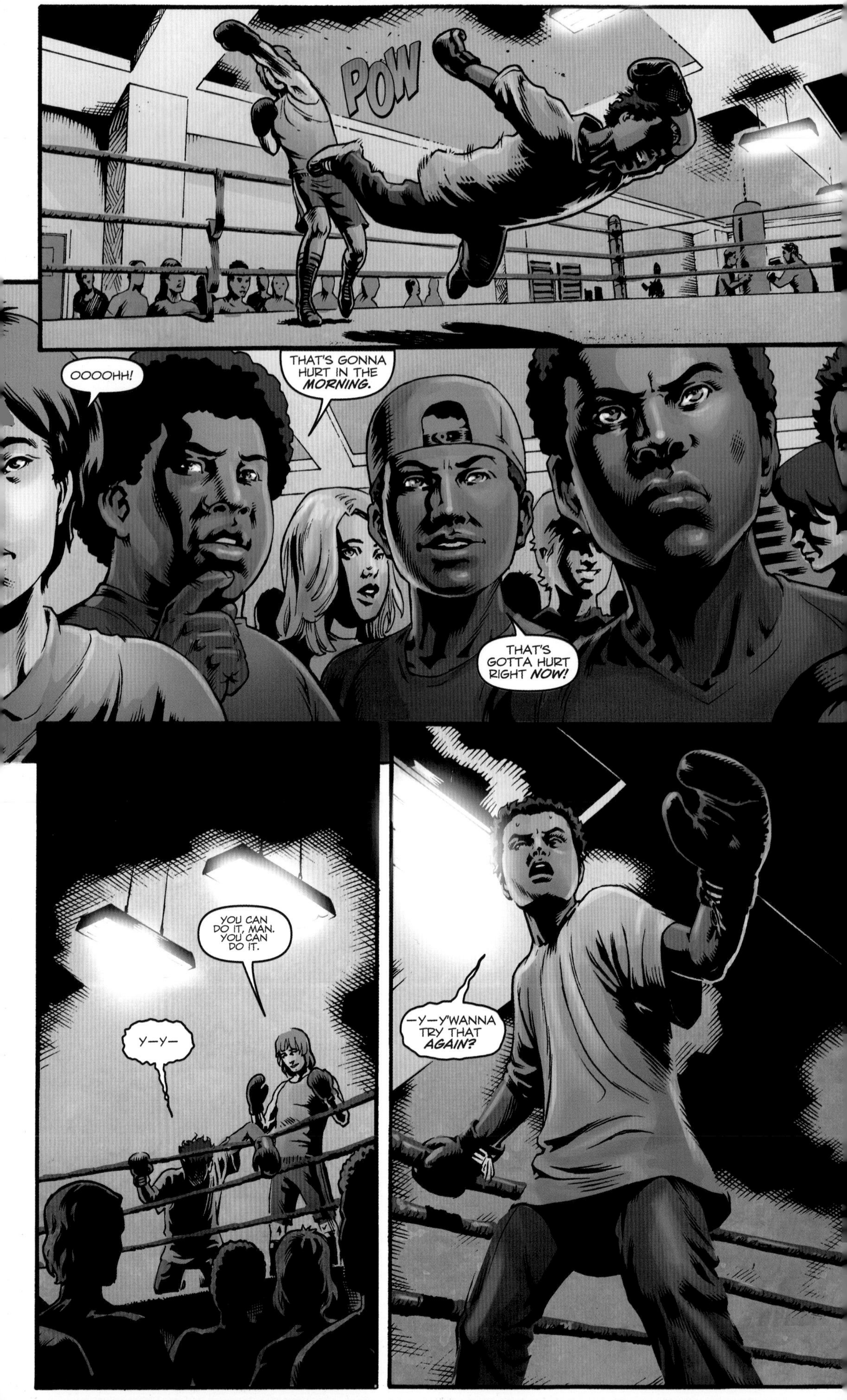
POW
OOOOHH!
THAT'S GONNA HURT IN THE MORNING.
THAT'S GOTTA HURT RIGHT NOW!
YOU CAN DO IT, MAN. YOU CAN DO IT.
Y—Y—
—Y—Y'WANNA TRY THAT AGAIN?

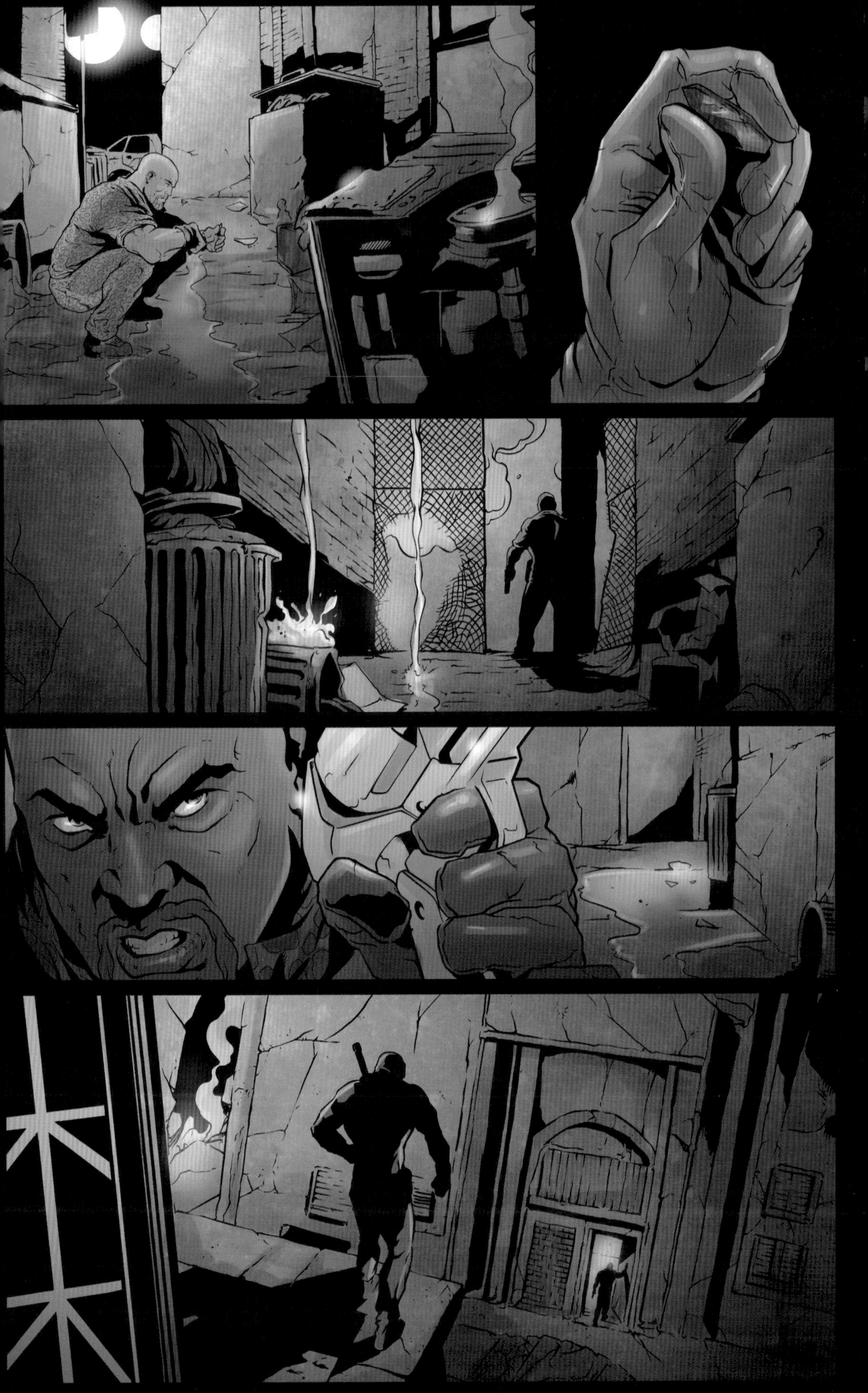

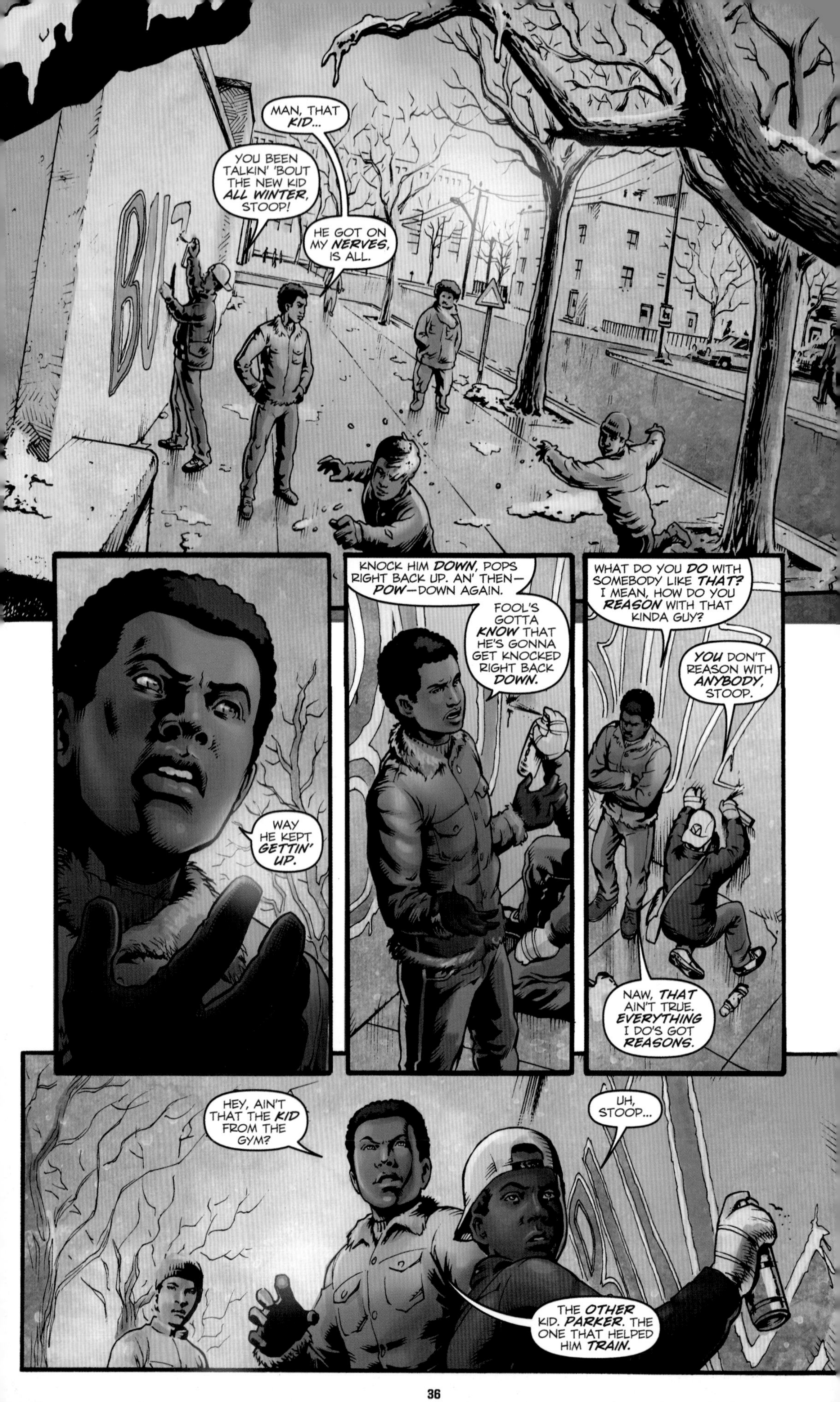

MAN, THAT KID...
YOU BEEN TALKIN' 'BOUT THE NEW KID ALL WINTER, STOOP!
HE GOT ON MY NERVES, IS ALL.
WAY HE KEPT GETTIN' UP.
KNOCK HIM DOWN, POPS RIGHT BACK UP. AN' THEN—POW—DOWN AGAIN.
FOOL'S GOTTA KNOW THAT HE'S GONNA GET KNOCKED RIGHT BACK DOWN.
WHAT DO YOU DO WITH SOMEBODY LIKE THAT? I MEAN, HOW DO YOU REASON WITH THAT KINDA GUY?
YOU DON'T REASON WITH ANYBODY, STOOP.
NAW, THAT AIN'T TRUE. EVERYTHING I DO'S GOT REASONS.
HEY, AIN'T THAT THE KID FROM THE GYM?
UH, STOOP...
THE OTHER KID. PARKER. THE ONE THAT HELPED HIM TRAIN.

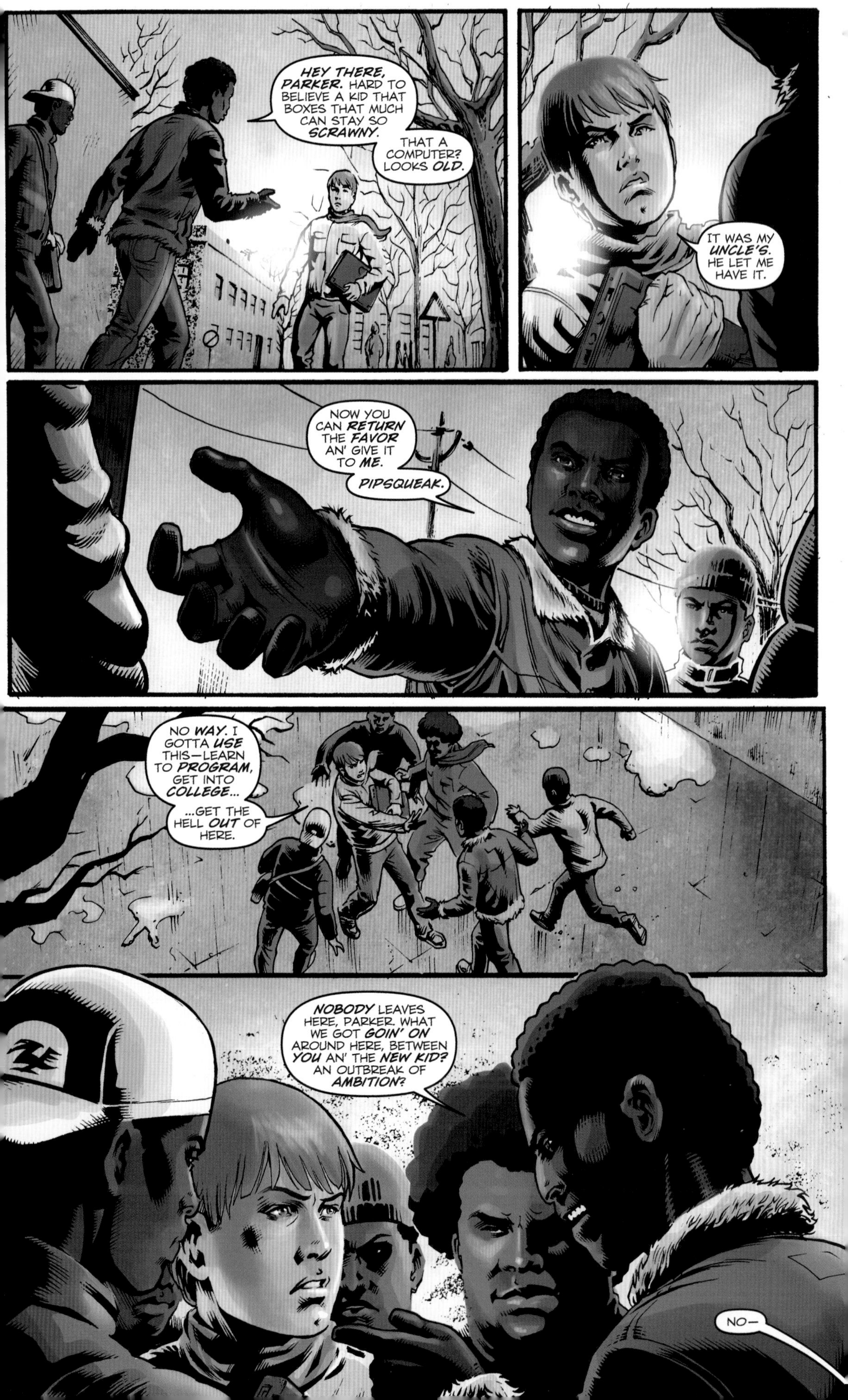
HEY THERE, PARKER. HARD TO BELIEVE A KID THAT BOXES THAT MUCH CAN STAY SO SCRAWNY.
THAT A COMPUTER? LOOKS OLD.
IT WAS MY UNCLE'S. HE LET ME HAVE IT.
NOW YOU CAN RETURN THE FAVOR AN' GIVE IT TO ME.
PIPSQUEAK.
NO WAY. I GOTTA USE THIS—LEARN TO PROGRAM, GET INTO COLLEGE...
...GET THE HELL OUT OF HERE.
NOBODY LEAVES HERE, PARKER. WHAT WE GOT GOIN' ON AROUND HERE, BETWEEN YOU AN' THE NEW KID? AN OUTBREAK OF AMBITION?
NO—

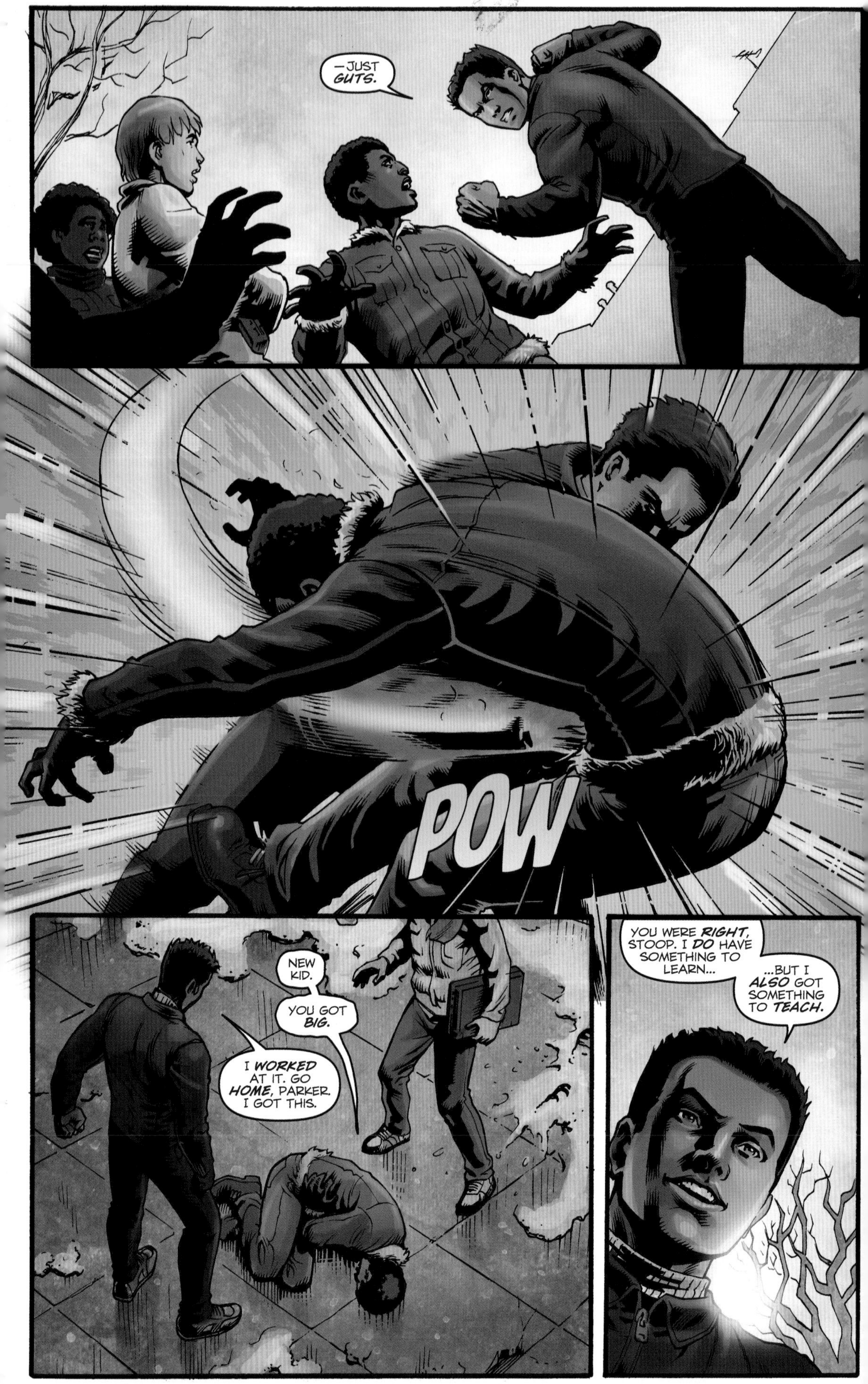
—JUST GUTS.
POW
NEW KID.
YOU GOT BIG.
I WORKED AT IT. GO HOME, PARKER. I GOT THIS.
YOU WERE RIGHT, STOOP. I DO HAVE SOMETHING TO LEARN...
...BUT I ALSO GOT SOMETHING TO TEACH.

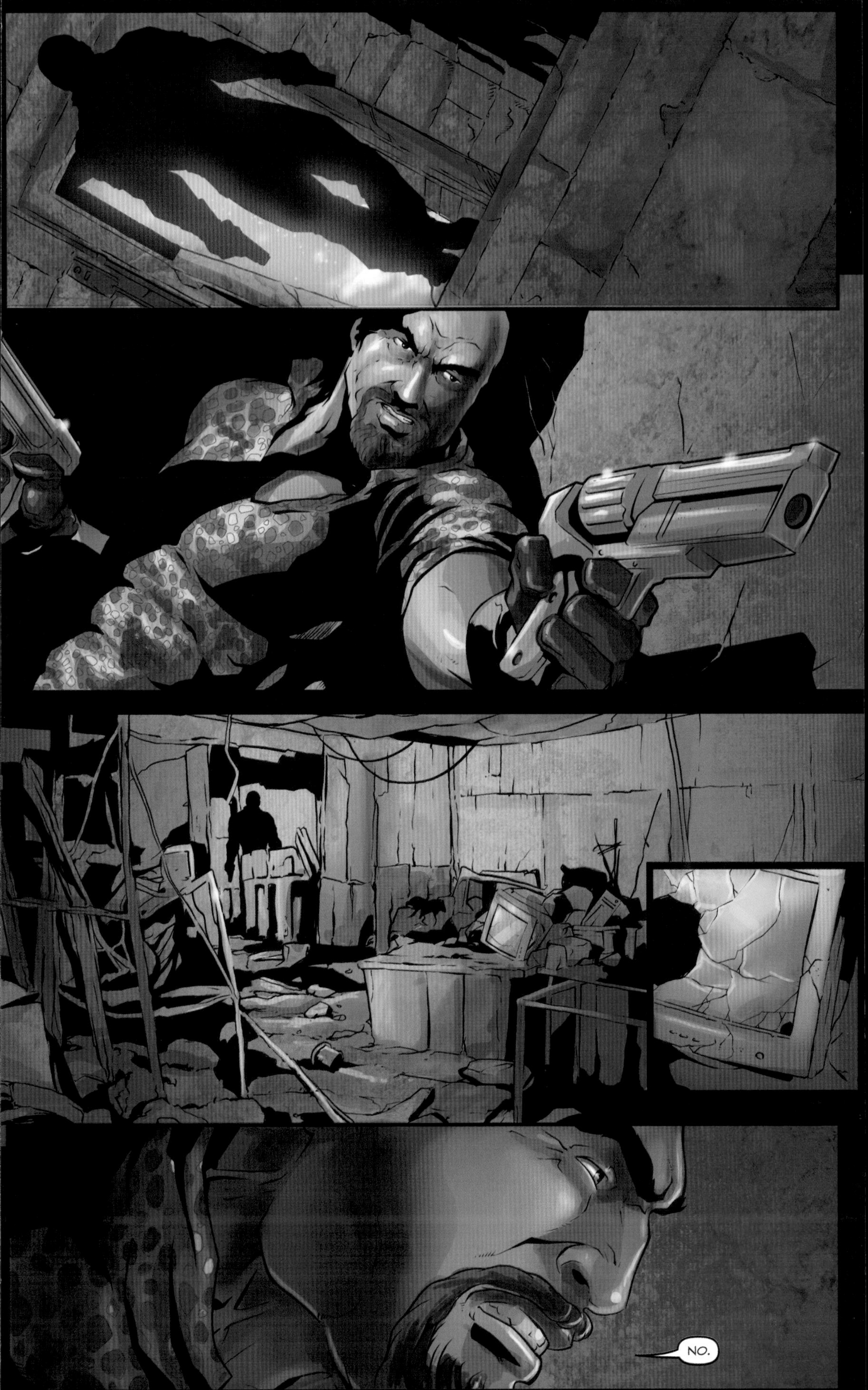
NO.

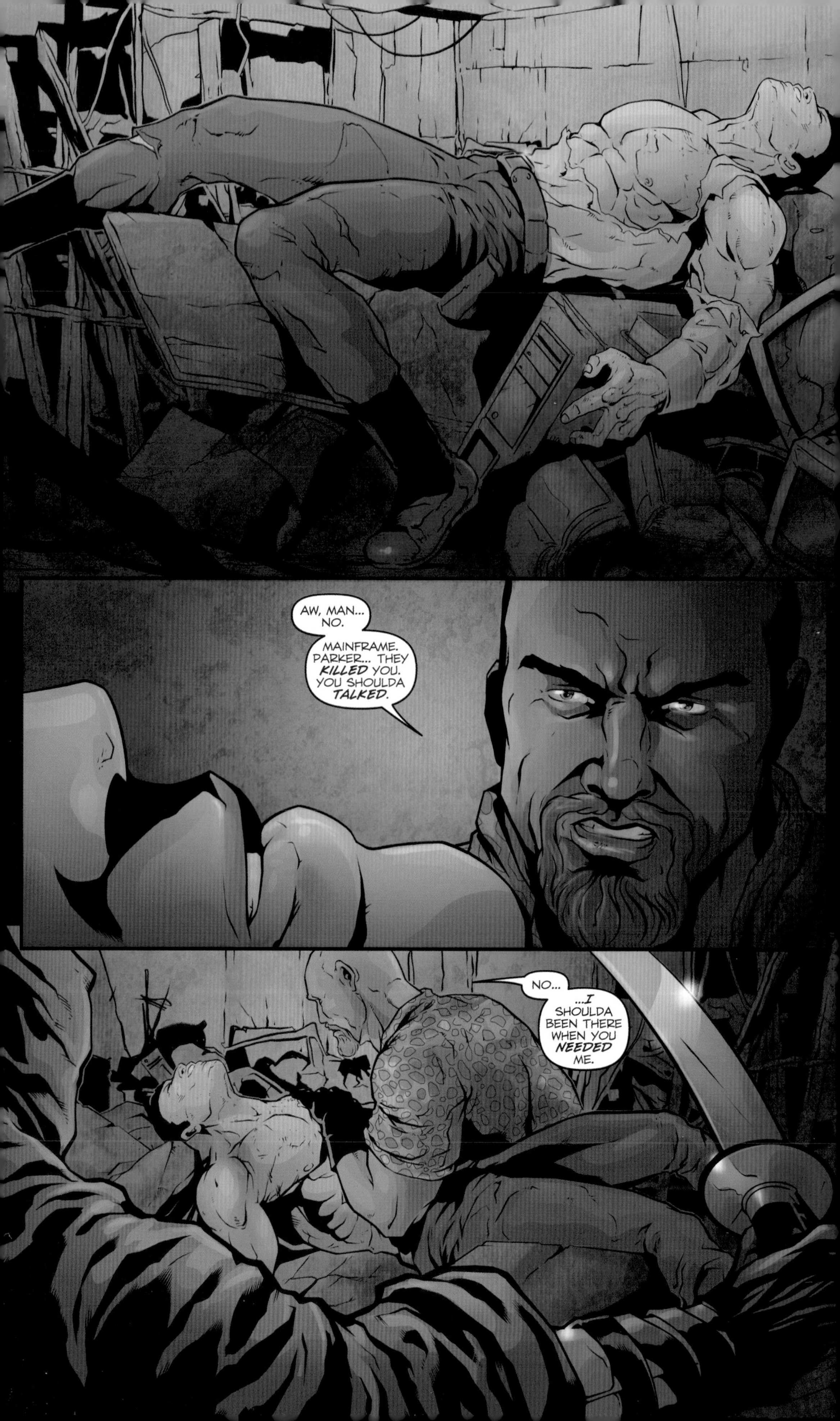
AW, MAN... NO.
MAINFRAME. PARKER... THEY **KILLED** YOU. YOU SHOULDA **TALKED**.
NO...
...**I** SHOULDA BEEN THERE WHEN YOU **NEEDED** ME.

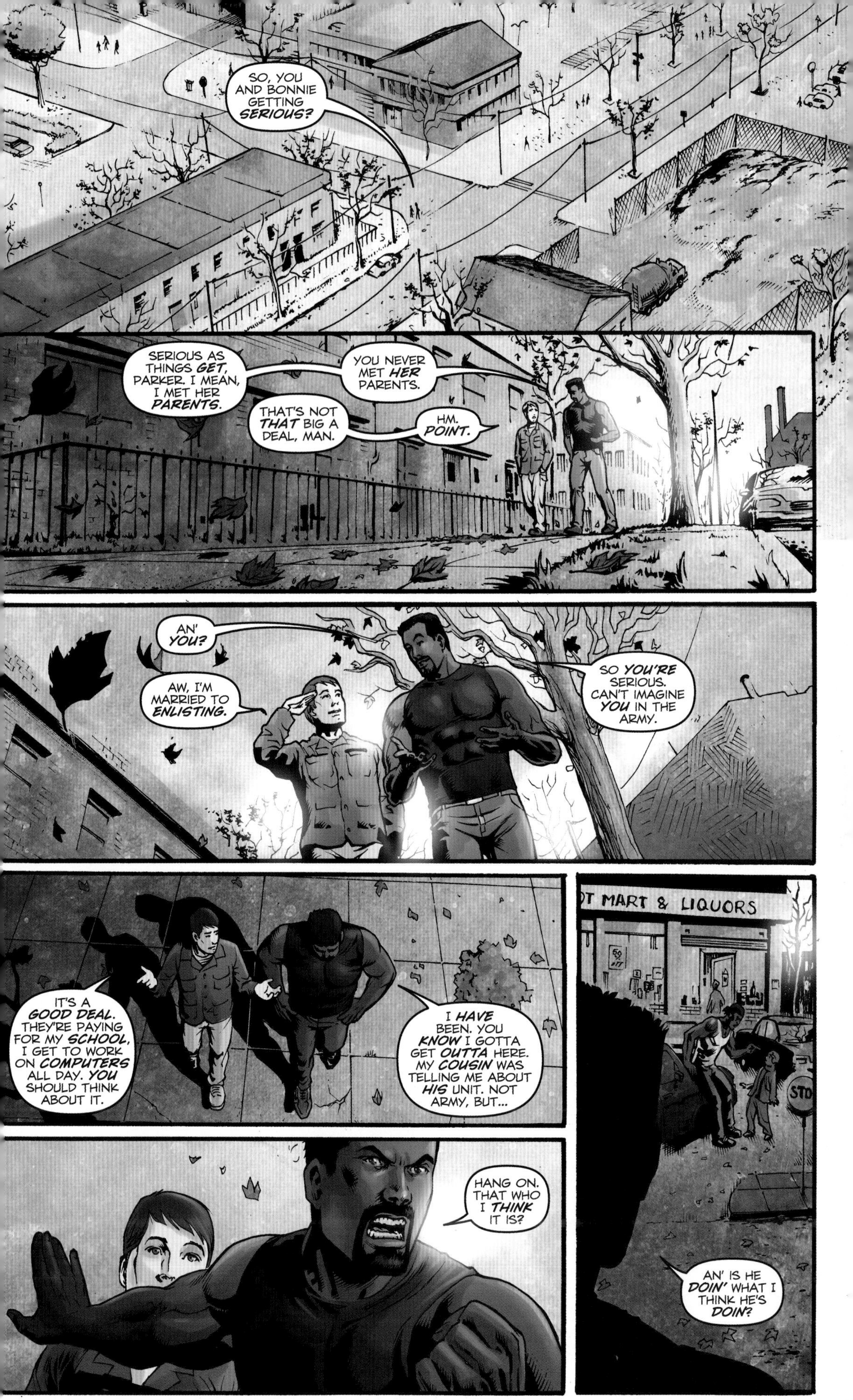
SO, YOU AND BONNIE GETTING SERIOUS?
SERIOUS AS THINGS GET, PARKER. I MEAN, I MET HER PARENTS.
YOU NEVER MET HER PARENTS.
THAT'S NOT THAT BIG A DEAL, MAN.
HM. POINT.
AN' YOU?
AW, I'M MARRIED TO ENLISTING.
SO YOU'RE SERIOUS. CAN'T IMAGINE YOU IN THE ARMY.
IT'S A GOOD DEAL. THEY'RE PAYING FOR MY SCHOOL, I GET TO WORK ON COMPUTERS ALL DAY. YOU SHOULD THINK ABOUT IT.
I HAVE BEEN. YOU KNOW I GOTTA GET OUTTA HERE. MY COUSIN WAS TELLING ME ABOUT HIS UNIT. NOT ARMY, BUT...
HANG ON. THAT WHO I THINK IT IS?
OT MART & LIQUORS
AN' IS HE DOIN' WHAT I THINK HE'S DOIN?

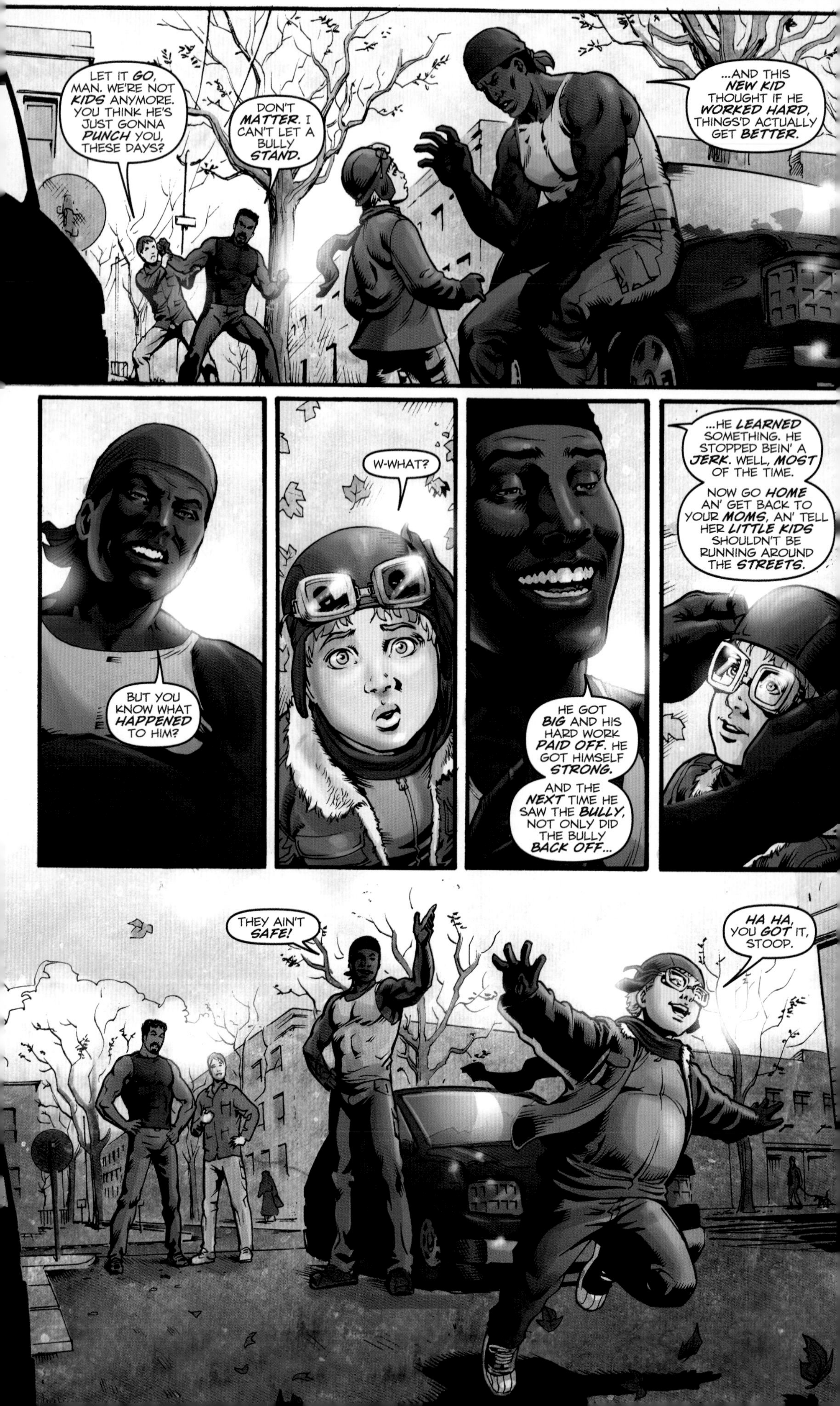

LET IT GO, MAN. WE'RE NOT KIDS ANYMORE. YOU THINK HE'S JUST GONNA PUNCH YOU, THESE DAYS?
DON'T MATTER. I CAN'T LET A BULLY STAND.
...AND THIS NEW KID THOUGHT IF HE WORKED HARD, THINGS'D ACTUALLY GET BETTER.
BUT YOU KNOW WHAT HAPPENED TO HIM?
W-WHAT?
HE GOT BIG AND HIS HARD WORK PAID OFF. HE GOT HIMSELF STRONG.
AND THE NEXT TIME HE SAW THE BULLY, NOT ONLY DID THE BULLY BACK OFF...
...HE LEARNED SOMETHING. HE STOPPED BEIN' A JERK. WELL, MOST OF THE TIME.
NOW GO HOME AN' GET BACK TO YOUR MOMS, AN' TELL HER LITTLE KIDS SHOULDN'T BE RUNNING AROUND THE STREETS.
THEY AIN'T SAFE!
HA HA, YOU GOT IT, STOOP.

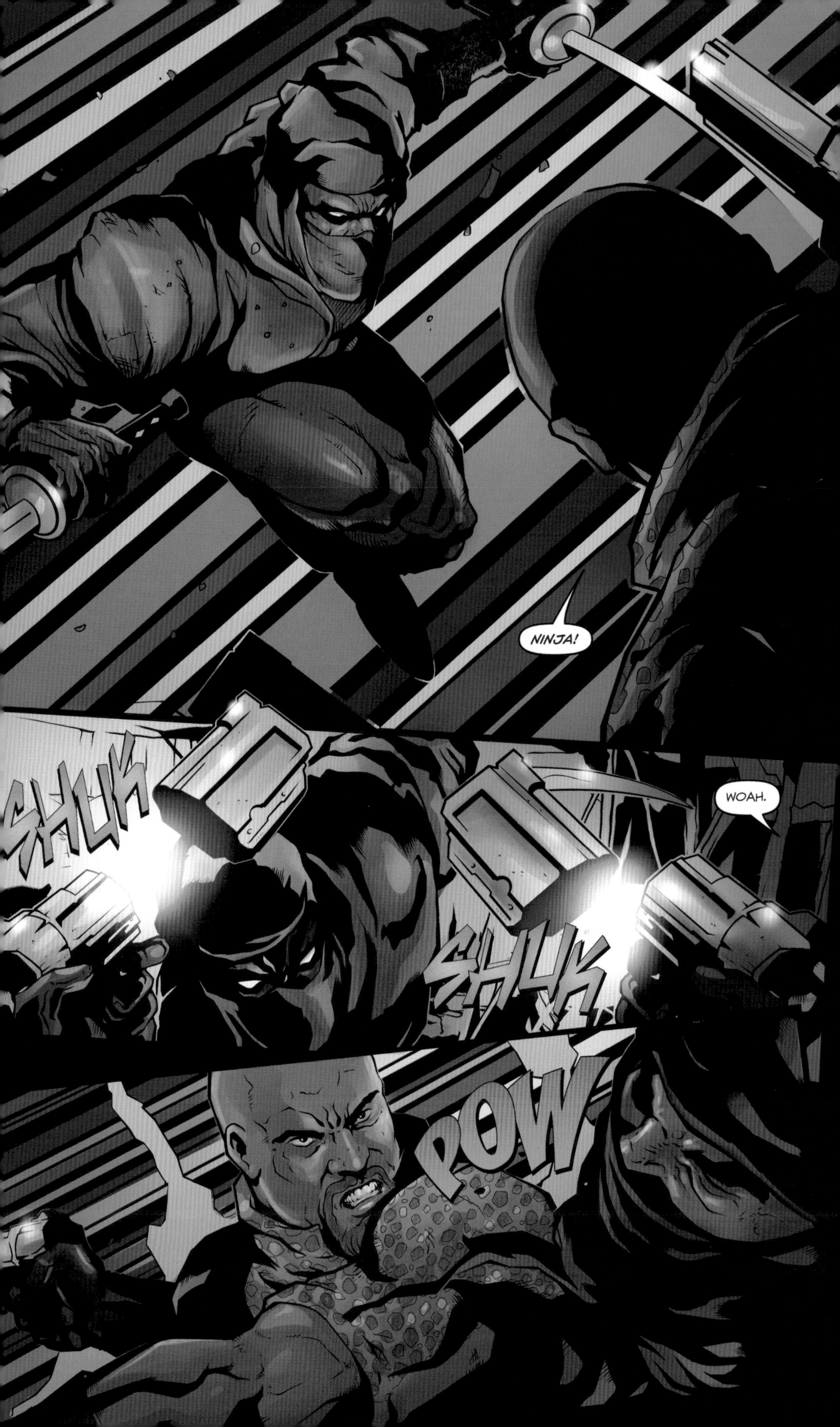
NINJA!
SHUK
WOAH.
SHUK
POW

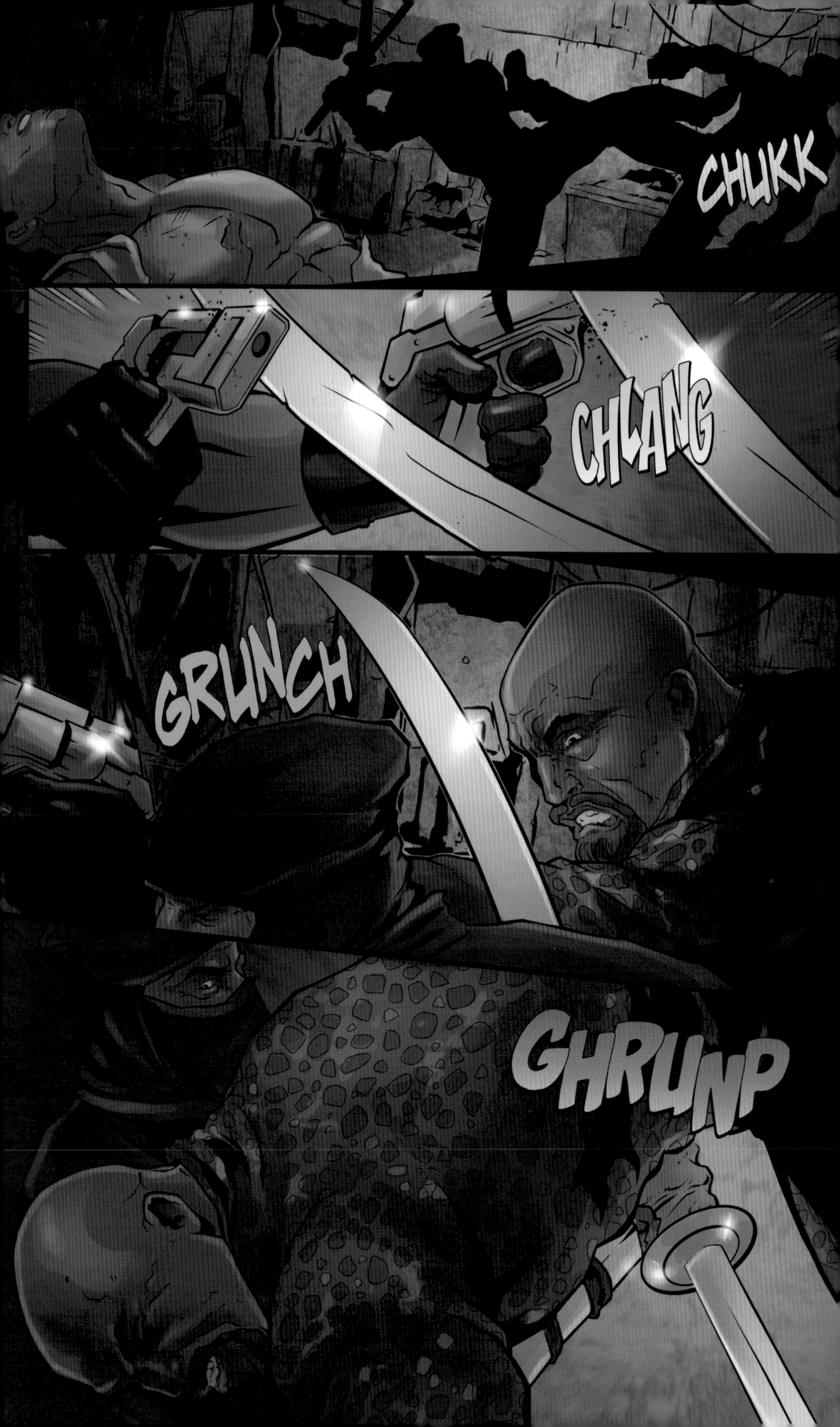
CHUKK
CHLANG
GRUNCH
GHRUNP

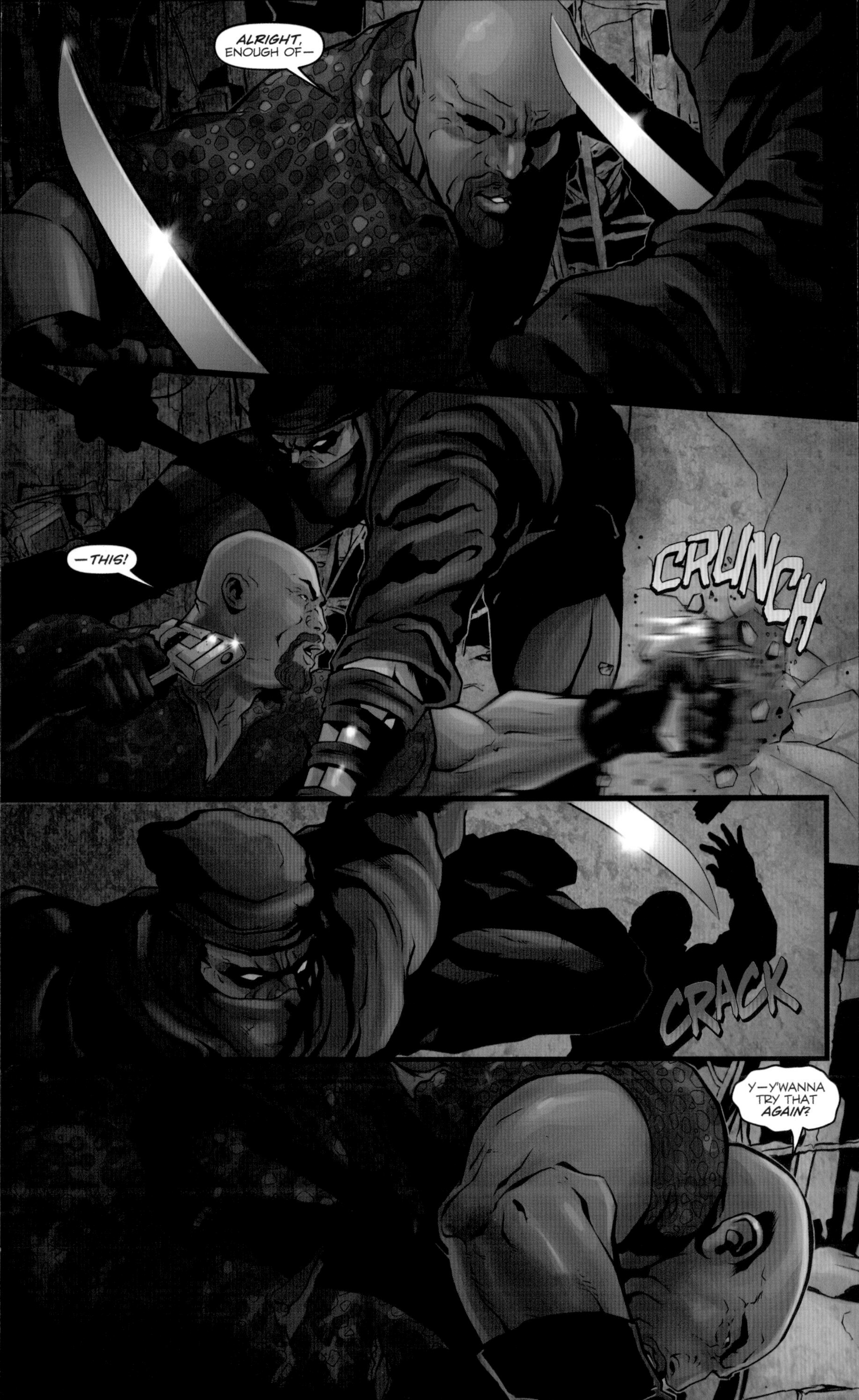
ALRIGHT, ENOUGH OF—
—THIS!
CRUNCH
CRACK
Y—Y'WANNA TRY THAT AGAIN?

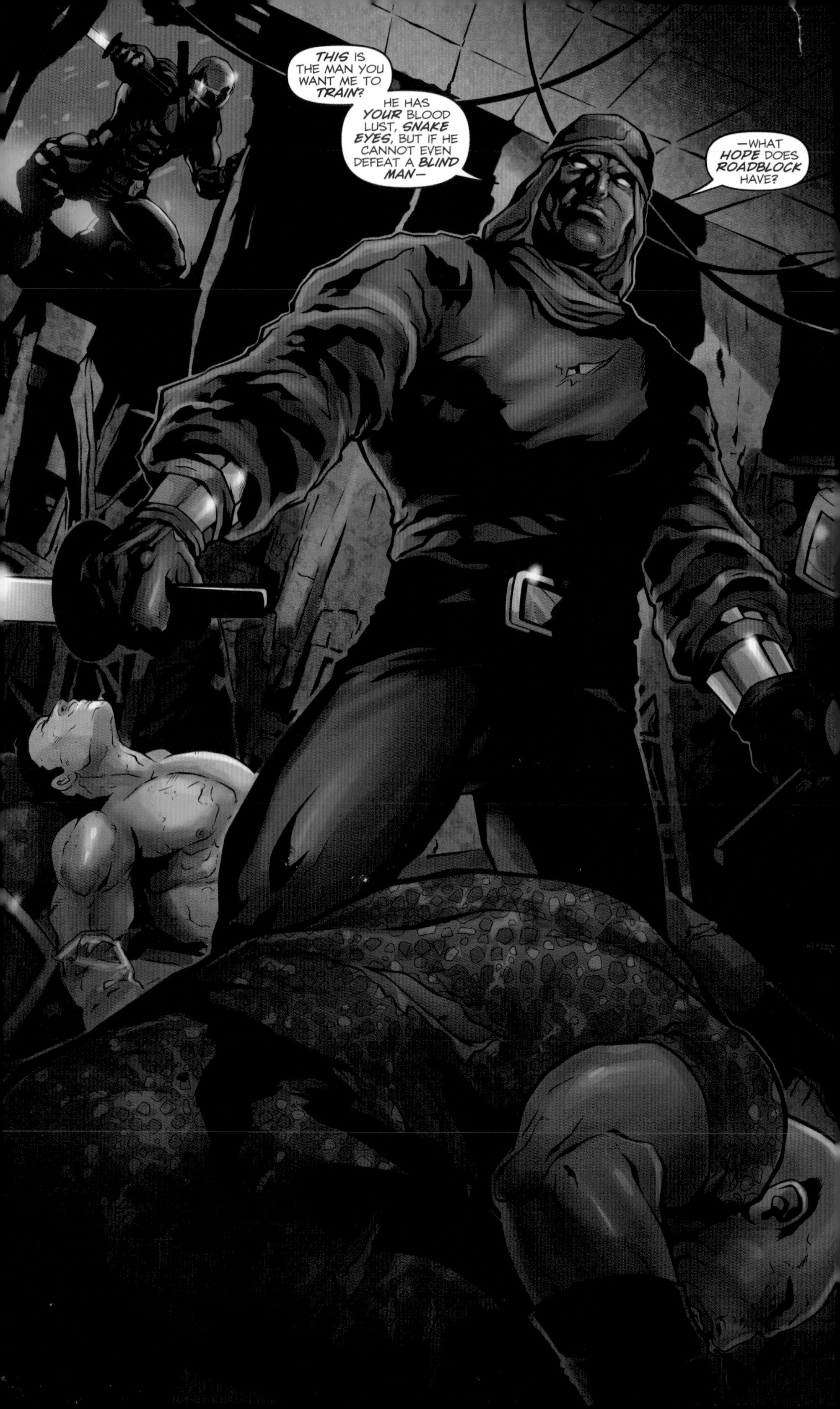
THIS IS THE MAN YOU WANT ME TO TRAIN?
HE HAS YOUR BLOOD LUST, SNAKE EYES, BUT IF HE CANNOT EVEN DEFEAT A BLIND MAN—
—WHAT HOPE DOES ROADBLOCK HAVE?

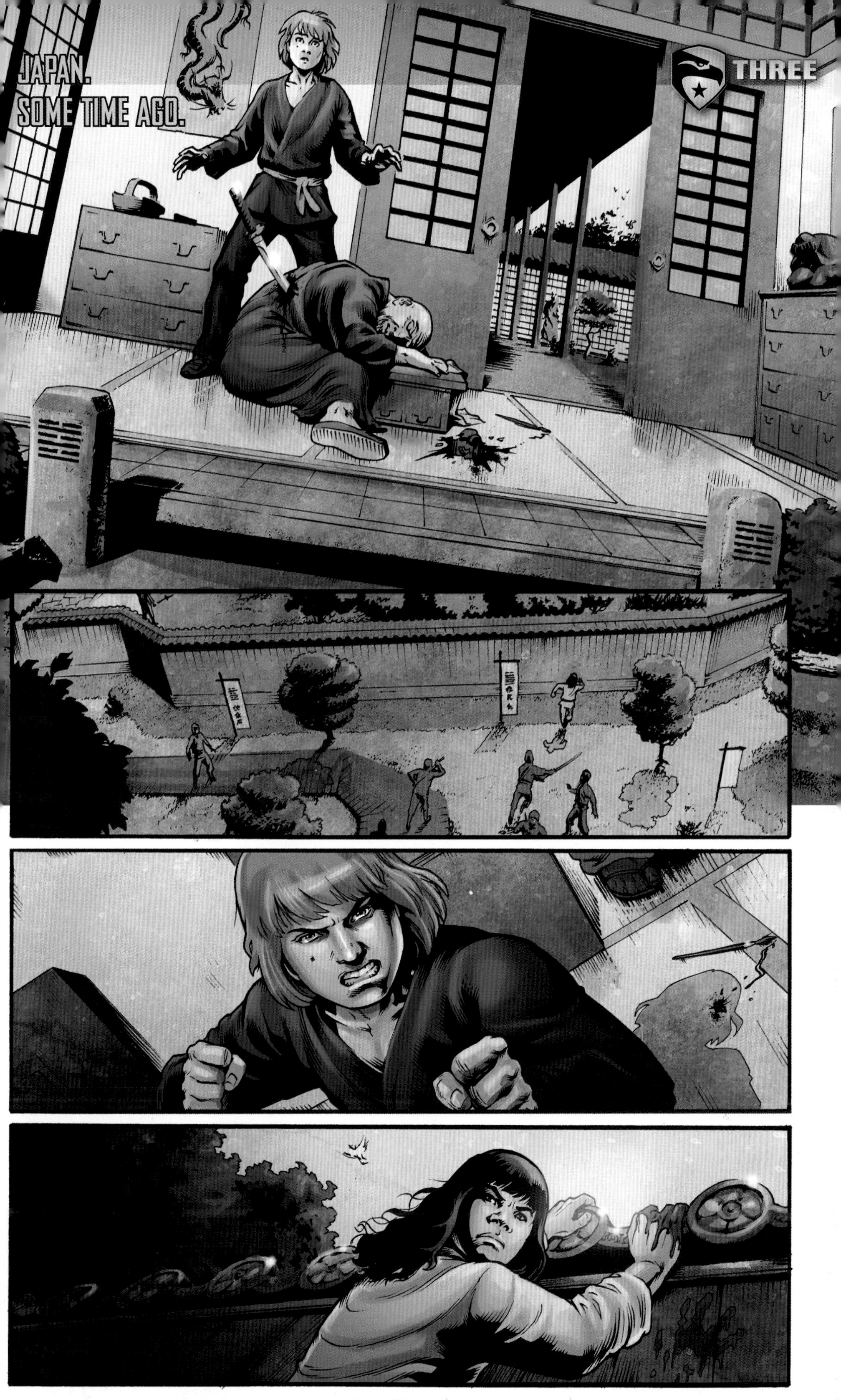
JAPAN.
SOME TIME AGO.
THREE

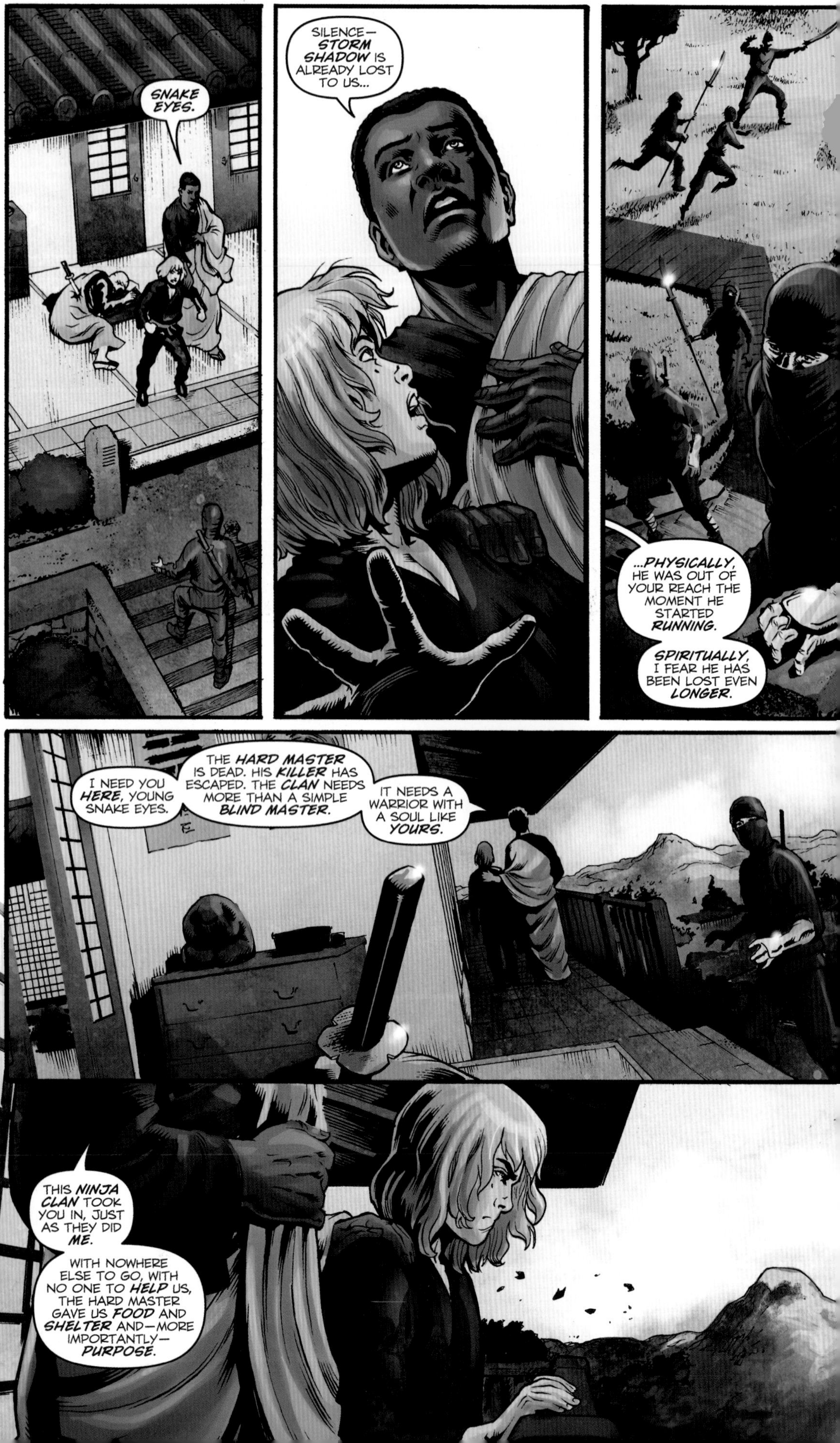
SNAKE EYES.
SILENCE— STORM SHADOW IS ALREADY LOST TO US...
...PHYSICALLY, HE WAS OUT OF YOUR REACH THE MOMENT HE STARTED RUNNING.
SPIRITUALLY, I FEAR HE HAS BEEN LOST EVEN LONGER.
I NEED YOU HERE, YOUNG SNAKE EYES.
THE HARD MASTER IS DEAD. HIS KILLER HAS ESCAPED. THE CLAN NEEDS MORE THAN A SIMPLE BLIND MASTER.
IT NEEDS A WARRIOR WITH A SOUL LIKE YOURS.
THIS NINJA CLAN TOOK YOU IN, JUST AS THEY DID ME.
WITH NOWHERE ELSE TO GO, WITH NO ONE TO HELP US, THE HARD MASTER GAVE US FOOD AND SHELTER AND—MORE IMPORTANTLY— PURPOSE.

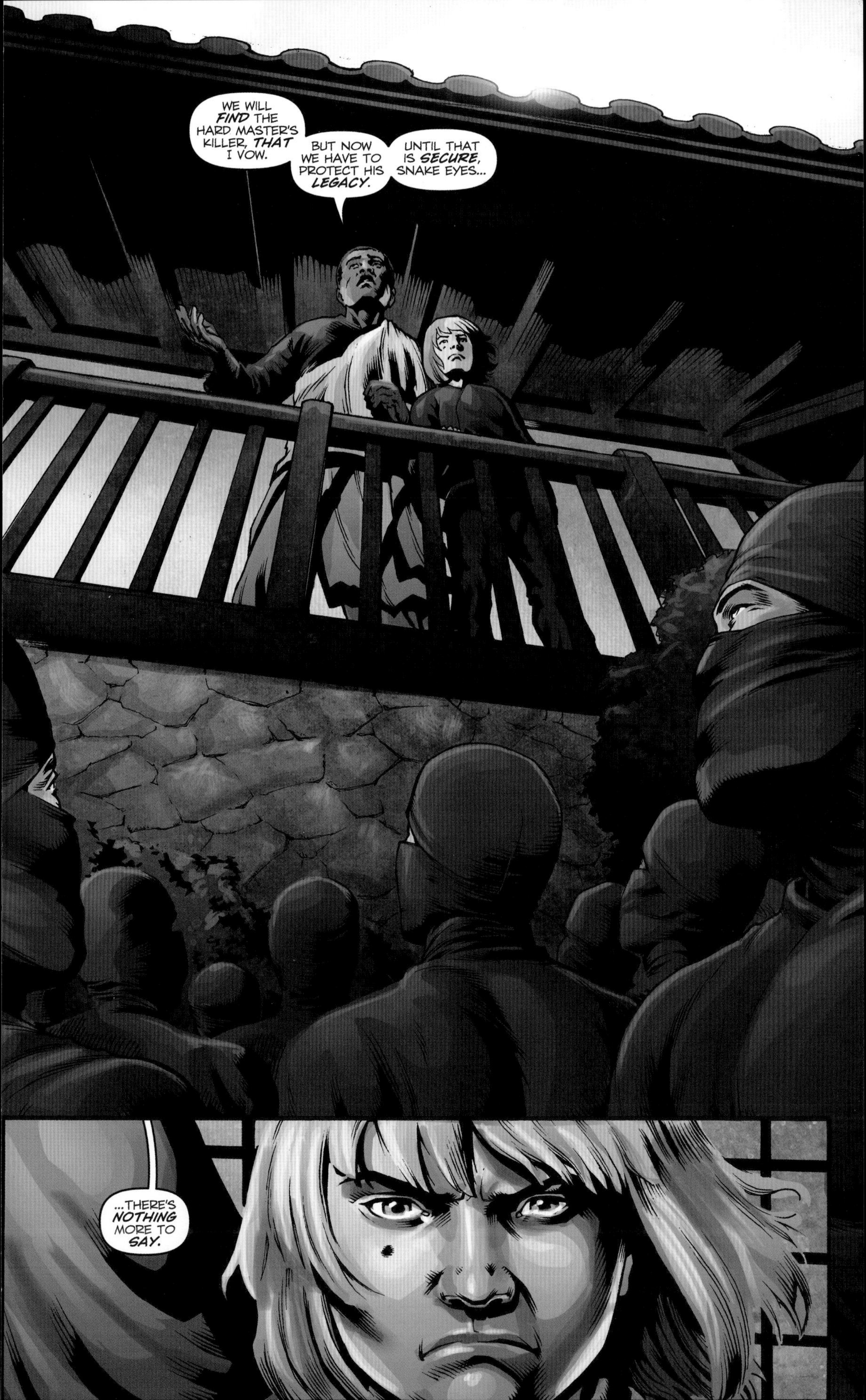

WE WILL FIND THE HARD MASTER'S KILLER, THAT I VOW.
BUT NOW WE HAVE TO PROTECT HIS LEGACY.
UNTIL THAT IS SECURE, SNAKE EYES...
...THERE'S NOTHING MORE TO SAY.

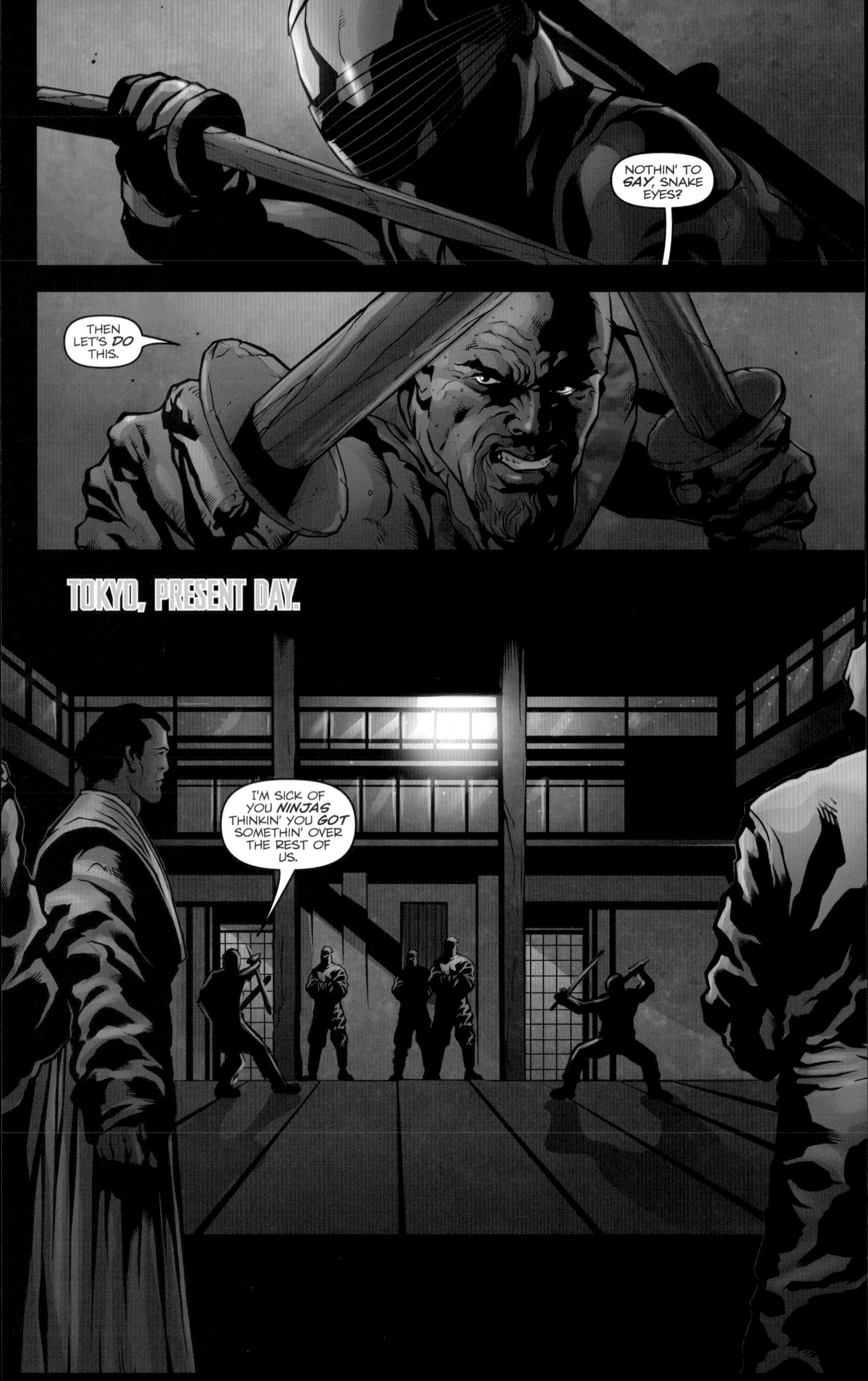
NOTHIN' TO SAY, SNAKE EYES?
THEN LET'S DO THIS.
TOKYO, PRESENT DAY.
I'M SICK OF YOU NINJAS THINKIN' YOU GOT SOMETHIN' OVER THE REST OF US.

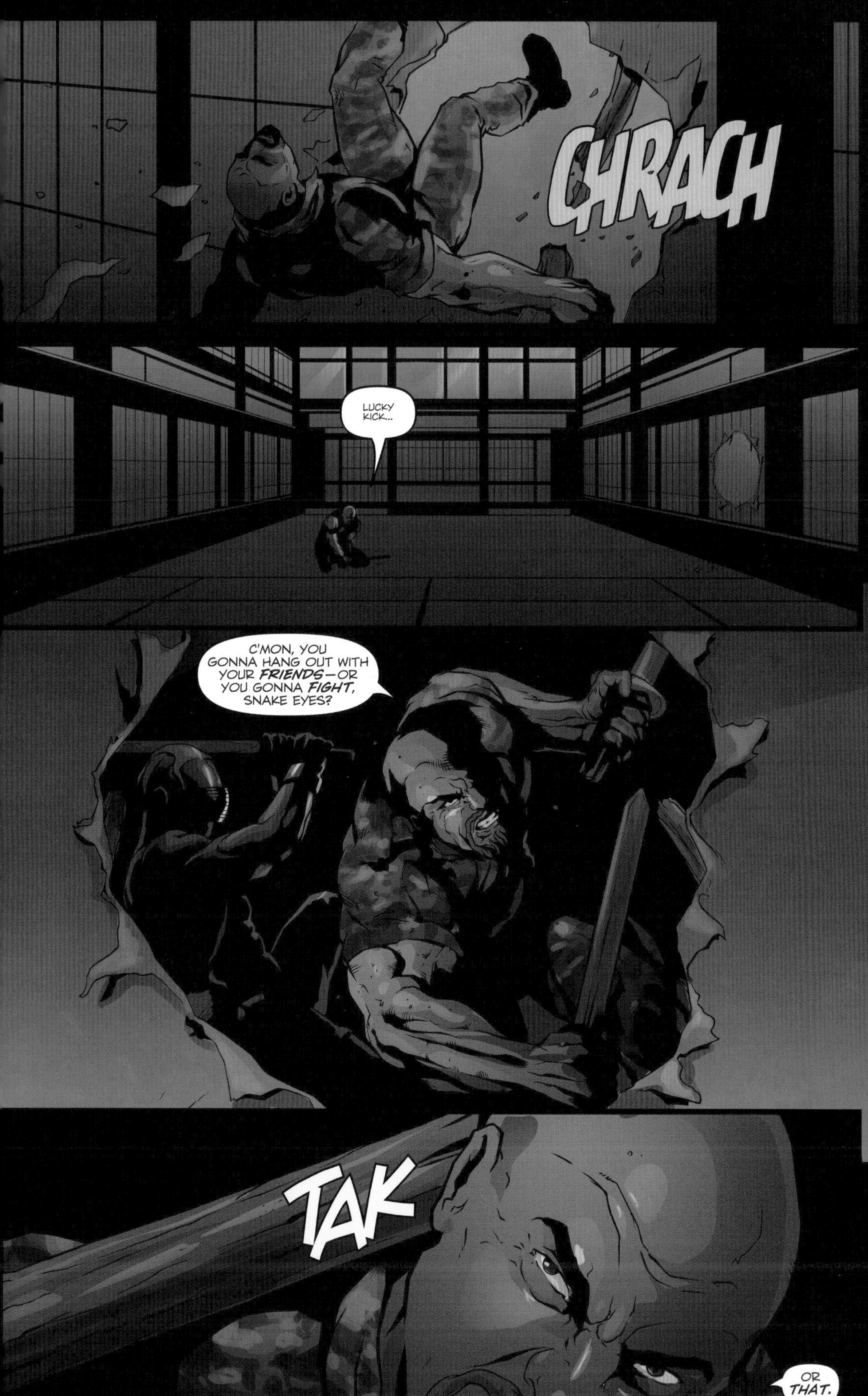
CHRACH
LUCKY KICK...
C'MON, YOU GONNA HANG OUT WITH YOUR *FRIENDS*—OR YOU GONNA *FIGHT*, SNAKE EYES?
TAK
OR *THAT.*

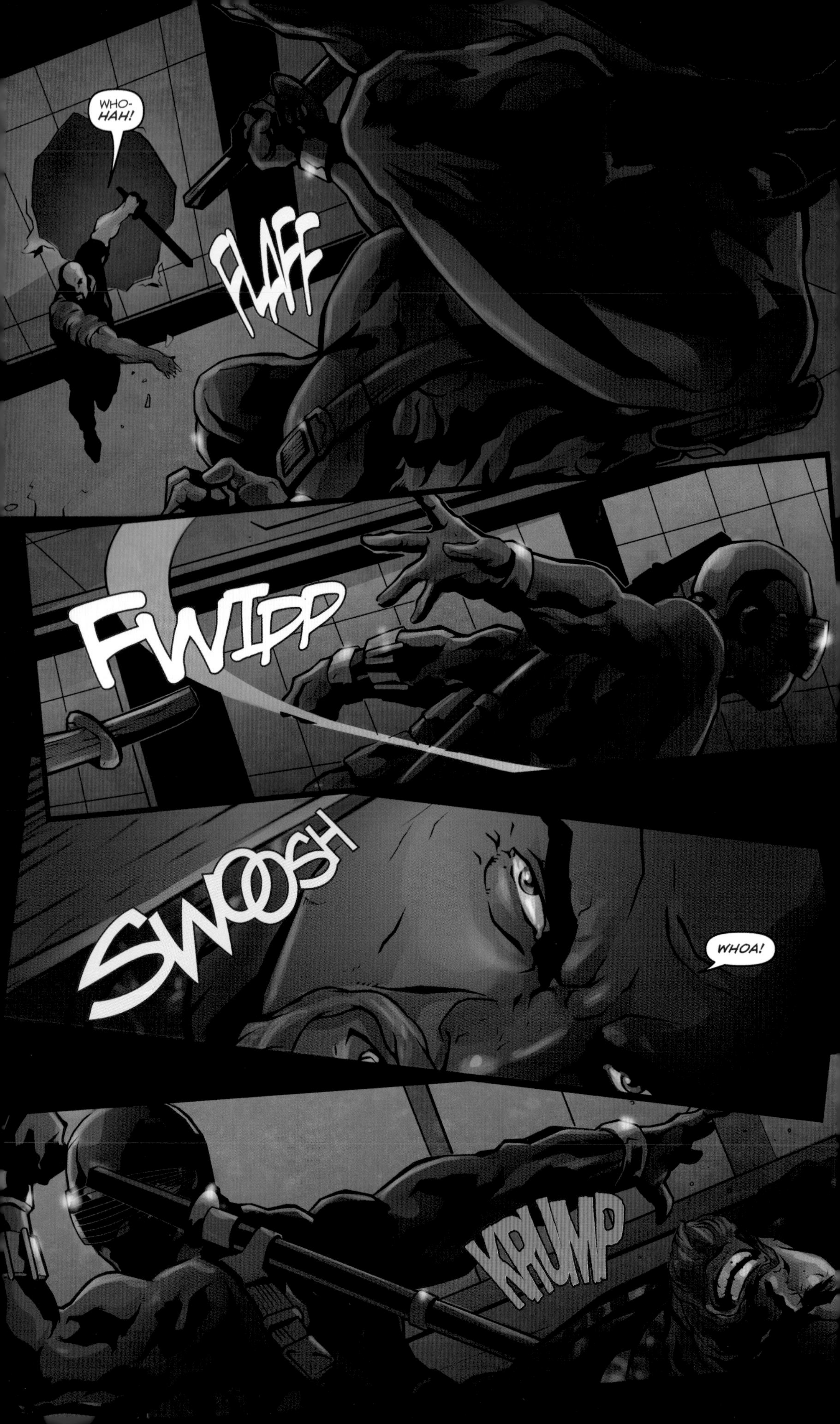
WHO-HAH!
PLAFF
FWIPP
SWOOSH
WHOA!
KRUMP

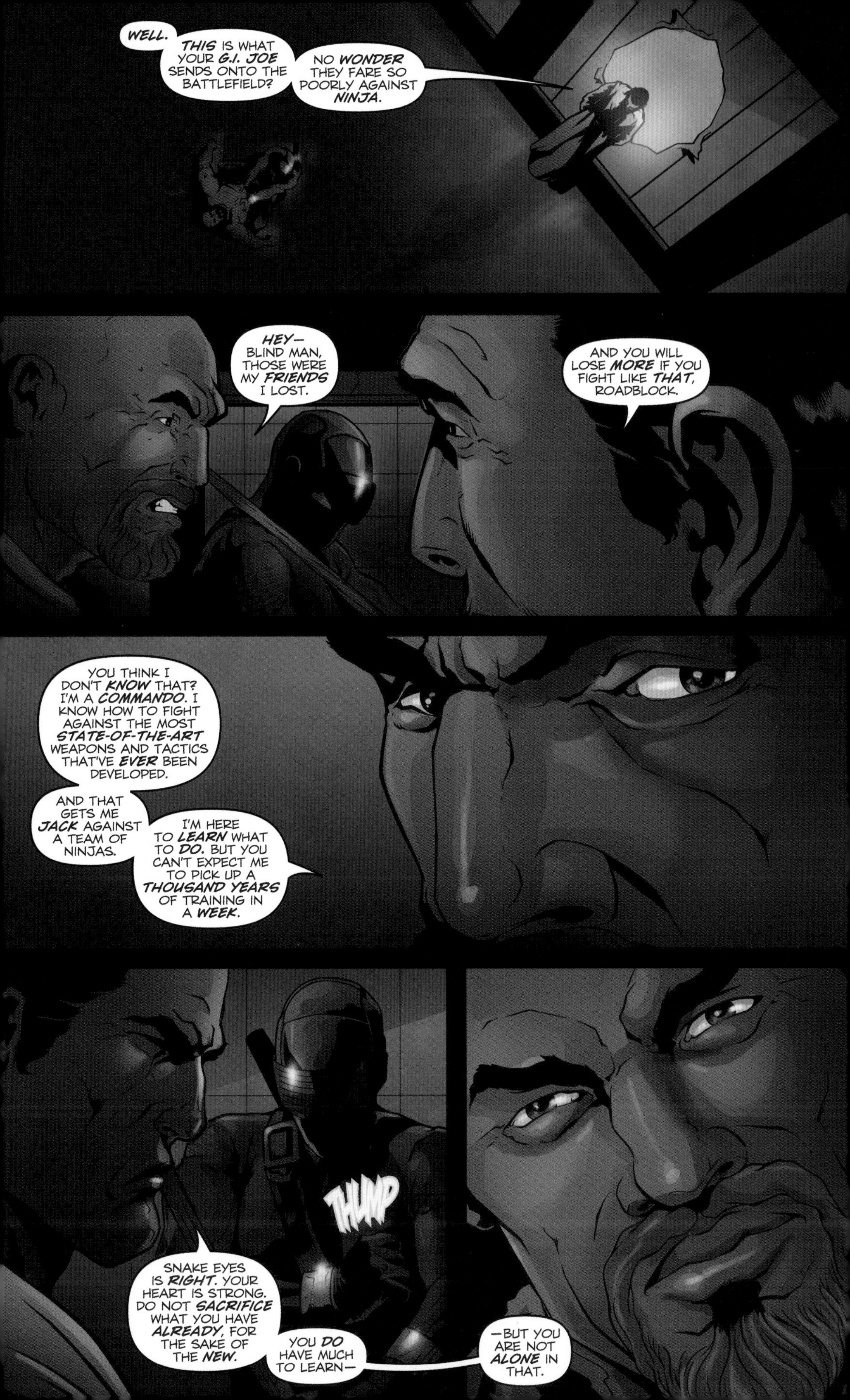
WELL.
THIS IS WHAT YOUR G.I. JOE SENDS ONTO THE BATTLEFIELD?
NO WONDER THEY FARE SO POORLY AGAINST NINJA.
HEY— BLIND MAN, THOSE WERE MY FRIENDS I LOST.
AND YOU WILL LOSE MORE IF YOU FIGHT LIKE THAT, ROADBLOCK.
YOU THINK I DON'T KNOW THAT? I'M A COMMANDO. I KNOW HOW TO FIGHT AGAINST THE MOST STATE-OF-THE-ART WEAPONS AND TACTICS THAT'VE EVER BEEN DEVELOPED.
AND THAT GETS ME JACK AGAINST A TEAM OF NINJAS.
I'M HERE TO LEARN WHAT TO DO. BUT YOU CAN'T EXPECT ME TO PICK UP A THOUSAND YEARS OF TRAINING IN A WEEK.
THUMP
SNAKE EYES IS RIGHT. YOUR HEART IS STRONG. DO NOT SACRIFICE WHAT YOU HAVE ALREADY, FOR THE SAKE OF THE NEW.
YOU DO HAVE MUCH TO LEARN—
—BUT YOU ARE NOT ALONE IN THAT.

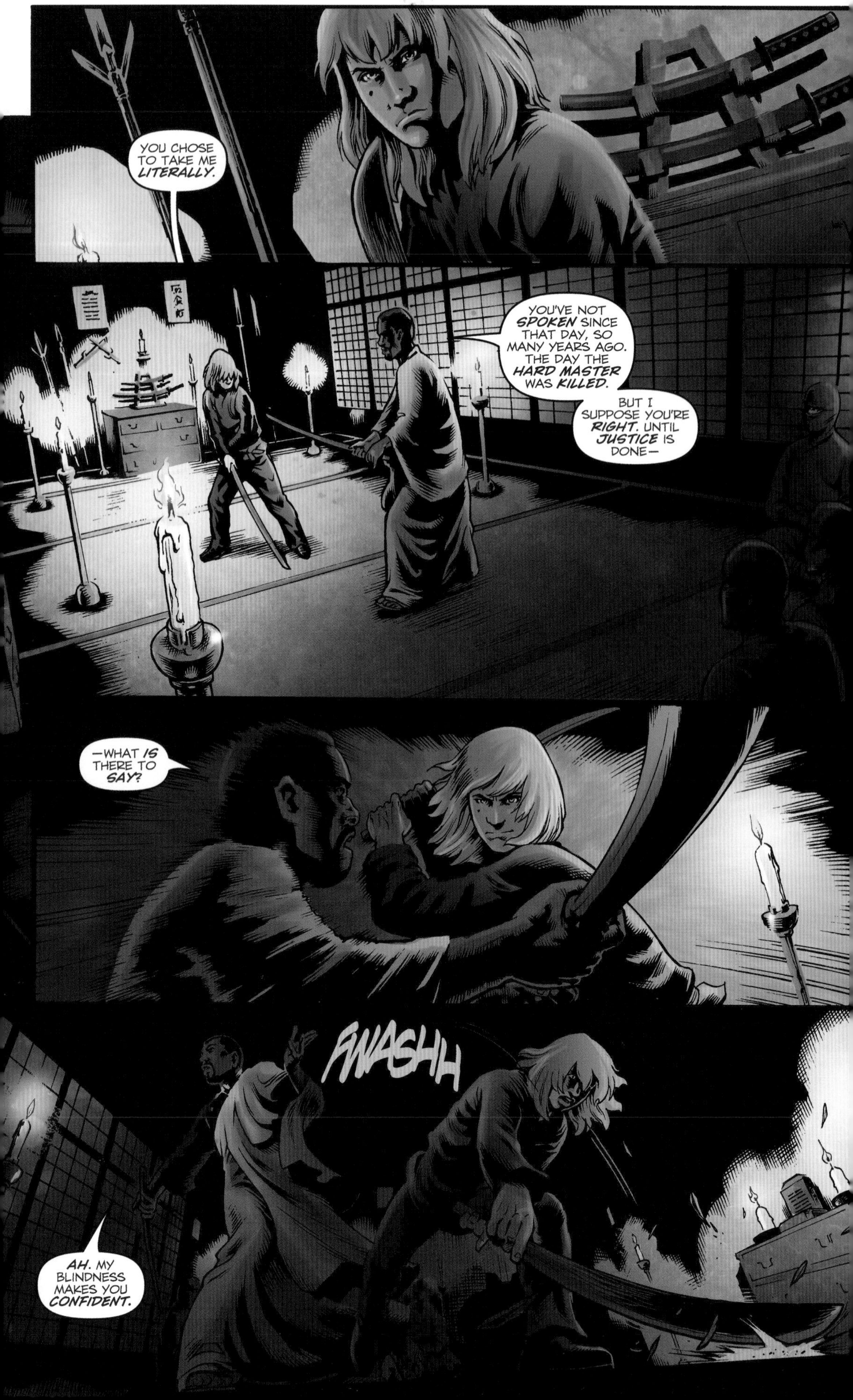
YOU CHOSE TO TAKE ME LITERALLY.
YOU'VE NOT SPOKEN SINCE THAT DAY, SO MANY YEARS AGO. THE DAY THE HARD MASTER WAS KILLED.
BUT I SUPPOSE YOU'RE RIGHT. UNTIL JUSTICE IS DONE—
—WHAT IS THERE TO SAY?
FWASHH
AH. MY BLINDNESS MAKES YOU CONFIDENT.

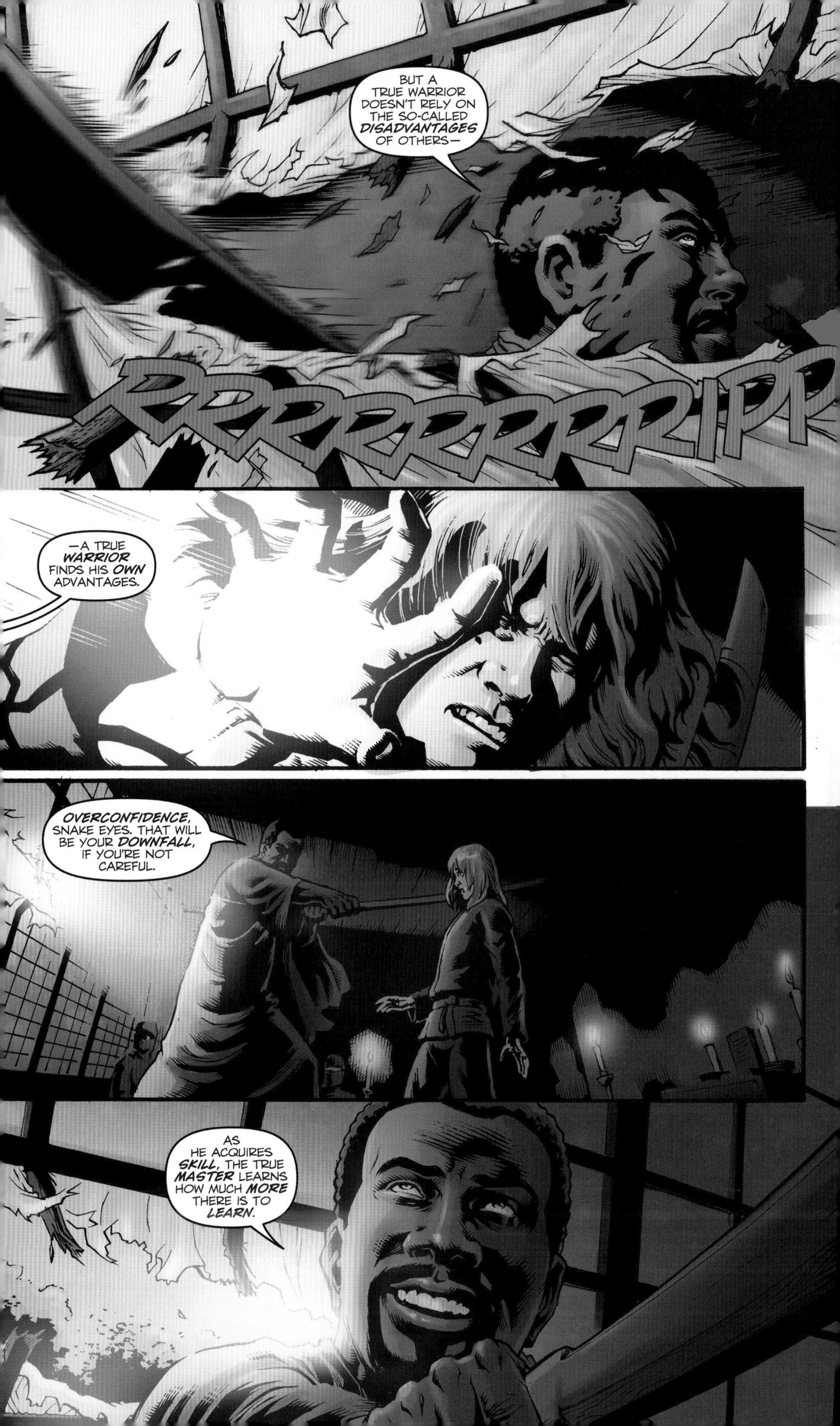
BUT A TRUE WARRIOR DOESN'T RELY ON THE SO-CALLED DISADVANTAGES OF OTHERS—
RRRRRRRRRRRIPP
—A TRUE WARRIOR FINDS HIS OWN ADVANTAGES.
OVERCONFIDENCE, SNAKE EYES. THAT WILL BE YOUR DOWNFALL, IF YOU'RE NOT CAREFUL.
AS HE ACQUIRES SKILL, THE TRUE MASTER LEARNS HOW MUCH MORE THERE IS TO LEARN.

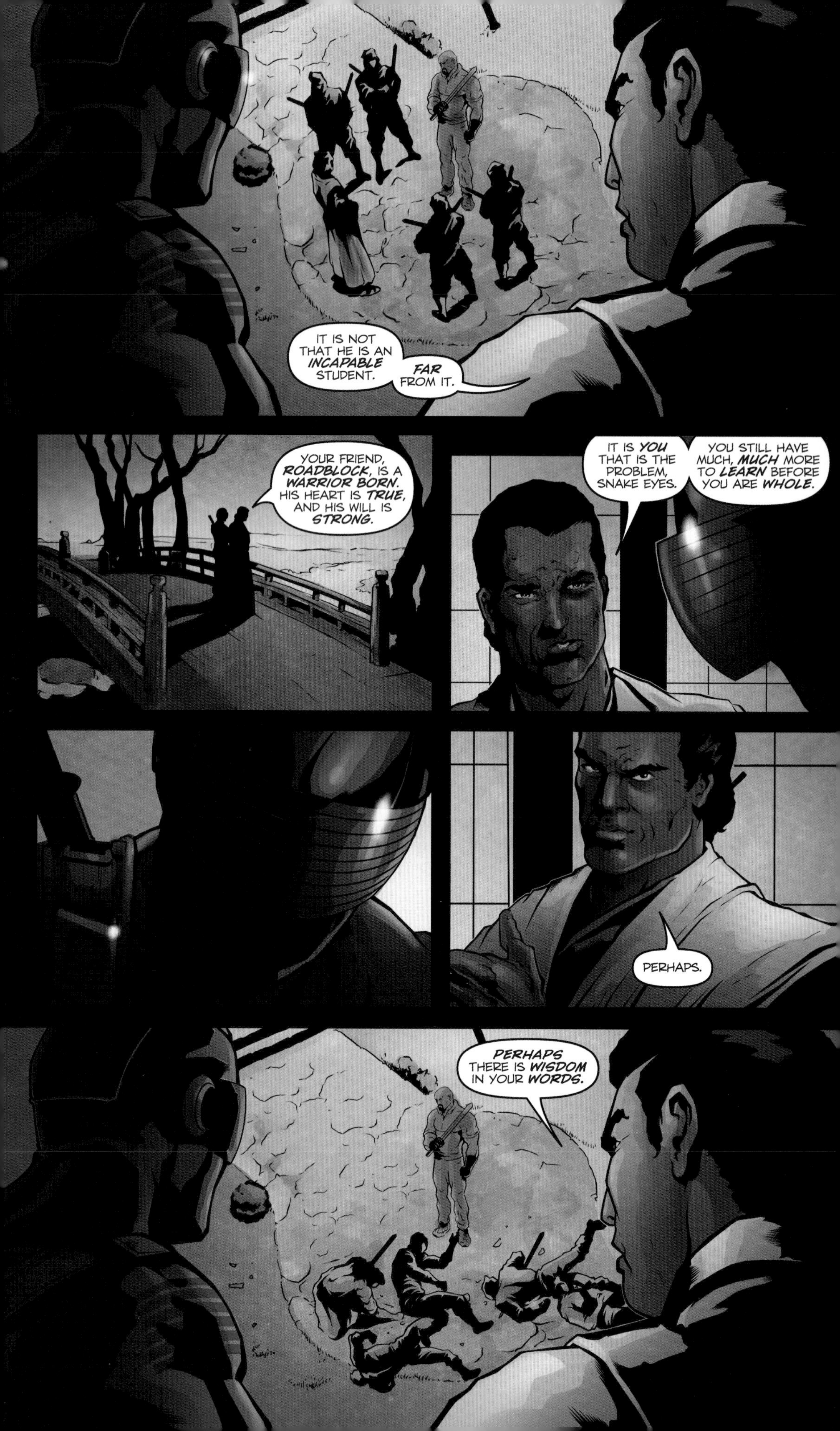
IT IS NOT THAT HE IS AN INCAPABLE STUDENT.
FAR FROM IT.
YOUR FRIEND, ROADBLOCK, IS A WARRIOR BORN. HIS HEART IS TRUE, AND HIS WILL IS STRONG.
IT IS YOU THAT IS THE PROBLEM, SNAKE EYES.
YOU STILL HAVE MUCH, MUCH MORE TO LEARN BEFORE YOU ARE WHOLE.
PERHAPS.
PERHAPS THERE IS WISDOM IN YOUR WORDS.

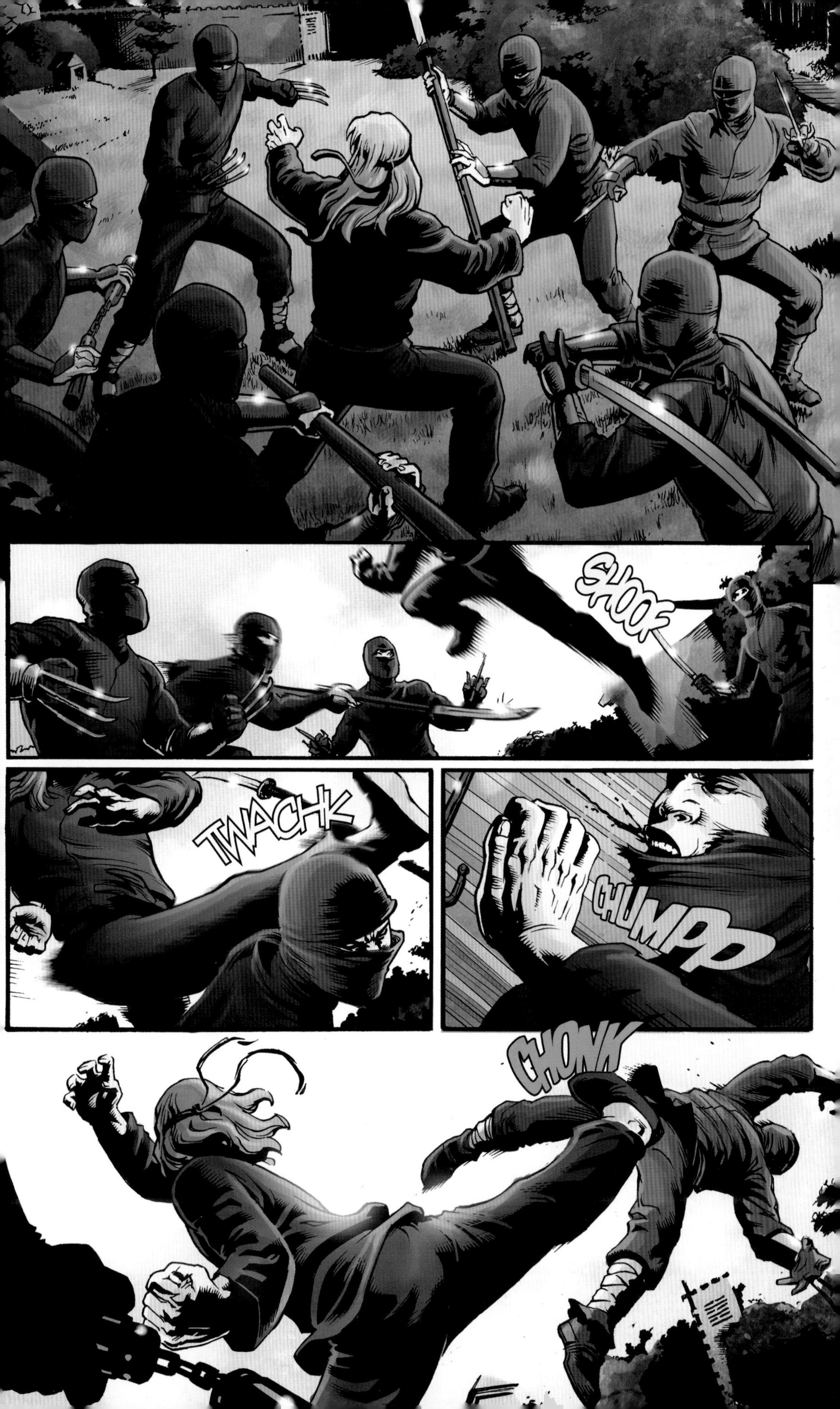
SHOOF
TWACHK
CHUMPP
CHONK

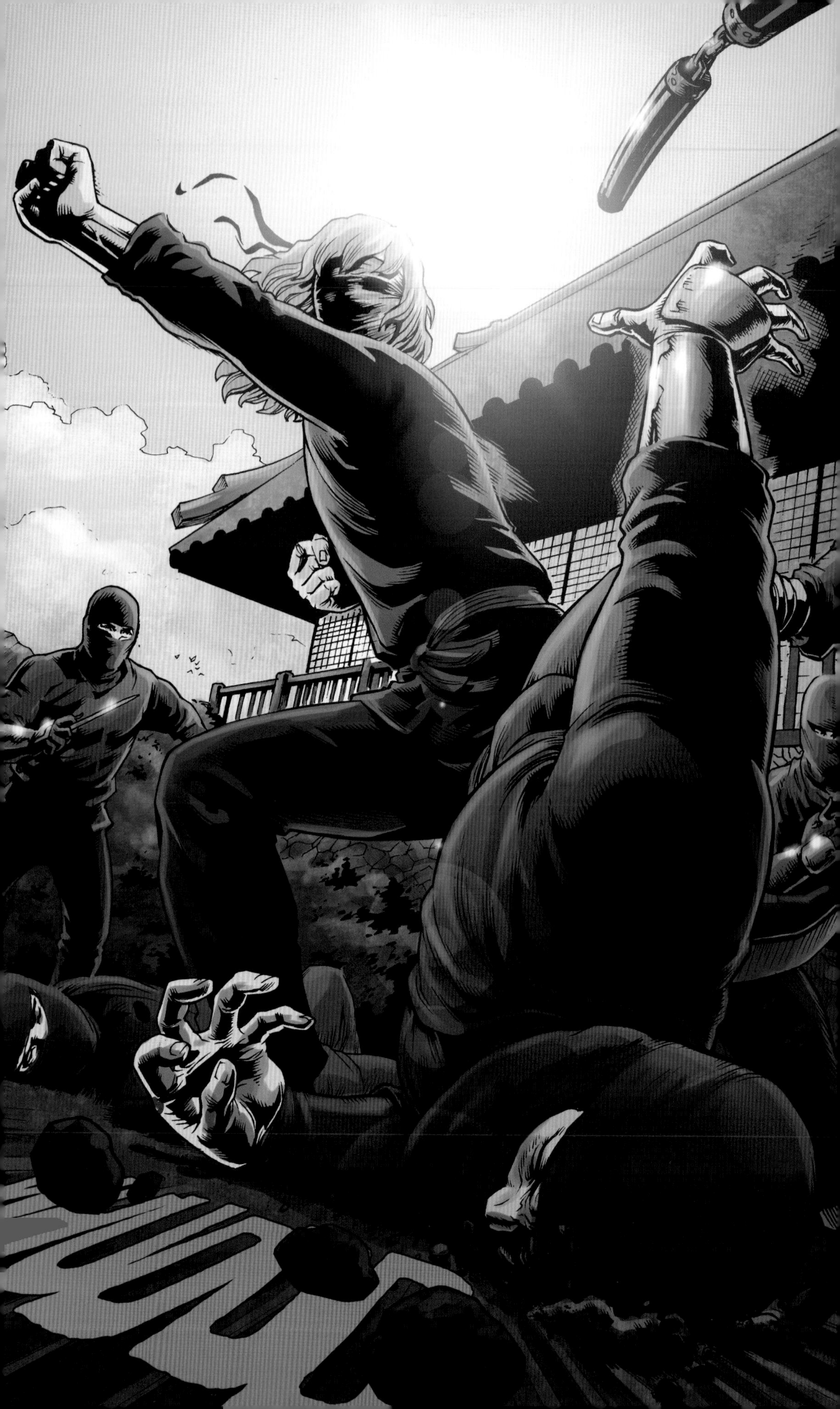

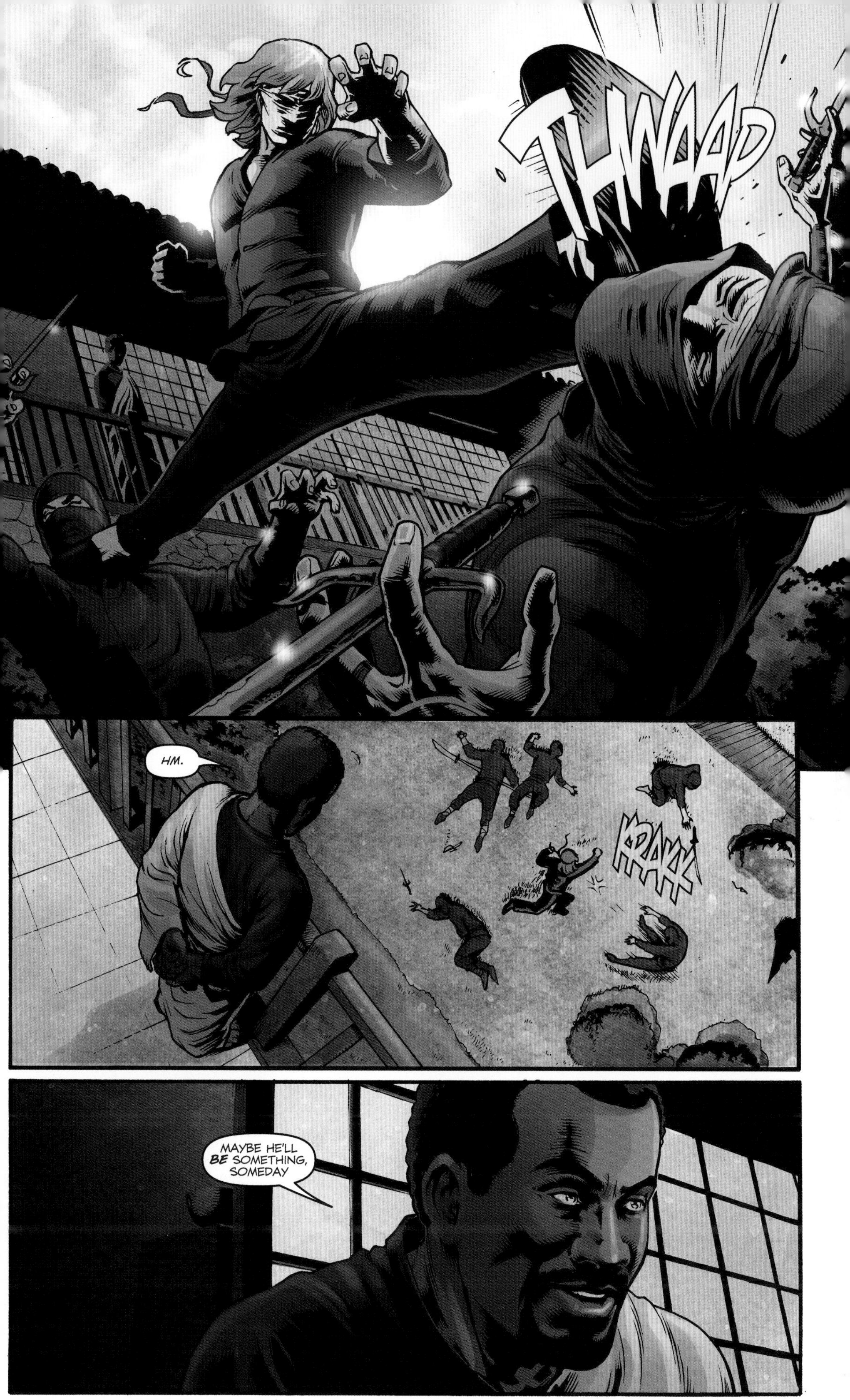
THWAAP
HM.
KRAKK
MAYBE HE'LL *BE* SOMETHING, SOMEDAY

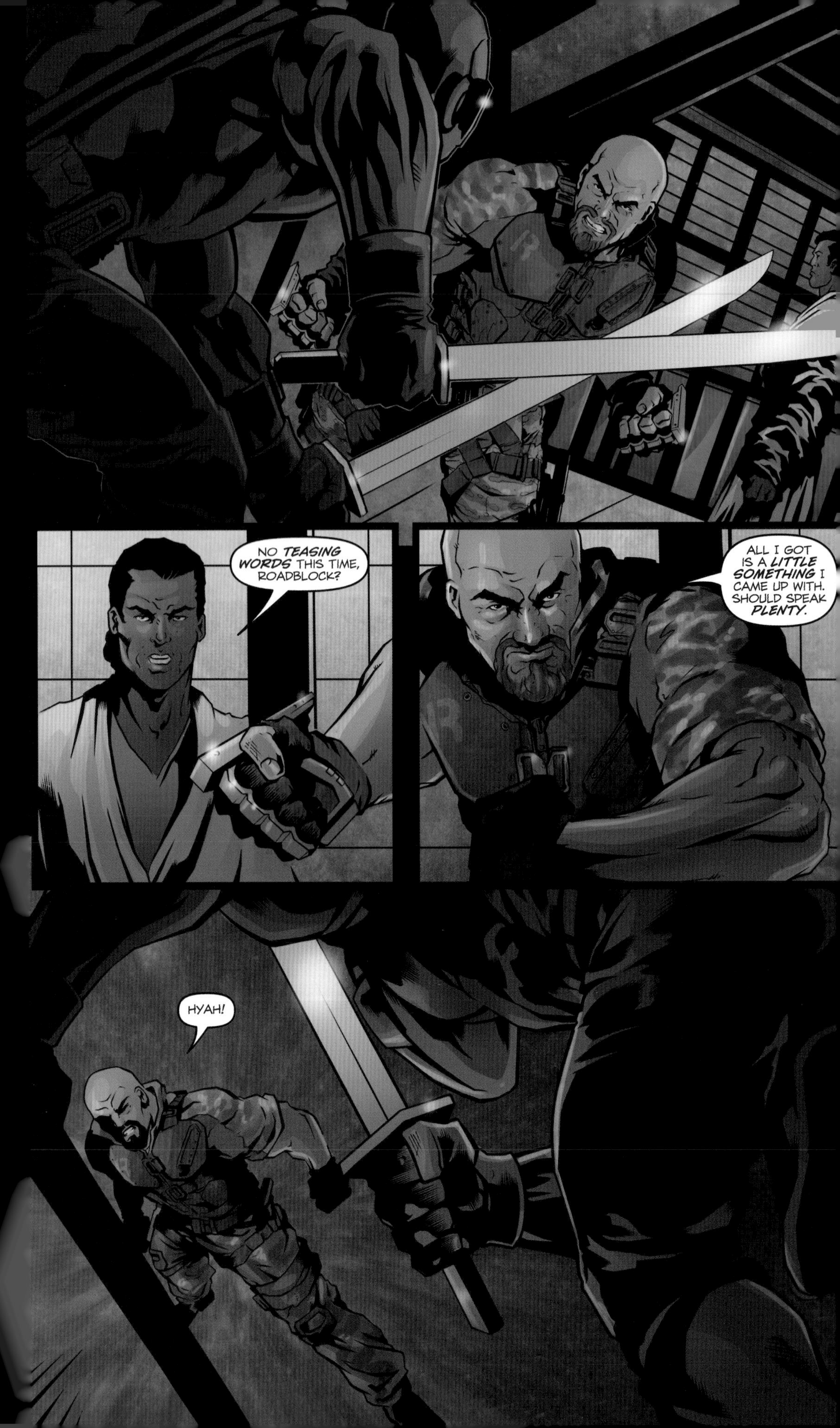
NO *TEASING WORDS* THIS TIME, ROADBLOCK?
ALL I GOT IS A *LITTLE SOMETHING* I CAME UP WITH. SHOULD SPEAK *PLENTY*.
HYAH!

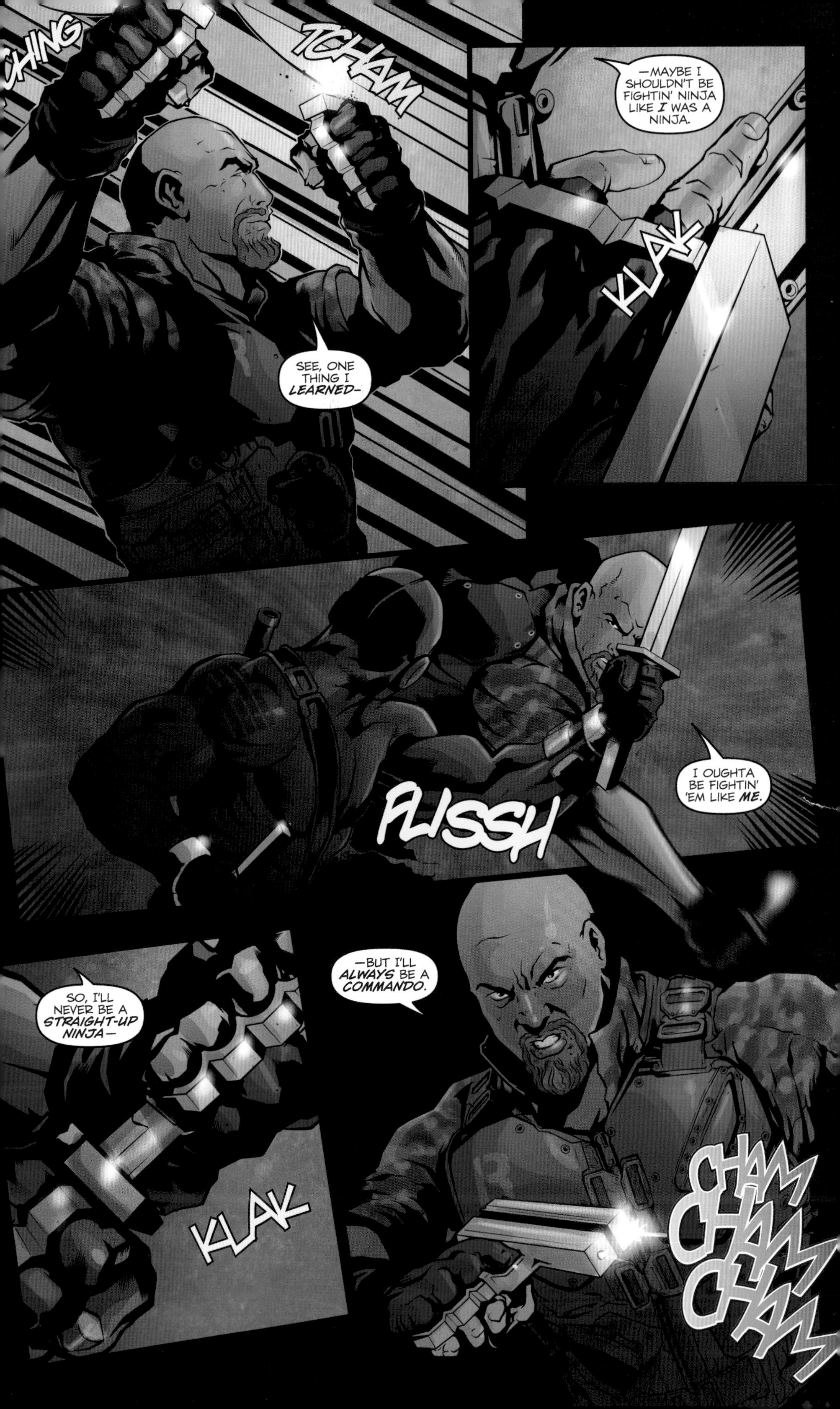
CHING
TCHAM
SEE, ONE THING I LEARNED—
—MAYBE I SHOULDN'T BE FIGHTIN' NINJA LIKE I WAS A NINJA.
KLAK
FLISSH
I OUGHTA BE FIGHTIN' 'EM LIKE ME.
SO, I'LL NEVER BE A STRAIGHT-UP NINJA—
KLAK
—BUT I'LL ALWAYS BE A COMMANDO.
CHAM CHAM CHAM CHAM

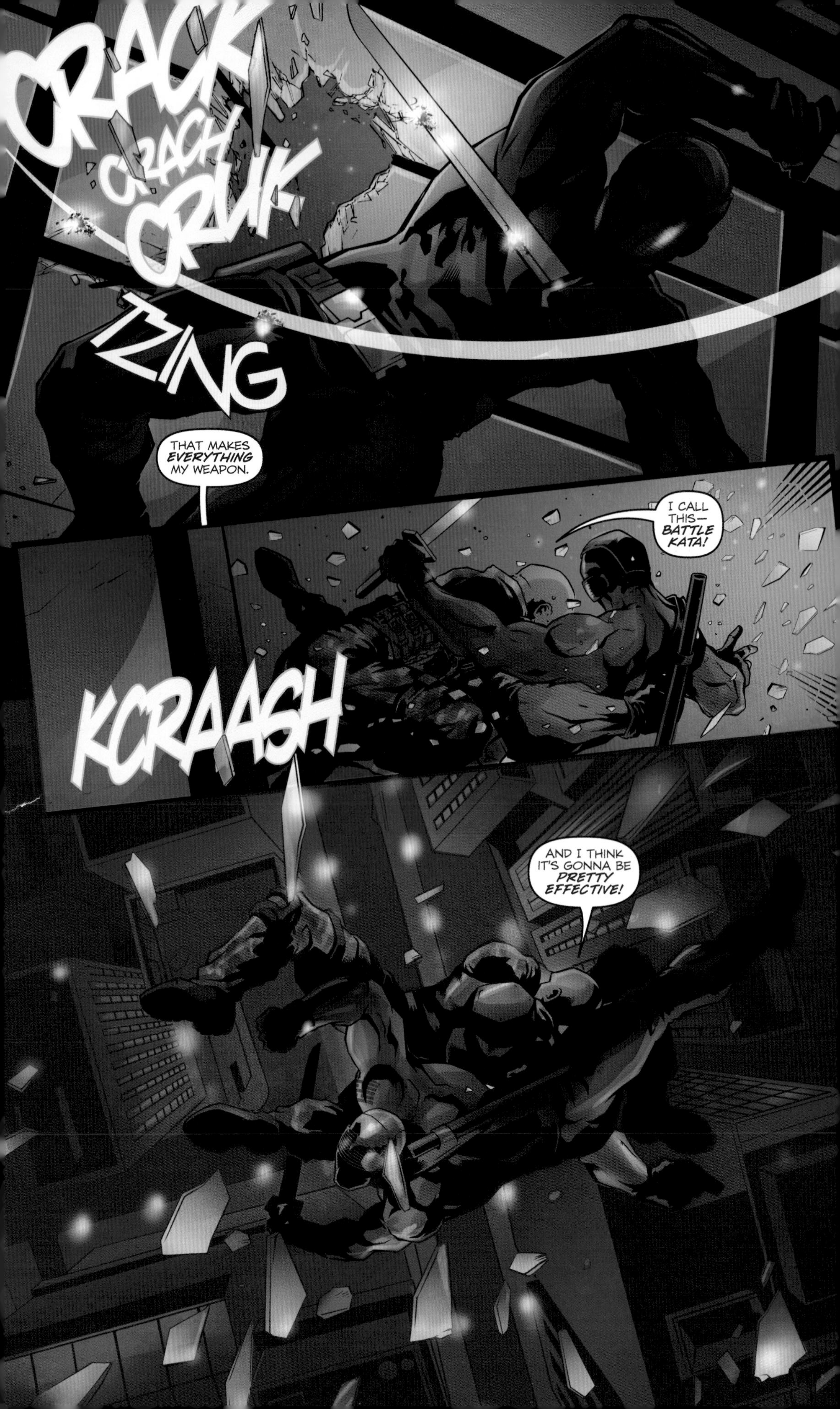
CRACK
CRACK
CRUK
TZING
THAT MAKES EVERYTHING MY WEAPON.
I CALL THIS— BATTLE KATA!
KRAASH
AND I THINK IT'S GONNA BE PRETTY EFFECTIVE!

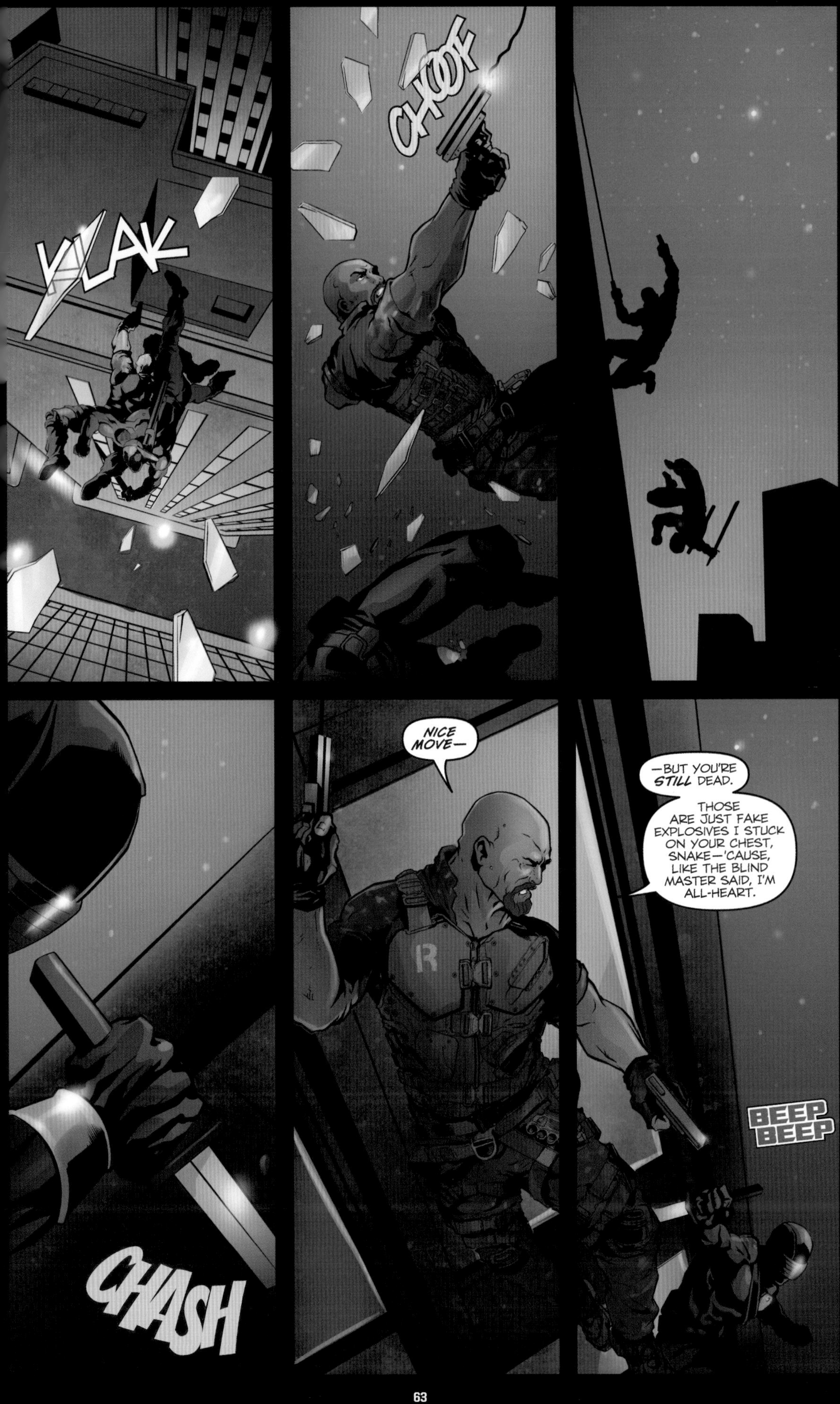

YLAK
CHOOF
CHASH
NICE MOVE—
—BUT YOU'RE STILL DEAD.
THOSE ARE JUST FAKE EXPLOSIVES I STUCK ON YOUR CHEST, SNAKE—'CAUSE, LIKE THE BLIND MASTER SAID, I'M ALL-HEART.
BEEP BEEP

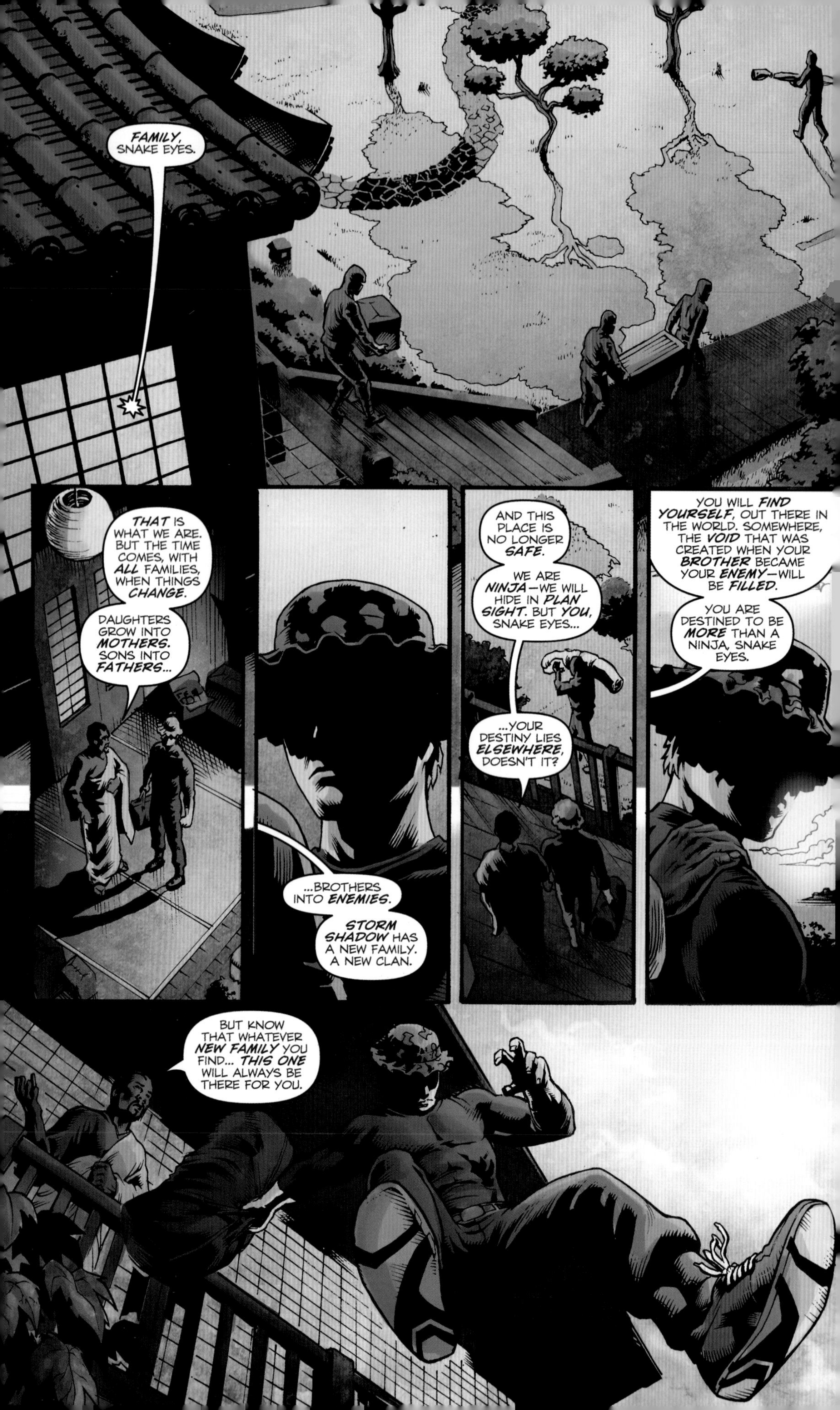

FAMILY, SNAKE EYES.
THAT IS WHAT WE ARE. BUT THE TIME COMES, WITH ALL FAMILIES, WHEN THINGS CHANGE.
DAUGHTERS GROW INTO MOTHERS. SONS INTO FATHERS...
...BROTHERS INTO ENEMIES.
STORM SHADOW HAS A NEW FAMILY. A NEW CLAN.
AND THIS PLACE IS NO LONGER SAFE.
WE ARE NINJA—WE WILL HIDE IN PLAN SIGHT. BUT YOU, SNAKE EYES...
...YOUR DESTINY LIES ELSEWHERE, DOESN'T IT?
YOU WILL FIND YOURSELF, OUT THERE IN THE WORLD. SOMEWHERE, THE VOID THAT WAS CREATED WHEN YOUR BROTHER BECAME YOUR ENEMY—WILL BE FILLED.
YOU ARE DESTINED TO BE MORE THAN A NINJA, SNAKE EYES.
BUT KNOW THAT WHATEVER NEW FAMILY YOU FIND... THIS ONE WILL ALWAYS BE THERE FOR YOU.

I GUESS YOU COULD CALL THAT A *DIRTY TRICK*, BUT... WELL, I DON'T KNOW IF YOU EVER LOST A *BROTHER*.

I DON'T MEAN SOMEBODY THAT HAPPENS TO BE *RELATED* TO YOU, Y'KNOW?

I MEAN THE GUY YOU *TRUST* WITH YOUR *LIFE*. THAT'S WHAT MY BUDDY, *MAINFRAME*, WAS. BEFORE THE NINJAS *GOT HIM* IN BOROVIA.

KOSS SNAK

YOU LOSE A *BROTHER*, AND A *DIRTY TRICK* TO GET AT *WHOEVER* PULLED THE TRIGGER—

—OR *STABBED* THE *SWORD*—

—WELL, YOU DO WHAT YOU GOTTA TO MAKE THINGS *RIGHT*. COMMANDO, NINJA—YOU JUST TAKE WHAT *WORKS*, AND YOU MAKE IT *HAPPEN*.

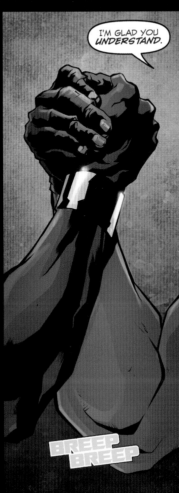

I'M GLAD YOU *UNDERSTAND*.

BREEP BREEP

SNAKE EYES FROM SCARLETT. CODE *ZERO*.

GEAR UP, BECAUSE I KNOW WHAT THE BAD GUYS ARE *AFTER*. THE PLANE LEAVES IN *TEN*.

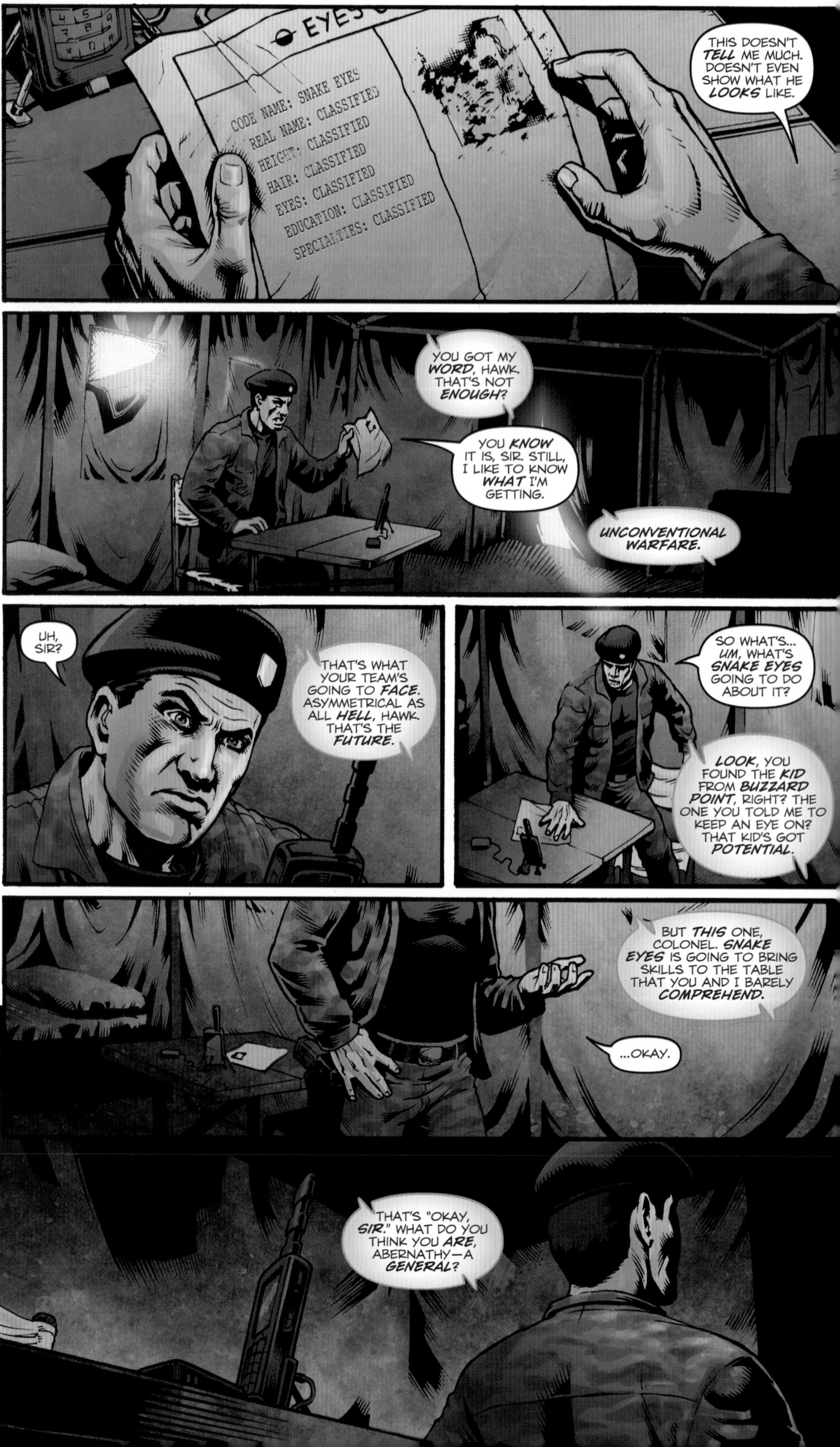
EYES
CODE NAME: SNAKE EYES
REAL NAME: CLASSIFIED
HEIGHT: CLASSIFIED
HAIR: CLASSIFIED
EYES: CLASSIFIED
EDUCATION: CLASSIFIED
SPECIALTIES: CLASSIFIED
THIS DOESN'T TELL ME MUCH. DOESN'T EVEN SHOW WHAT HE LOOKS LIKE.
YOU GOT MY WORD, HAWK. THAT'S NOT ENOUGH?
YOU KNOW IT IS, SIR. STILL, I LIKE TO KNOW WHAT I'M GETTING.
UNCONVENTIONAL WARFARE.
UH, SIR?
THAT'S WHAT YOUR TEAM'S GOING TO FACE. ASYMMETRICAL AS ALL HELL, HAWK. THAT'S THE FUTURE.
SO WHAT'S... UM, WHAT'S SNAKE EYES GOING TO DO ABOUT IT?
LOOK, YOU FOUND THE KID FROM BUZZARD POINT, RIGHT? THE ONE YOU TOLD ME TO KEEP AN EYE ON? THAT KID'S GOT POTENTIAL.
BUT THIS ONE, COLONEL. SNAKE EYES IS GOING TO BRING SKILLS TO THE TABLE THAT YOU AND I BARELY COMPREHEND.
...OKAY.
THAT'S "OKAY, SIR." WHAT DO YOU THINK YOU ARE, ABERNATHY—A GENERAL?

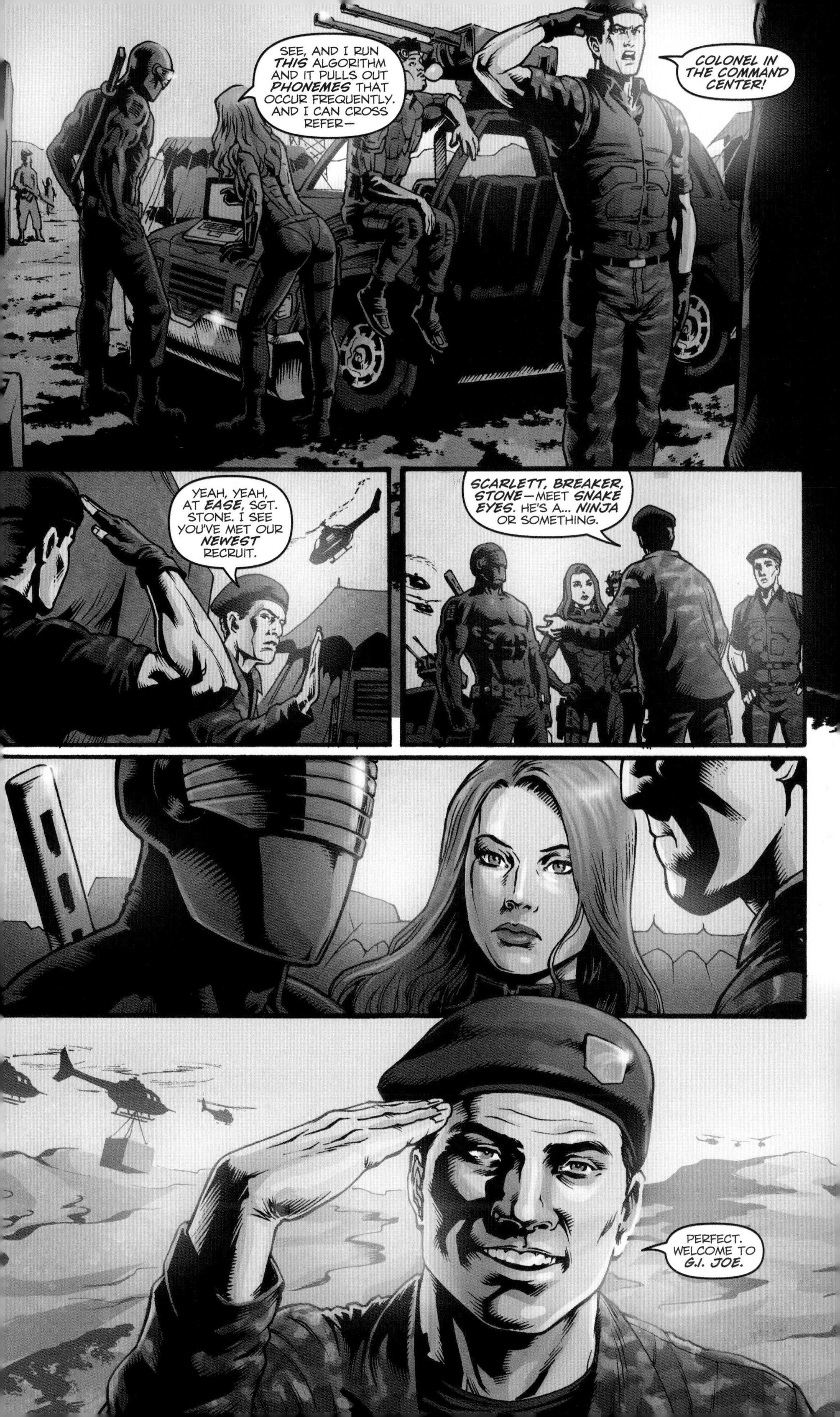
SEE, AND I RUN THIS ALGORITHM AND IT PULLS OUT PHONEMES THAT OCCUR FREQUENTLY. AND I CAN CROSS REFER—
COLONEL IN THE COMMAND CENTER!
YEAH, YEAH, AT EASE, SGT. STONE. I SEE YOU'VE MET OUR NEWEST RECRUIT.
SCARLETT, BREAKER, STONE—MEET SNAKE EYES. HE'S A... NINJA OR SOMETHING.
PERFECT. WELCOME TO G.I. JOE.

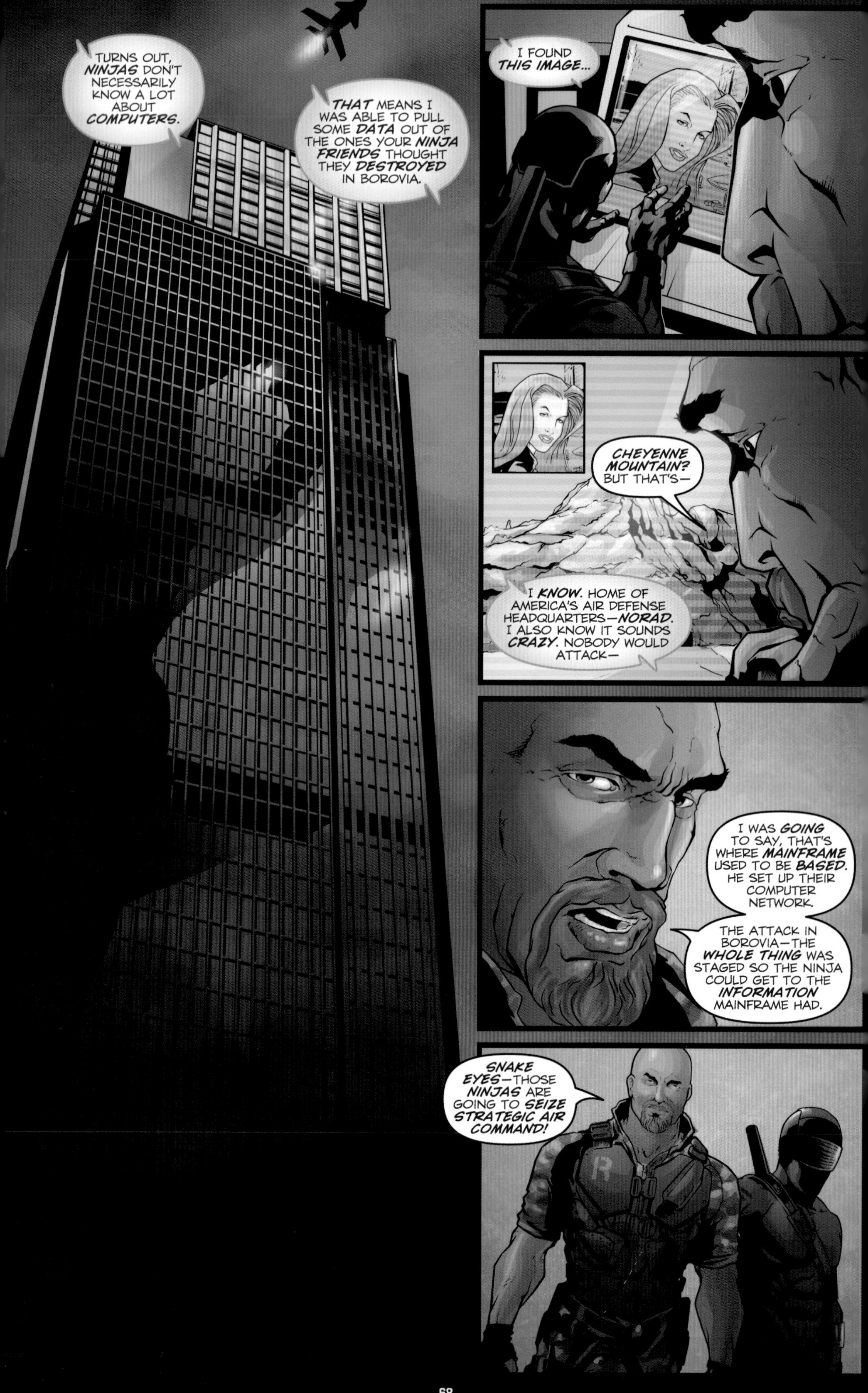
TURNS OUT, NINJAS DON'T NECESSARILY KNOW A LOT ABOUT COMPUTERS.
THAT MEANS I WAS ABLE TO PULL SOME DATA OUT OF THE ONES YOUR NINJA FRIENDS THOUGHT THEY DESTROYED IN BOROVIA.
I FOUND THIS IMAGE...
CHEYENNE MOUNTAIN? BUT THAT'S—
I KNOW. HOME OF AMERICA'S AIR DEFENSE HEADQUARTERS—NORAD. I ALSO KNOW IT SOUNDS CRAZY. NOBODY WOULD ATTACK—
I WAS GOING TO SAY, THAT'S WHERE MAINFRAME USED TO BE BASED. HE SET UP THEIR COMPUTER NETWORK.
THE ATTACK IN BOROVIA—THE WHOLE THING WAS STAGED SO THE NINJA COULD GET TO THE INFORMATION MAINFRAME HAD.
SNAKE EYES—THOSE NINJAS ARE GOING TO SEIZE STRATEGIC AIR COMMAND!

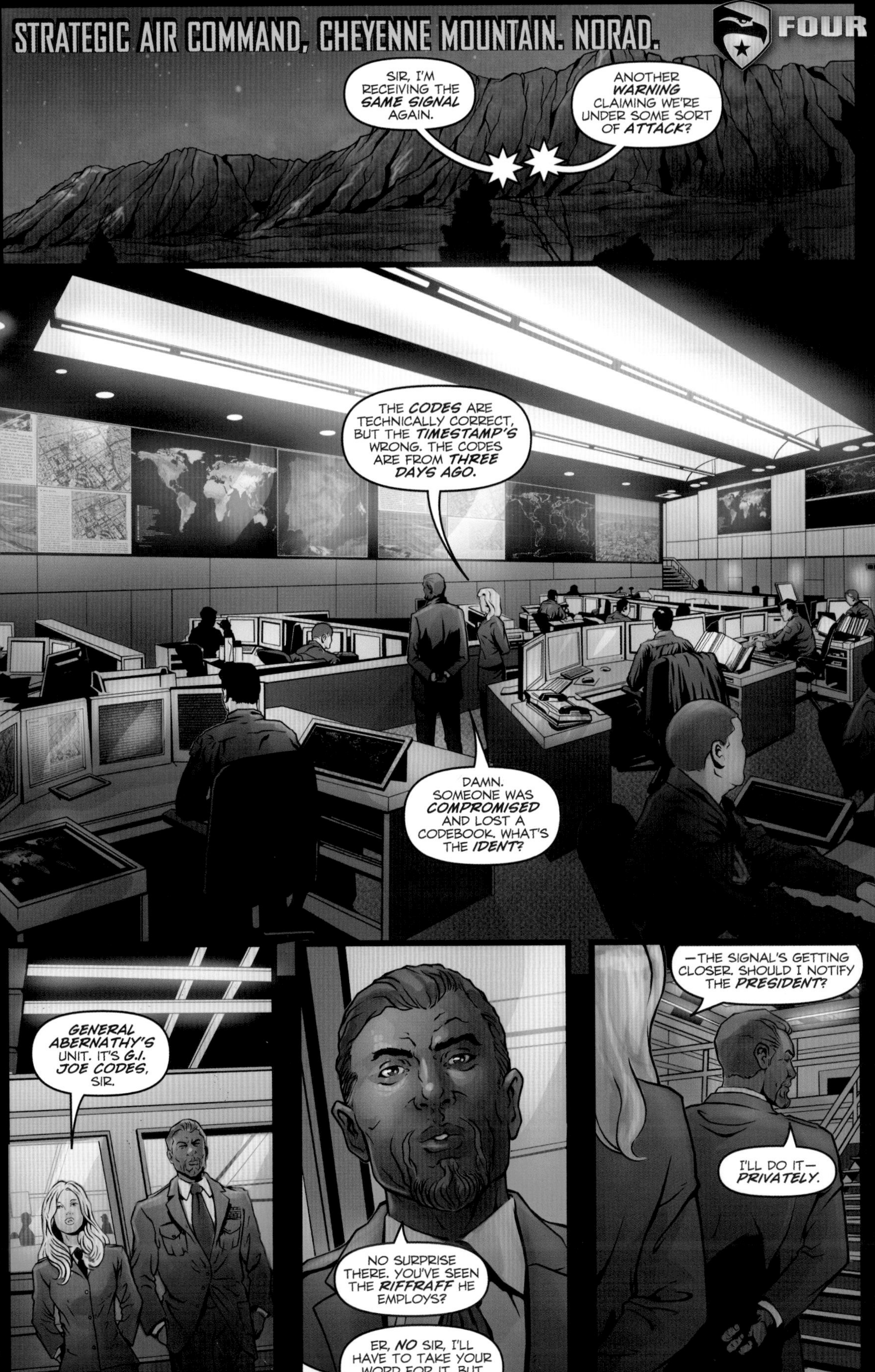
STRATEGIC AIR COMMAND, CHEYENNE MOUNTAIN. NORAD.
FOUR
SIR, I'M RECEIVING THE SAME SIGNAL AGAIN.
ANOTHER WARNING CLAIMING WE'RE UNDER SOME SORT OF ATTACK?
THE CODES ARE TECHNICALLY CORRECT, BUT THE TIMESTAMP'S WRONG. THE CODES ARE FROM THREE DAYS AGO.
DAMN. SOMEONE WAS COMPROMISED AND LOST A CODEBOOK. WHAT'S THE IDENT?
GENERAL ABERNATHY'S UNIT. IT'S G.I. JOE CODES, SIR.
NO SURPRISE THERE. YOU'VE SEEN THE RIFFRAFF HE EMPLOYS?
ER, NO SIR, I'LL HAVE TO TAKE YOUR WORD FOR IT. BUT THERE'S SOMETHING ELSE—
—THE SIGNAL'S GETTING CLOSER. SHOULD I NOTIFY THE PRESIDENT?
I'LL DO IT—PRIVATELY.

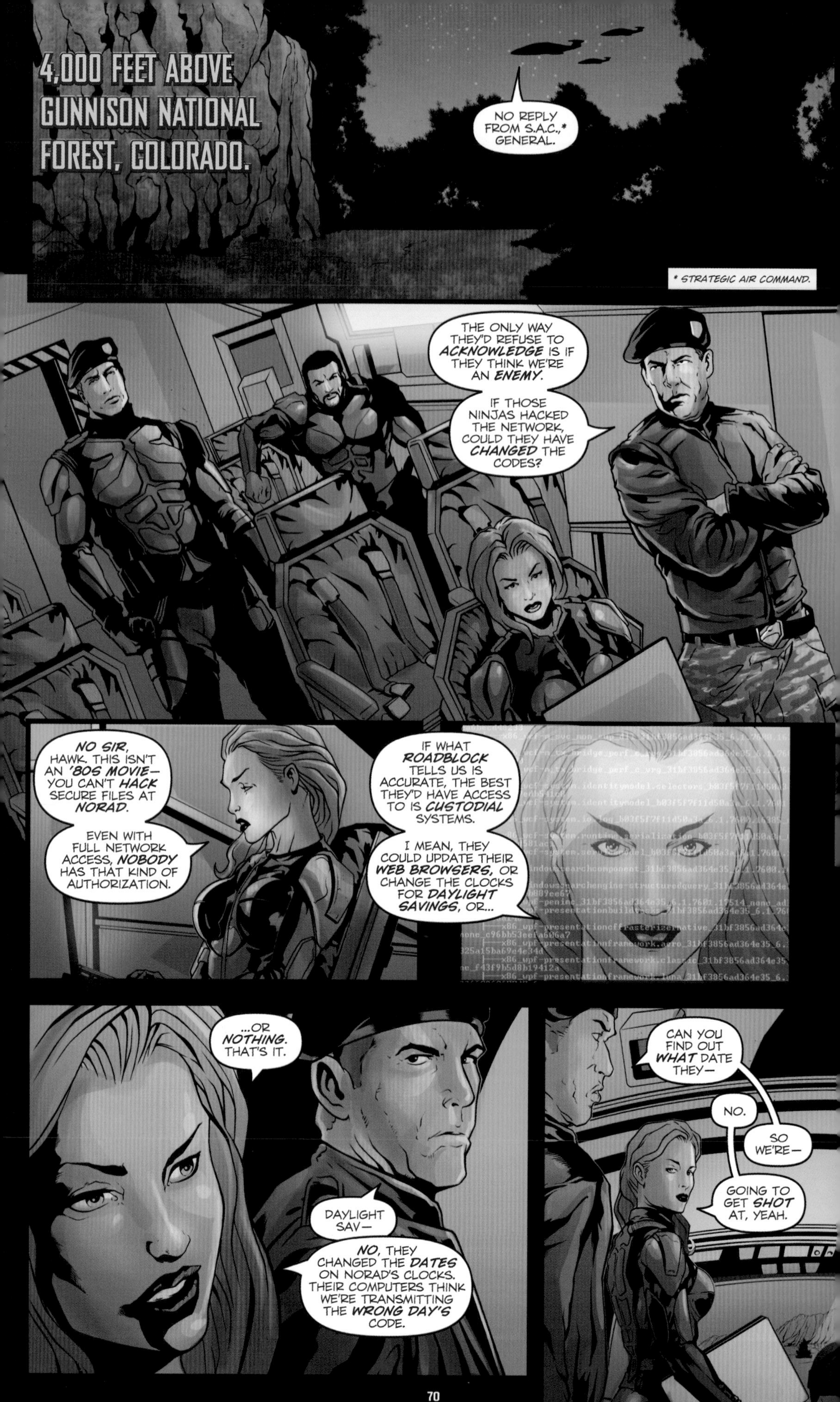
4,000 FEET ABOVE GUNNISON NATIONAL FOREST, COLORADO.
NO REPLY FROM S.A.C.,* GENERAL.
* STRATEGIC AIR COMMAND.
THE ONLY WAY THEY'D REFUSE TO ACKNOWLEDGE IS IF THEY THINK WE'RE AN ENEMY.
IF THOSE NINJAS HACKED THE NETWORK, COULD THEY HAVE CHANGED THE CODES?
NO SIR, HAWK. THIS ISN'T AN '80S MOVIE— YOU CAN'T HACK SECURE FILES AT NORAD.
EVEN WITH FULL NETWORK ACCESS, NOBODY HAS THAT KIND OF AUTHORIZATION.
IF WHAT ROADBLOCK TELLS US IS ACCURATE, THE BEST THEY'D HAVE ACCESS TO IS CUSTODIAL SYSTEMS.
I MEAN, THEY COULD UPDATE THEIR WEB BROWSERS, OR CHANGE THE CLOCKS FOR DAYLIGHT SAVINGS, OR...
...OR NOTHING. THAT'S IT.
DAYLIGHT SAV—
NO, THEY CHANGED THE DATES ON NORAD'S CLOCKS. THEIR COMPUTERS THINK WE'RE TRANSMITTING THE WRONG DAY'S CODE.
CAN YOU FIND OUT WHAT DATE THEY—
NO.
SO WE'RE—
GOING TO GET SHOT AT, YEAH.

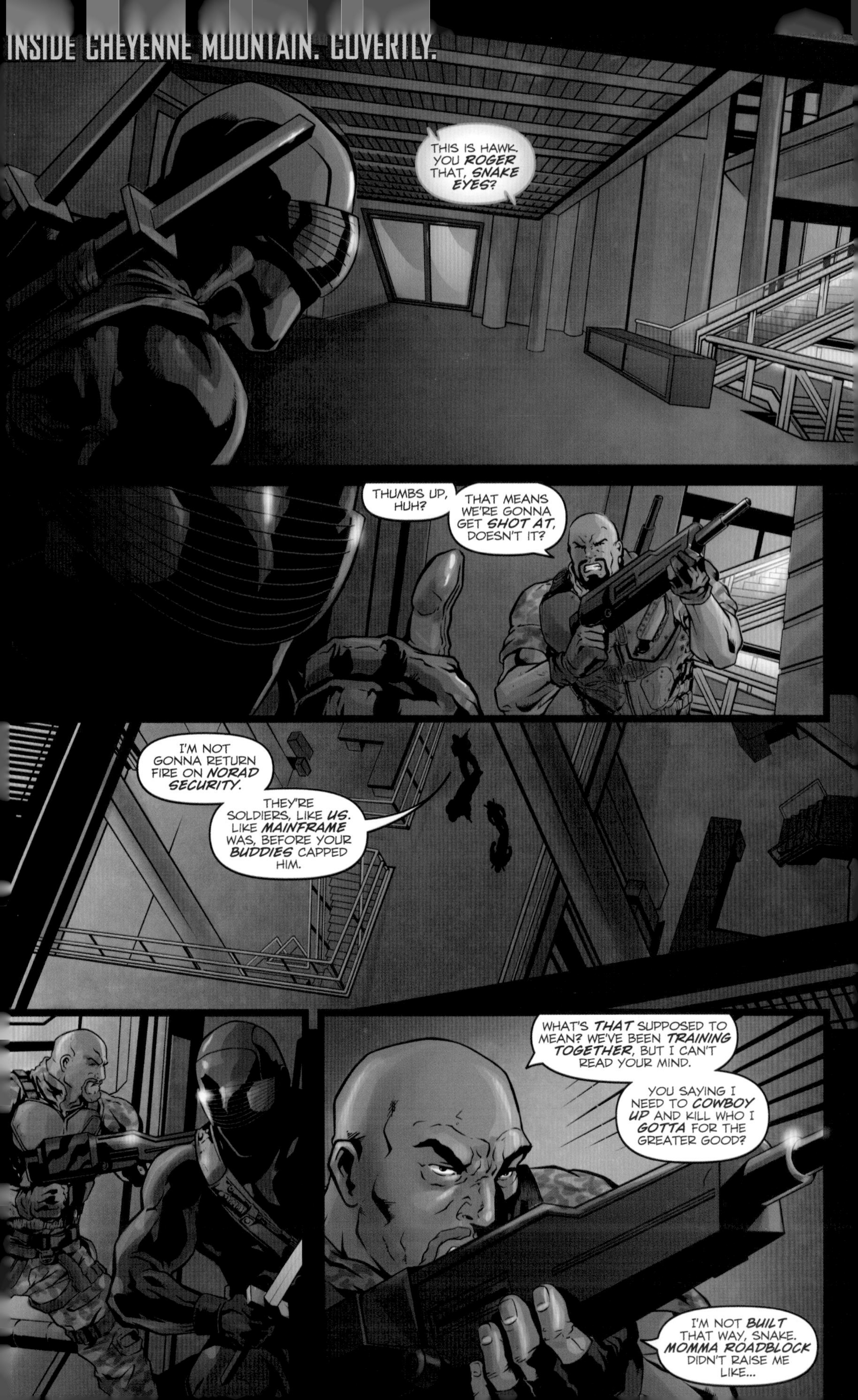
INSIDE CHEYENNE MOUNTAIN. COVERTLY.
THIS IS HAWK. YOU ROGER THAT, SNAKE EYES?
THUMBS UP, HUH?
THAT MEANS WE'RE GONNA GET SHOT AT, DOESN'T IT?
I'M NOT GONNA RETURN FIRE ON NORAD SECURITY.
THEY'RE SOLDIERS, LIKE US. LIKE MAINFRAME WAS, BEFORE YOUR BUDDIES CAPPED HIM.
WHAT'S THAT SUPPOSED TO MEAN? WE'VE BEEN TRAINING TOGETHER, BUT I CAN'T READ YOUR MIND.
YOU SAYING I NEED TO COWBOY UP AND KILL WHO I GOTTA FOR THE GREATER GOOD?
I'M NOT BUILT THAT WAY, SNAKE. MOMMA ROADBLOCK DIDN'T RAISE ME LIKE...

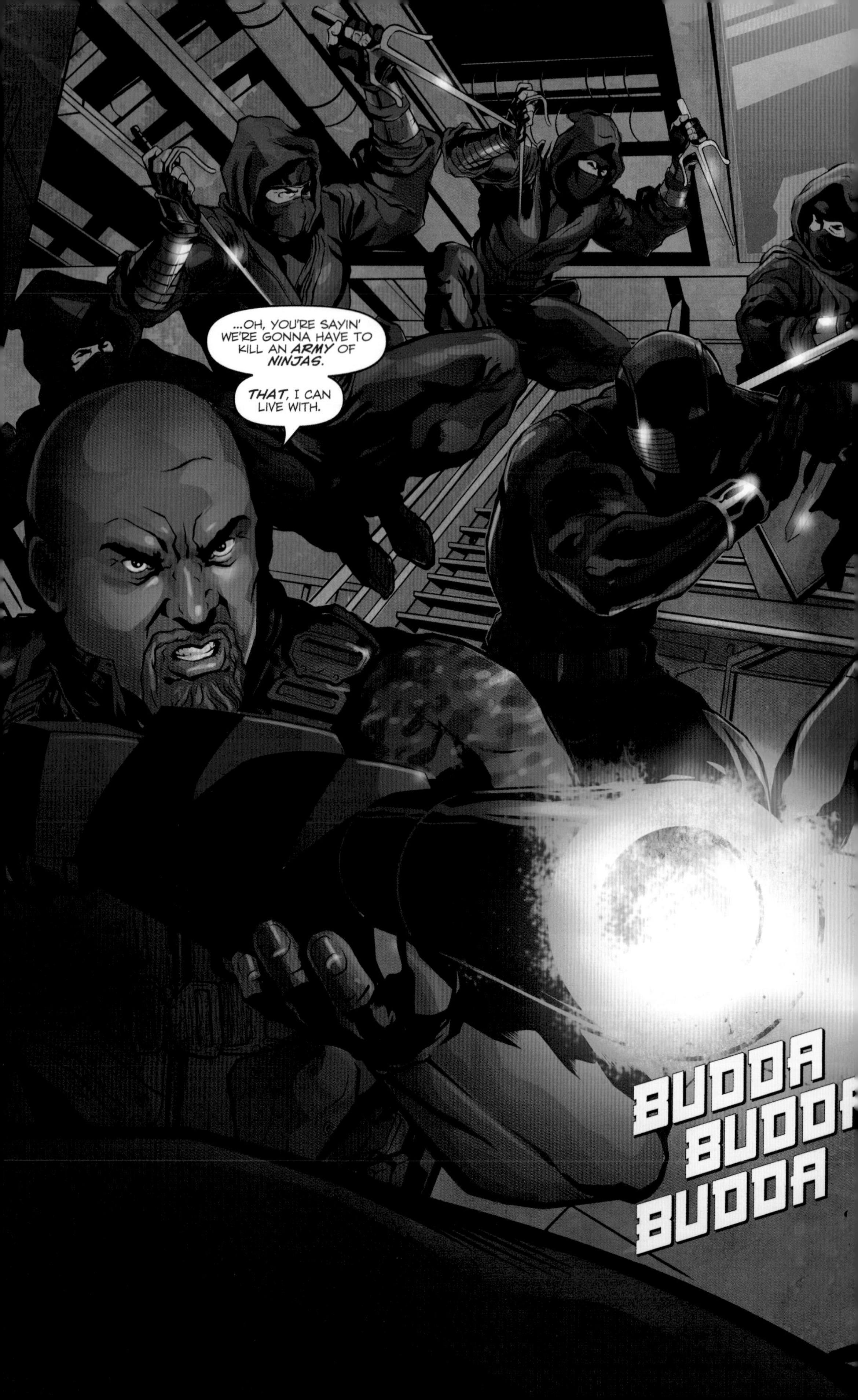
...OH, YOU'RE SAYIN' WE'RE GONNA HAVE TO KILL AN ARMY OF NINJAS.
THAT, I CAN LIVE WITH.
BUDDA BUDDA BUDDA

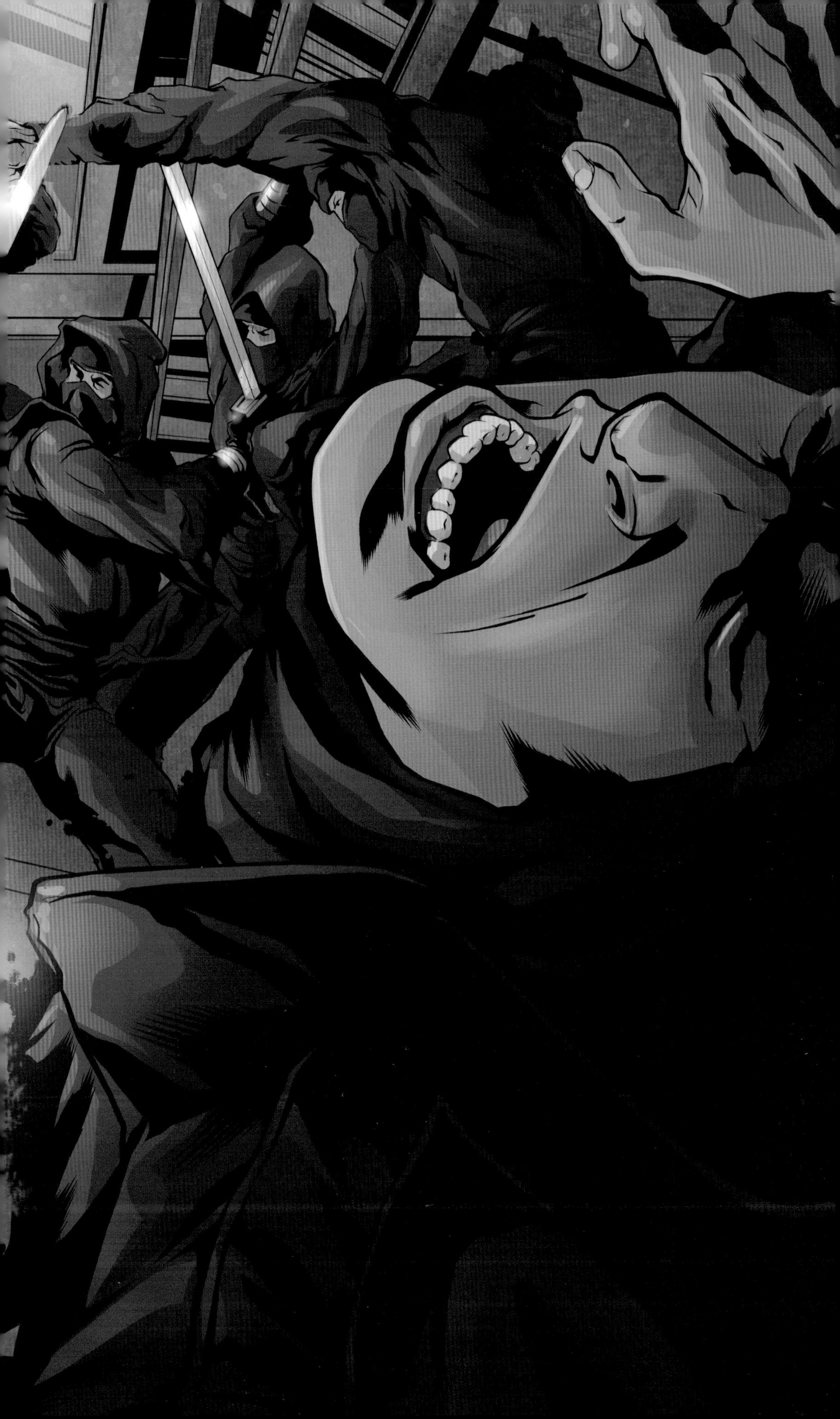

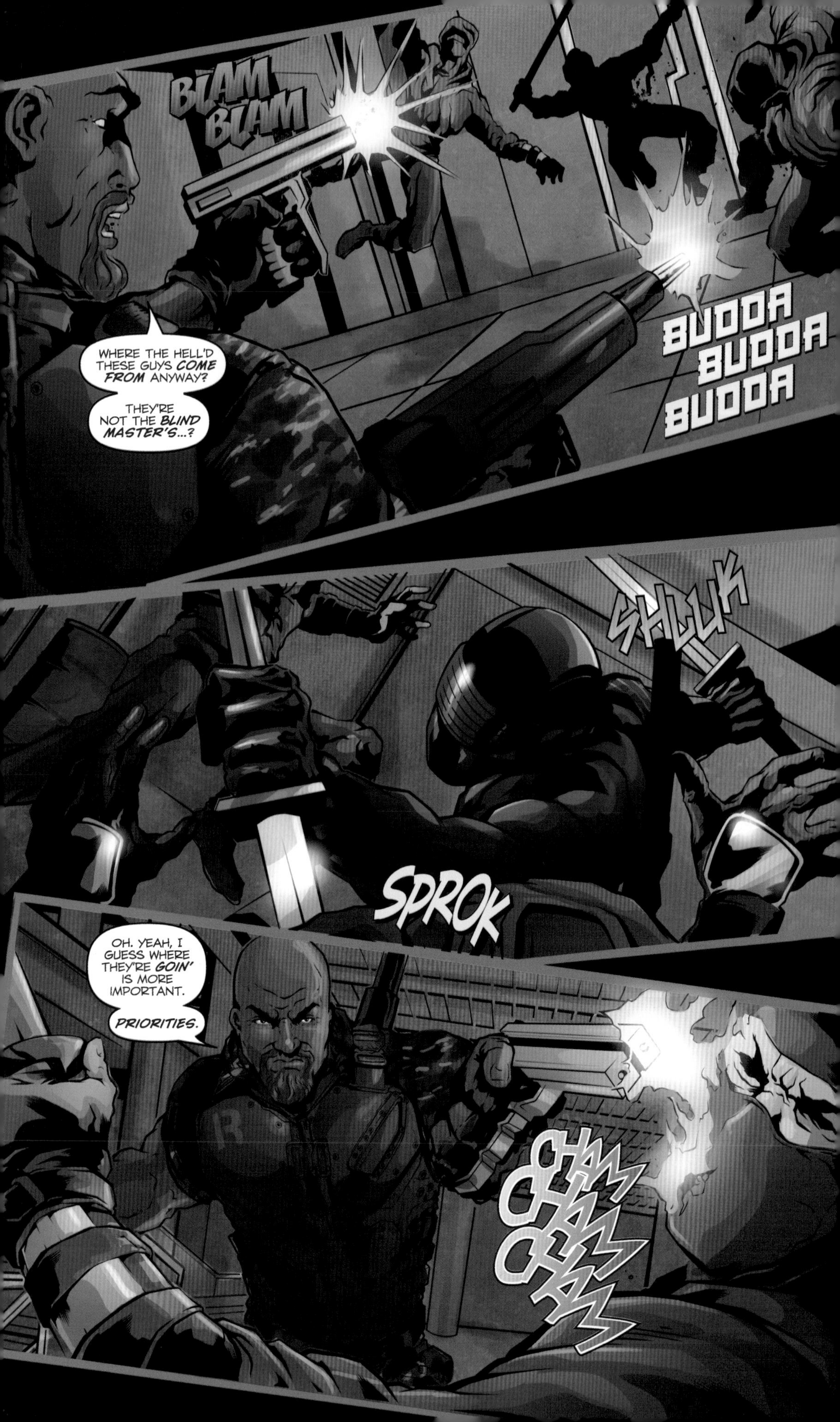
BLAM BLAM
WHERE THE HELL'D THESE GUYS COME FROM ANYWAY?
THEY'RE NOT THE BLIND MASTER'S...?
BUDDA BUDDA BUDDA
SHUK
SPROK
OH. YEAH, I GUESS WHERE THEY'RE GOIN' IS MORE IMPORTANT.
PRIORITIES.
CHAM CHAM CHAM CHAM

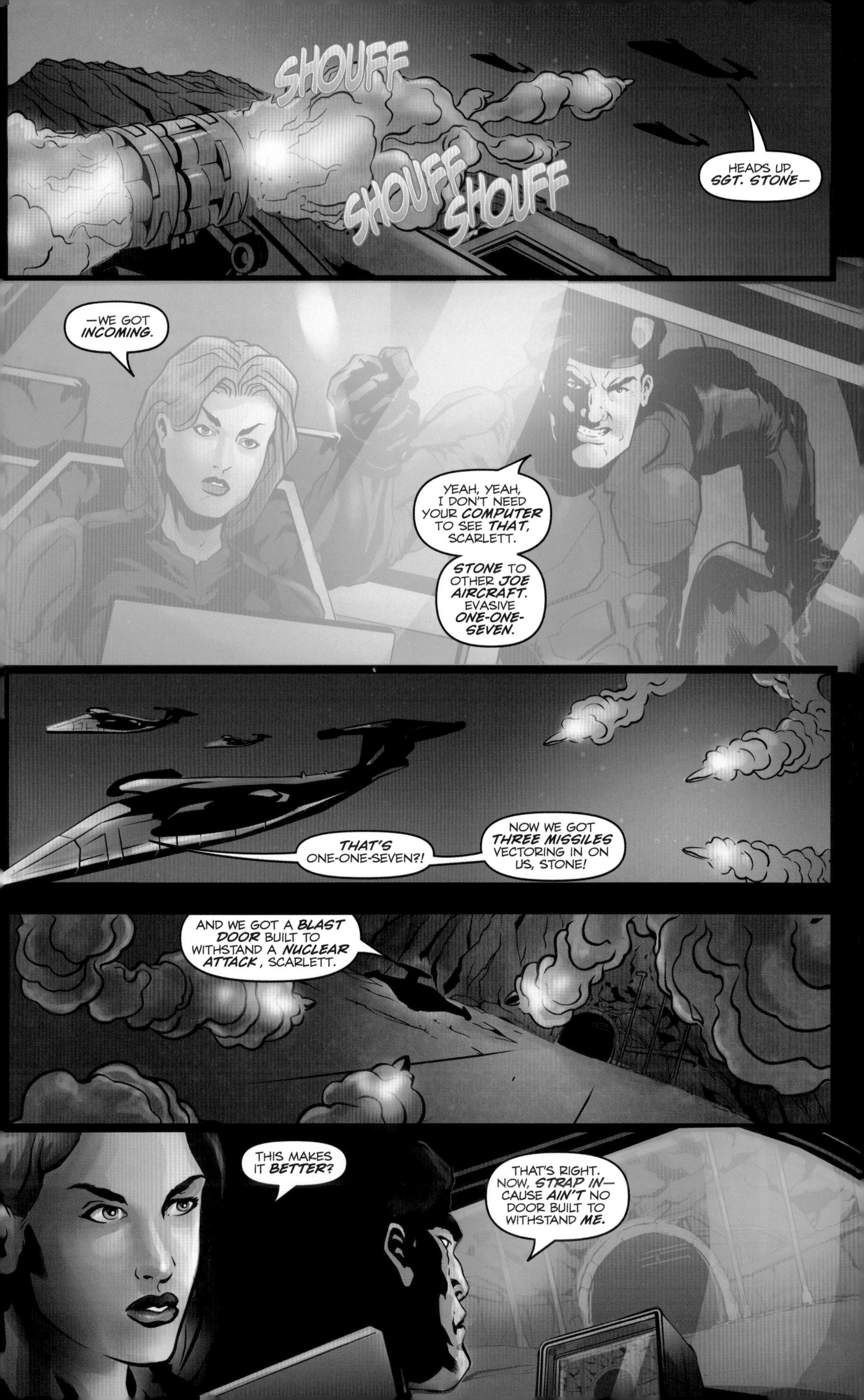
SHOUFF
SHOUFF
SHOUFF
HEADS UP, SGT. STONE—
—WE GOT INCOMING.
YEAH, YEAH, I DON'T NEED YOUR COMPUTER TO SEE THAT, SCARLETT.
STONE TO OTHER JOE AIRCRAFT. EVASIVE ONE-ONE-SEVEN.
THAT'S ONE-ONE-SEVEN?!
NOW WE GOT THREE MISSILES VECTORING IN ON US, STONE!
AND WE GOT A BLAST DOOR BUILT TO WITHSTAND A NUCLEAR ATTACK, SCARLETT.
THIS MAKES IT BETTER?
THAT'S RIGHT. NOW, STRAP IN— CAUSE AIN'T NO DOOR BUILT TO WITHSTAND ME.

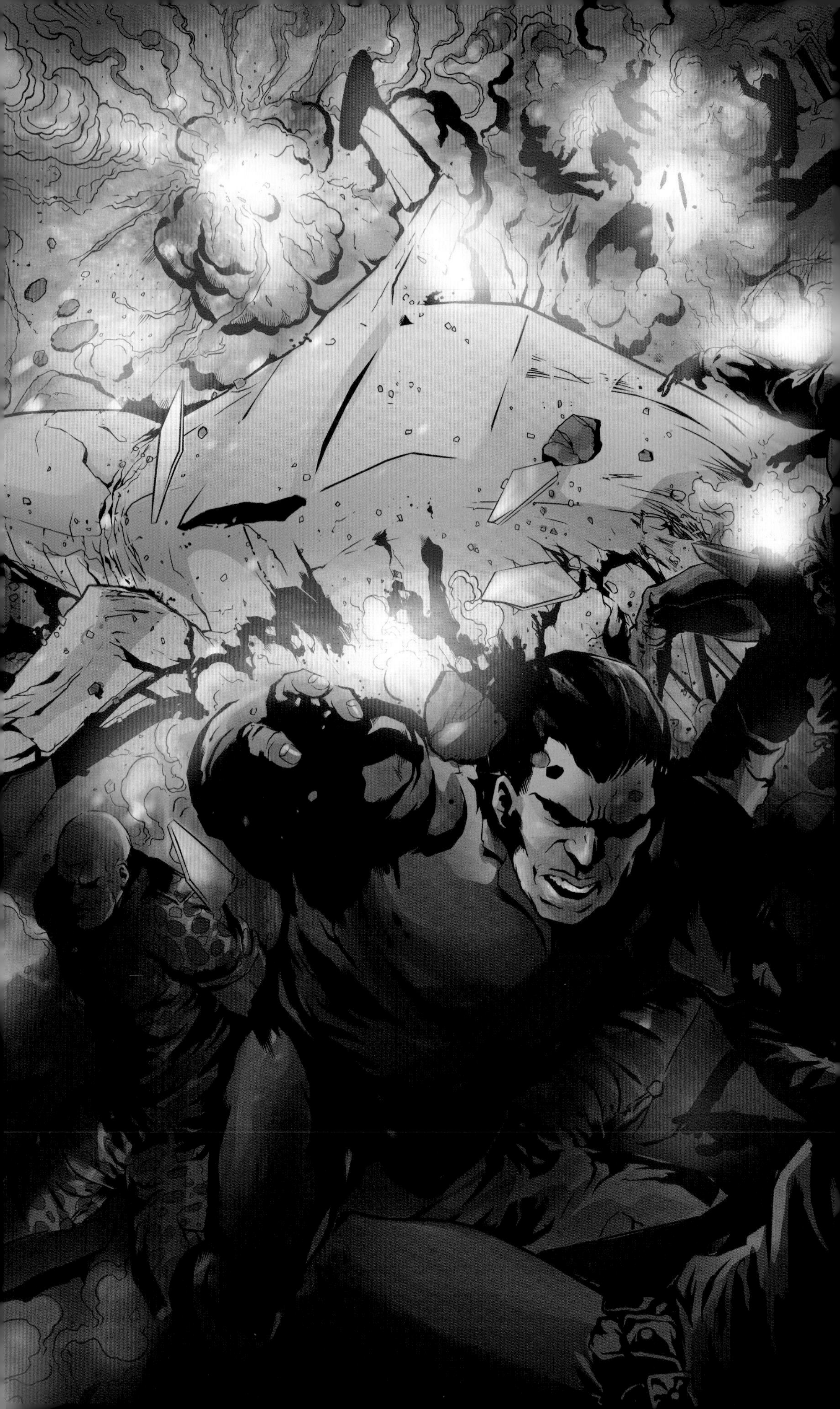

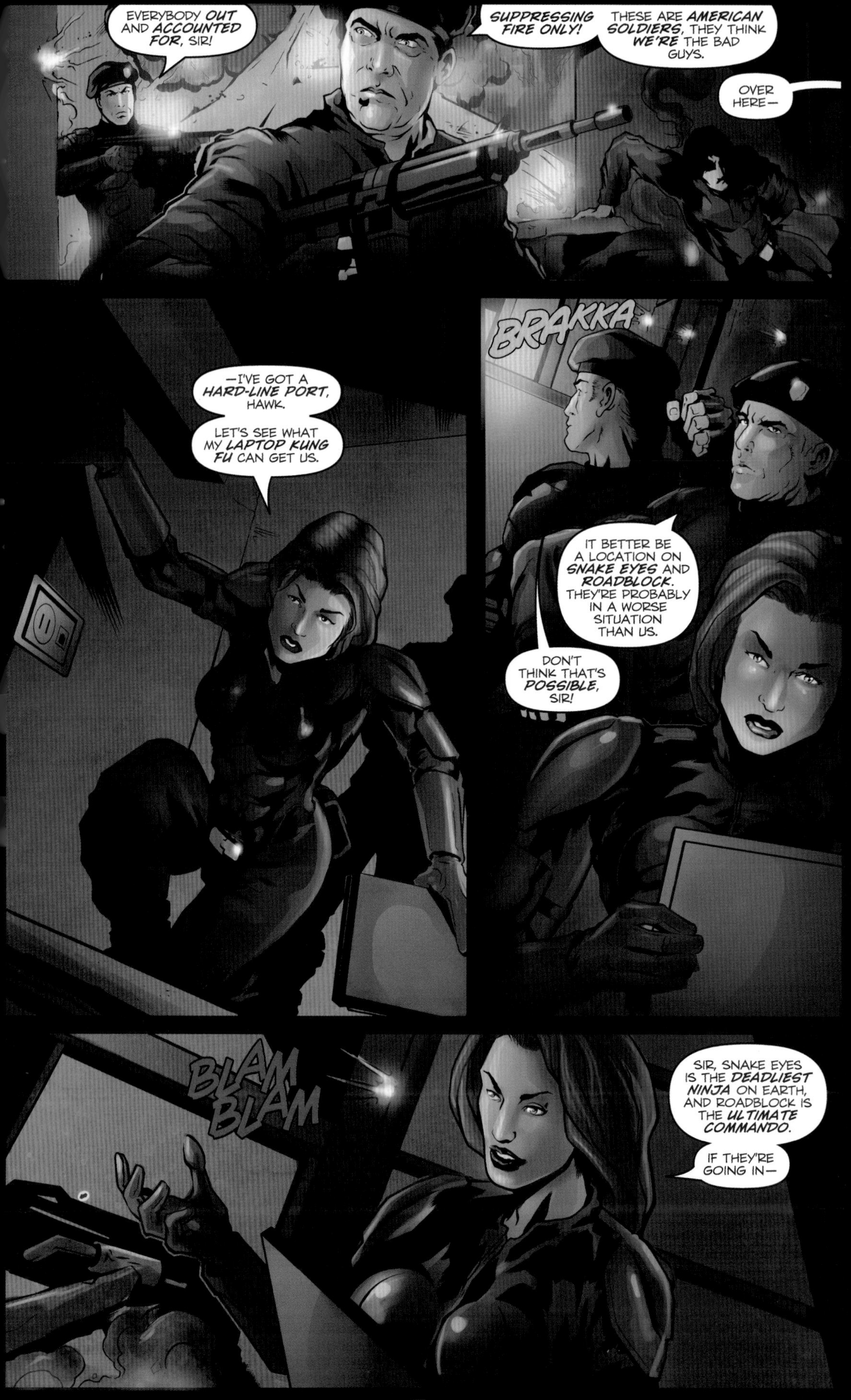
EVERYBODY OUT AND ACCOUNTED FOR, SIR!
SUPPRESSING FIRE ONLY!
THESE ARE AMERICAN SOLDIERS, THEY THINK WE'RE THE BAD GUYS.
OVER HERE—
—I'VE GOT A HARD-LINE PORT, HAWK.
LET'S SEE WHAT MY LAPTOP KUNG FU CAN GET US.
BRAKKA
IT BETTER BE A LOCATION ON SNAKE EYES AND ROADBLOCK. THEY'RE PROBABLY IN A WORSE SITUATION THAN US.
DON'T THINK THAT'S POSSIBLE, SIR!
BLAM BLAM
SIR, SNAKE EYES IS THE DEADLIEST NINJA ON EARTH, AND ROADBLOCK IS THE ULTIMATE COMMANDO.
IF THEY'RE GOING IN—

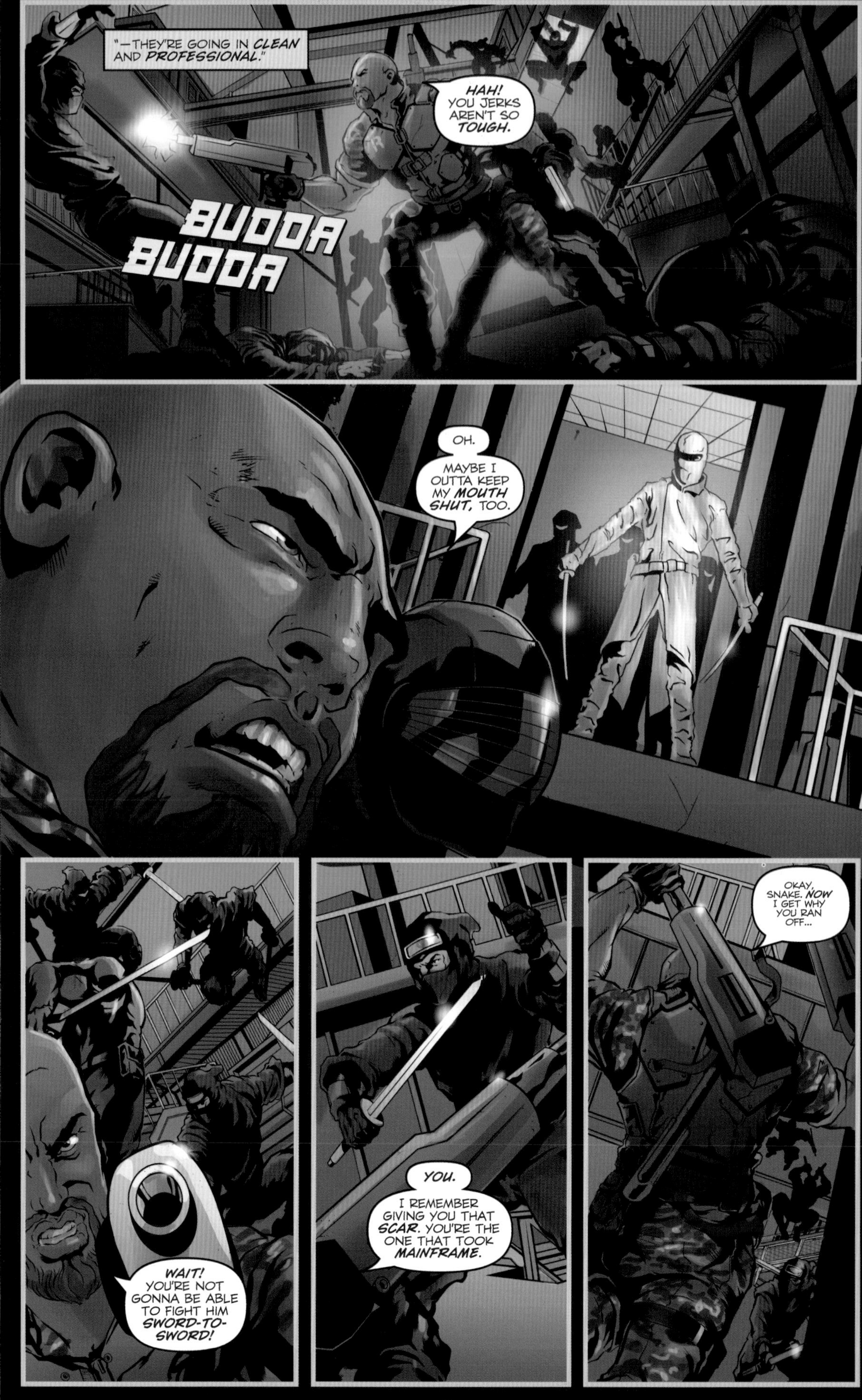
"—THEY'RE GOING IN CLEAN AND PROFESSIONAL."
HAH! YOU JERKS AREN'T SO TOUGH.
BUDDA BUDDA
OH.
MAYBE I OUTTA KEEP MY MOUTH SHUT, TOO.
WAIT! YOU'RE NOT GONNA BE ABLE TO FIGHT HIM SWORD-TO-SWORD!
YOU.
I REMEMBER GIVING YOU THAT SCAR. YOU'RE THE ONE THAT TOOK MAINFRAME.
OKAY, SNAKE. NOW I GET WHY YOU RAN OFF...

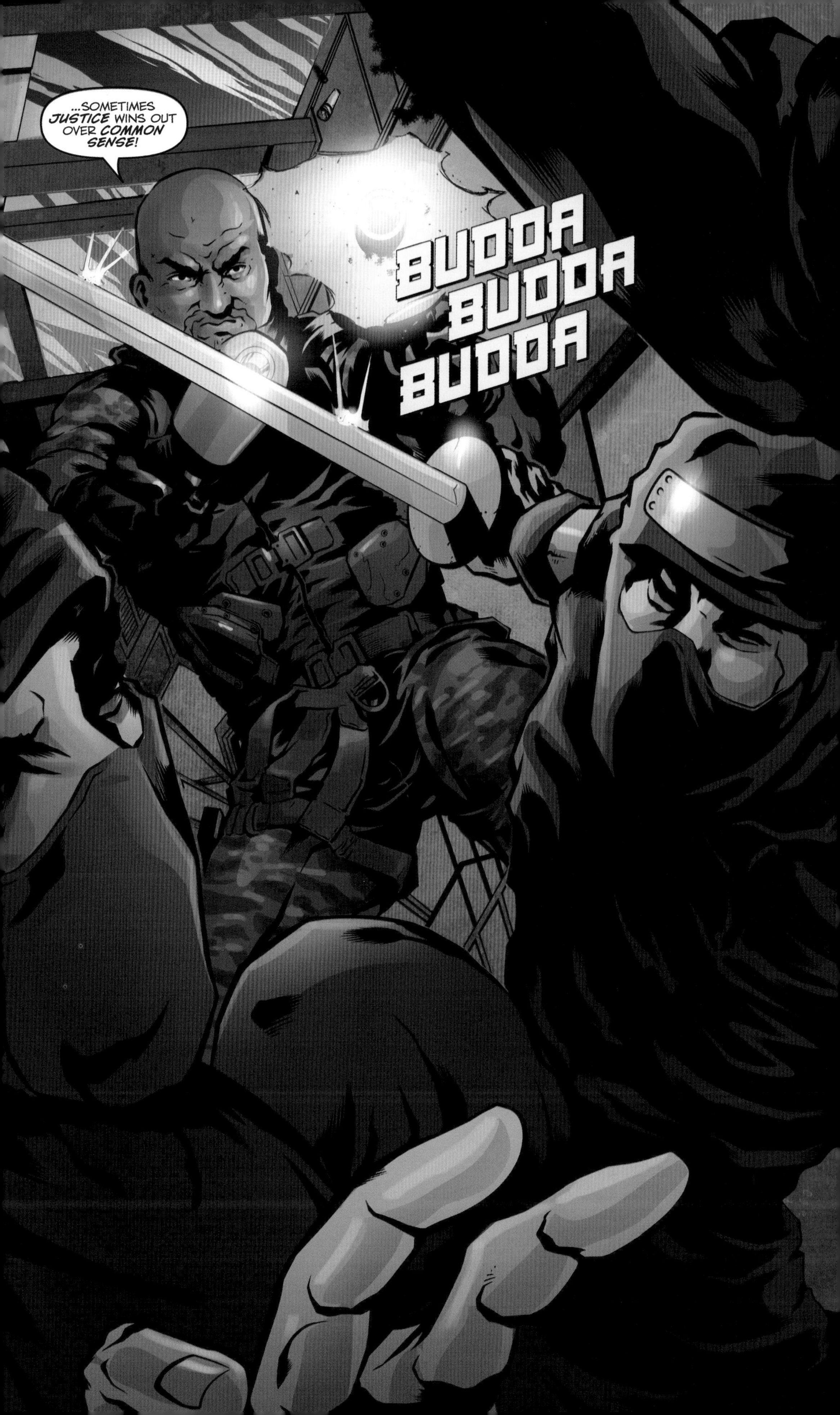
...SOMETIMES JUSTICE WINS OUT OVER COMMON SENSE!
BUDDA BUDDA BUDDA

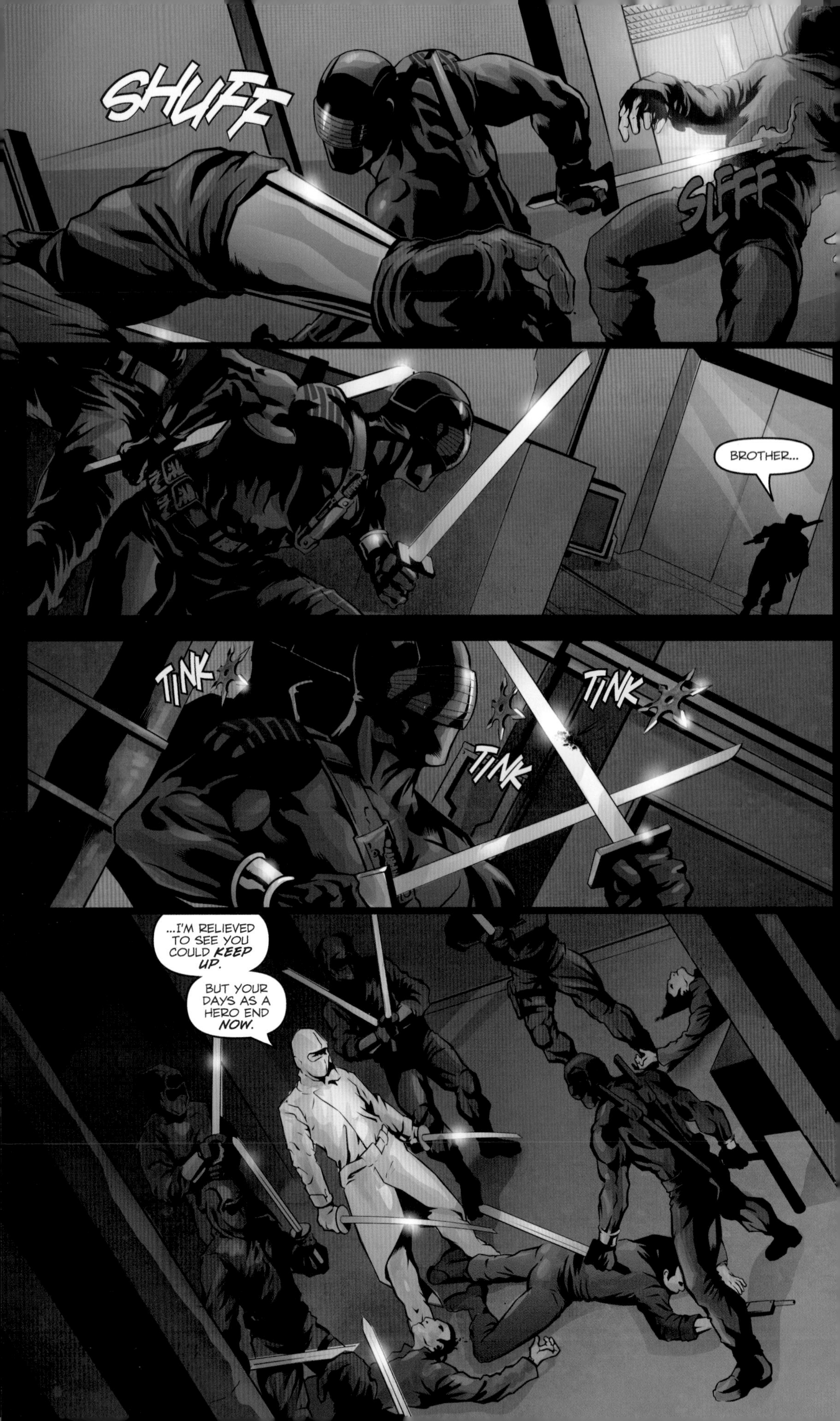
SHUFF
SLFFF
BROTHER...
TINK
TINK
TINK
...I'M RELIEVED TO SEE YOU COULD KEEP UP.
BUT YOUR DAYS AS A HERO END NOW.

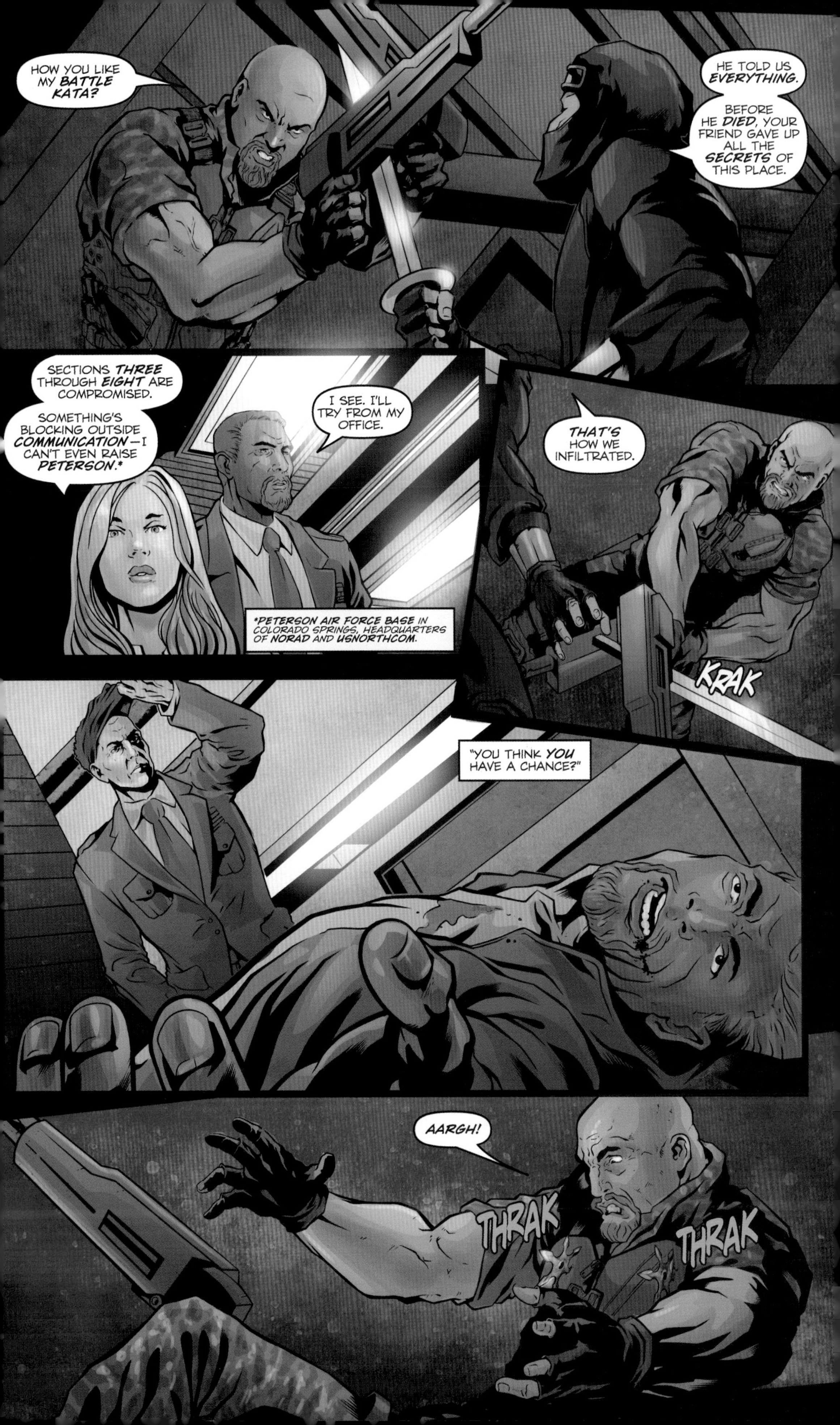
HOW YOU LIKE MY BATTLE KATA?
HE TOLD US EVERYTHING.
BEFORE HE DIED, YOUR FRIEND GAVE UP ALL THE SECRETS OF THIS PLACE.
SECTIONS THREE THROUGH EIGHT ARE COMPROMISED.
SOMETHING'S BLOCKING OUTSIDE COMMUNICATION—I CAN'T EVEN RAISE PETERSON.*
I SEE. I'LL TRY FROM MY OFFICE.
*PETERSON AIR FORCE BASE IN COLORADO SPRINGS, HEADQUARTERS OF NORAD AND USNORTHCOM.
THAT'S HOW WE INFILTRATED.
KRAK
"YOU THINK YOU HAVE A CHANCE?"
AARGH!
THRAK
THRAK

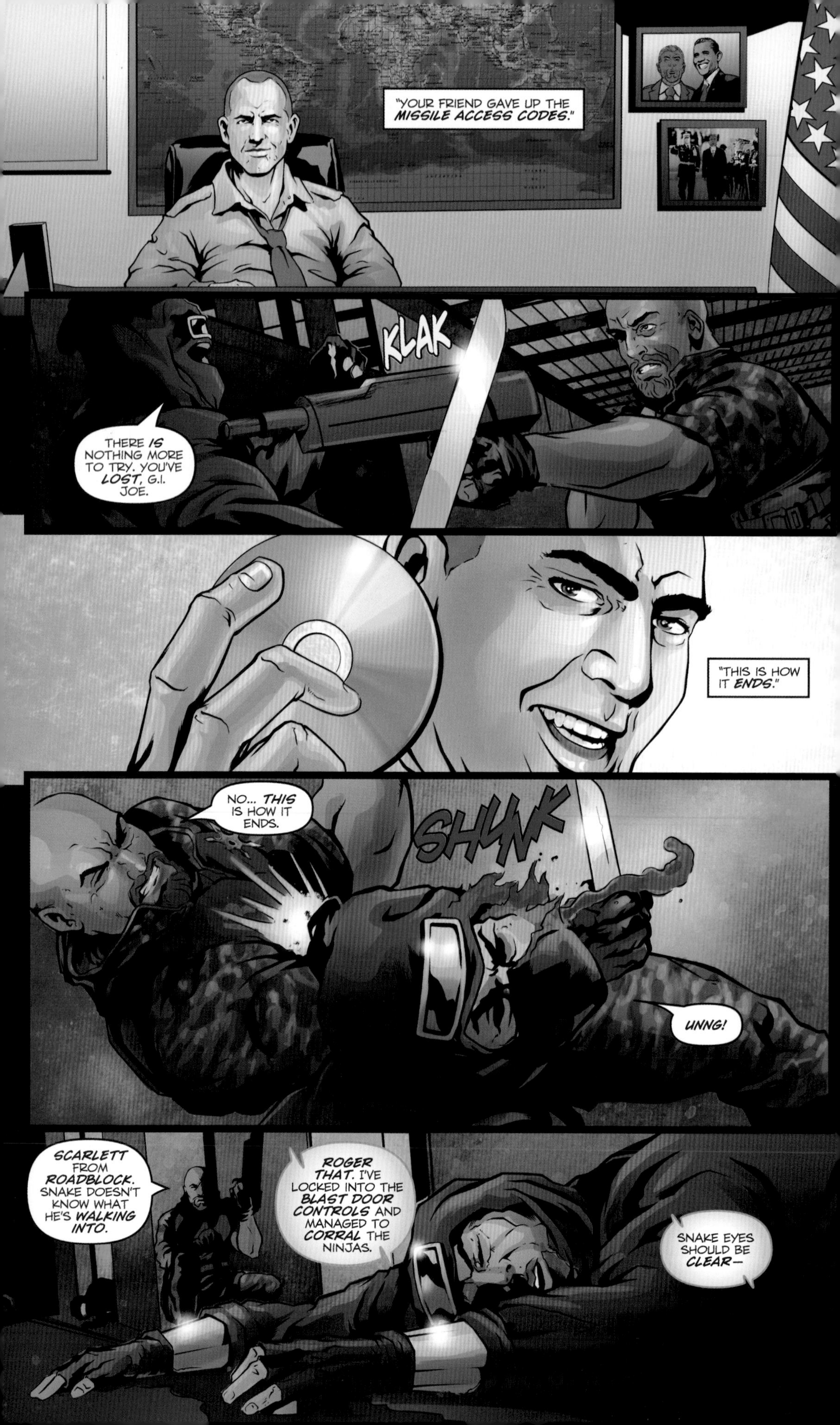
"YOUR FRIEND GAVE UP THE MISSILE ACCESS CODES."
KLAK
THERE IS NOTHING MORE TO TRY. YOU'VE LOST, G.I. JOE.
"THIS IS HOW IT ENDS."
NO... THIS IS HOW IT ENDS.
SHUNK
UNNG!
SCARLETT FROM ROADBLOCK. SNAKE DOESN'T KNOW WHAT HE'S WALKING INTO.
ROGER THAT. I'VE LOCKED INTO THE BLAST DOOR CONTROLS AND MANAGED TO CORRAL THE NINJAS.
SNAKE EYES SHOULD BE CLEAR—

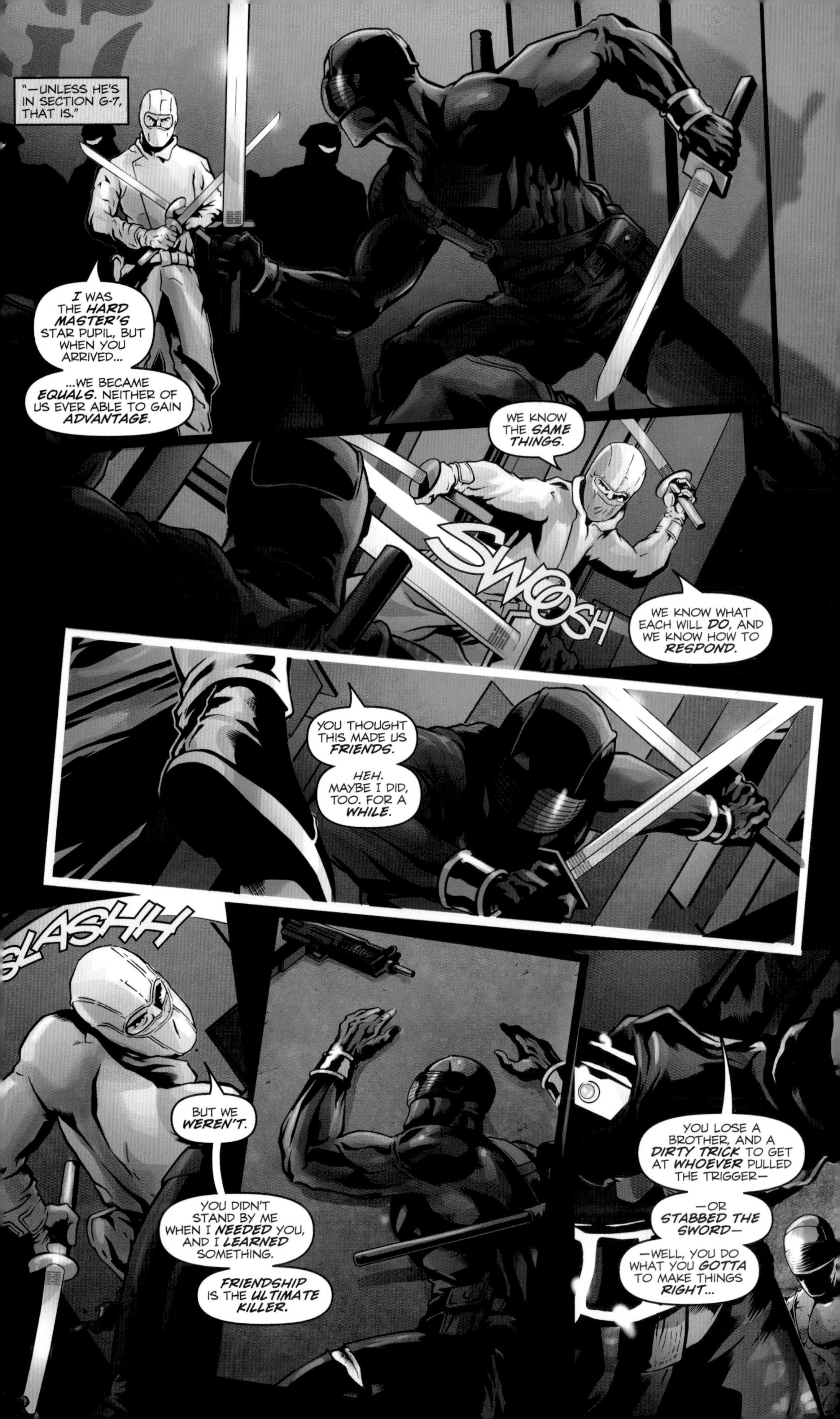
"—UNLESS HE'S IN SECTION G-7, THAT IS."
I WAS THE HARD MASTER'S STAR PUPIL, BUT WHEN YOU ARRIVED...
...WE BECAME EQUALS. NEITHER OF US EVER ABLE TO GAIN ADVANTAGE.
WE KNOW THE SAME THINGS.
SWOOSH
WE KNOW WHAT EACH WILL DO, AND WE KNOW HOW TO RESPOND.
YOU THOUGHT THIS MADE US FRIENDS.
HEH. MAYBE I DID, TOO. FOR A WHILE.
SLASHH
BUT WE WEREN'T.
YOU DIDN'T STAND BY ME WHEN I NEEDED YOU, AND I LEARNED SOMETHING.
FRIENDSHIP IS THE ULTIMATE KILLER.
YOU LOSE A BROTHER, AND A DIRTY TRICK TO GET AT WHOEVER PULLED THE TRIGGER—
—OR STABBED THE SWORD—
—WELL, YOU DO WHAT YOU GOTTA TO MAKE THINGS RIGHT...

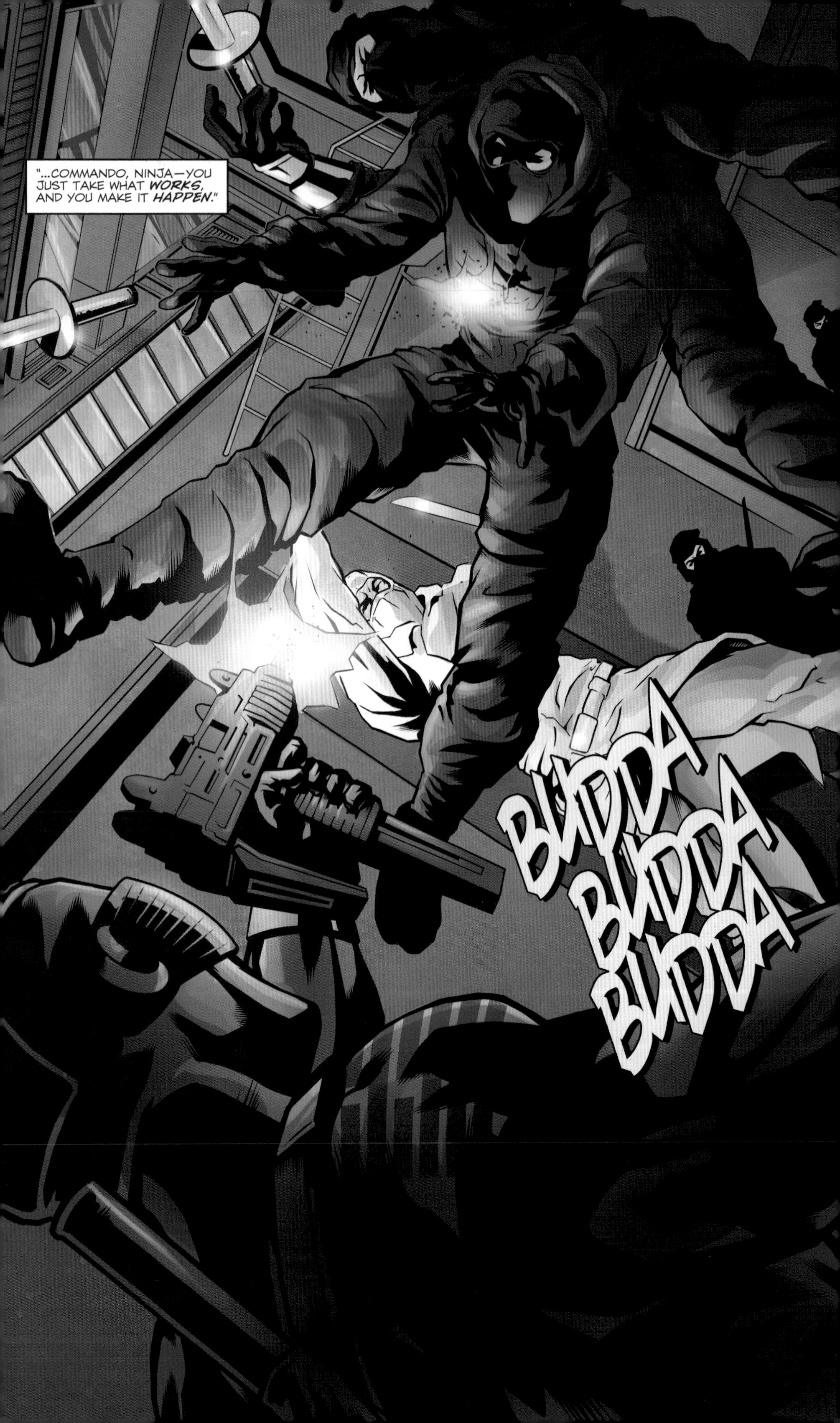
"...COMMANDO, NINJA—YOU JUST TAKE WHAT WORKS, AND YOU MAKE IT HAPPEN."
BUDDA BUDDA BUDDA

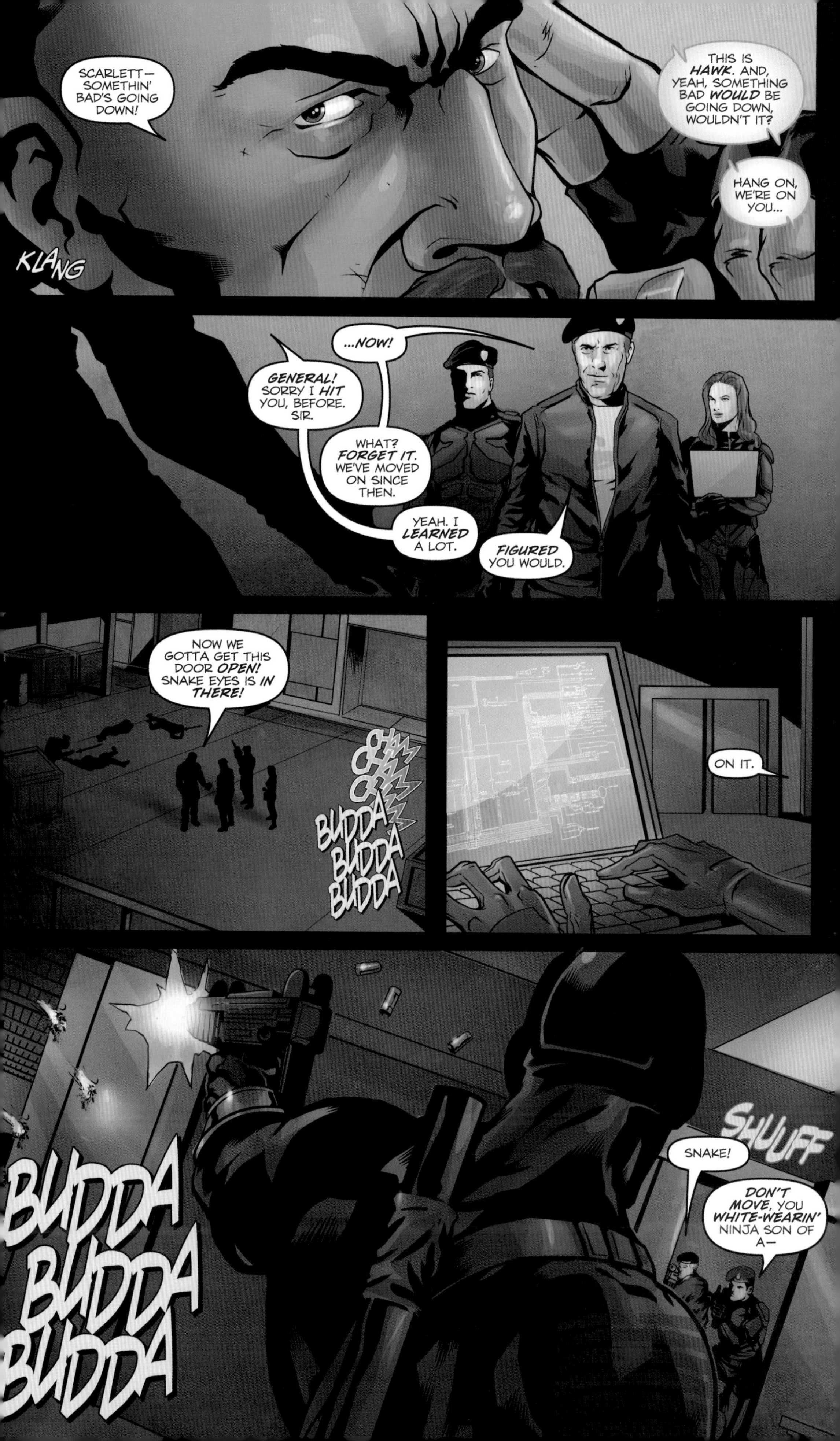
SCARLETT—SOMETHIN' BAD'S GOING DOWN!
THIS IS HAWK. AND, YEAH, SOMETHING BAD WOULD BE GOING DOWN, WOULDN'T IT?
HANG ON, WE'RE ON YOU...
KLANG
GENERAL! SORRY I HIT YOU, BEFORE. SIR.
...NOW!
WHAT? FORGET IT. WE'VE MOVED ON SINCE THEN.
YEAH. I LEARNED A LOT.
FIGURED YOU WOULD.
NOW WE GOTTA GET THIS DOOR OPEN! SNAKE EYES IS IN THERE!
CHAM CHAM CHAM
BUDDA BUDDA BUDDA
ON IT.
BUDDA BUDDA BUDDA
SHUUFF
SNAKE!
DON'T MOVE, YOU WHITE-WEARIN' NINJA SON OF A—

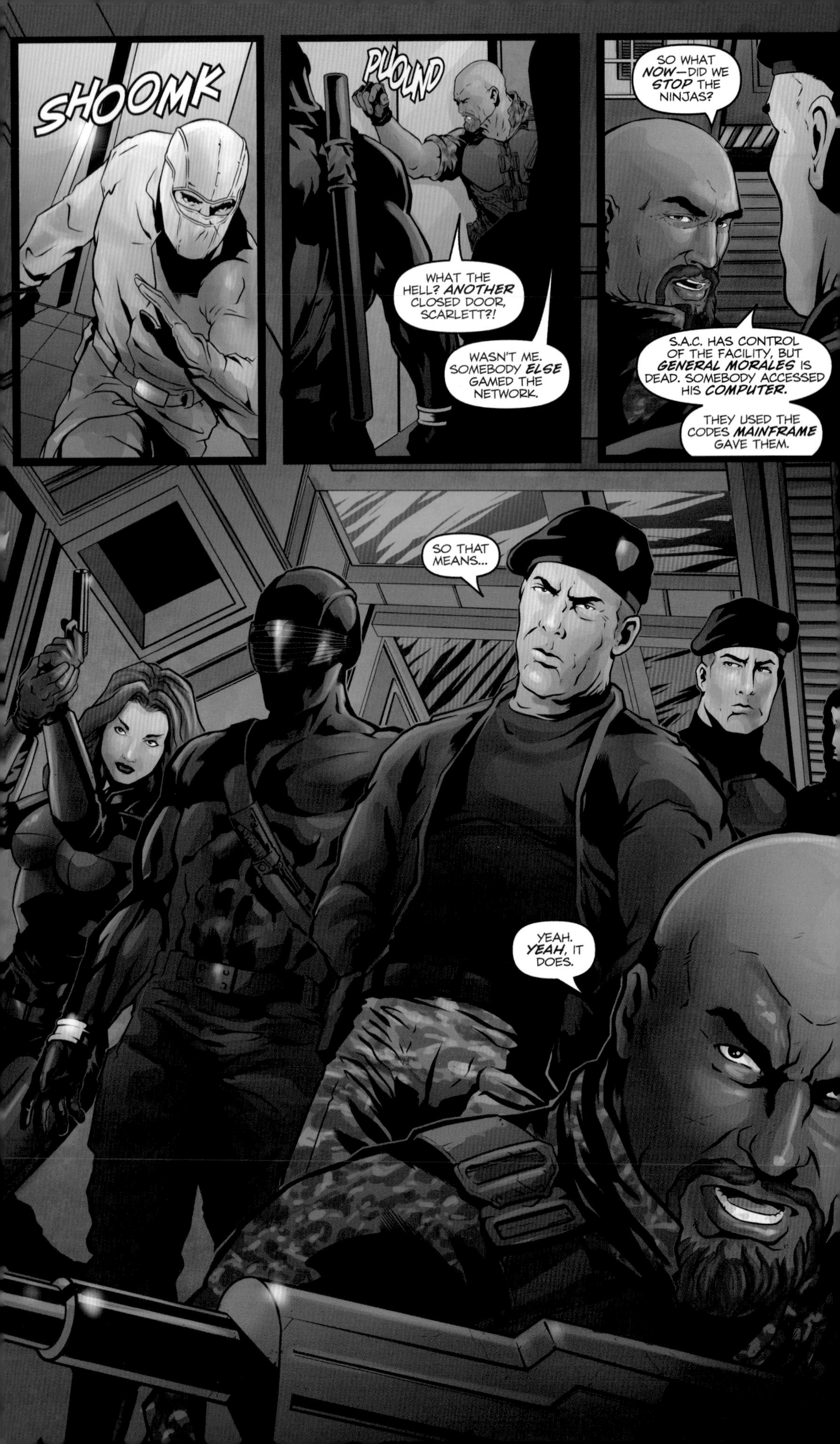
SHOOMK
PUOUND
WHAT THE HELL? ANOTHER CLOSED DOOR, SCARLETT?!
WASN'T ME. SOMEBODY ELSE GAMED THE NETWORK.
SO WHAT NOW—DID WE STOP THE NINJAS?
S.A.C. HAS CONTROL OF THE FACILITY, BUT GENERAL MORALES IS DEAD. SOMEBODY ACCESSED HIS COMPUTER.
THEY USED THE CODES MAINFRAME GAVE THEM.
SO THAT MEANS...
YEAH. YEAH, IT DOES.

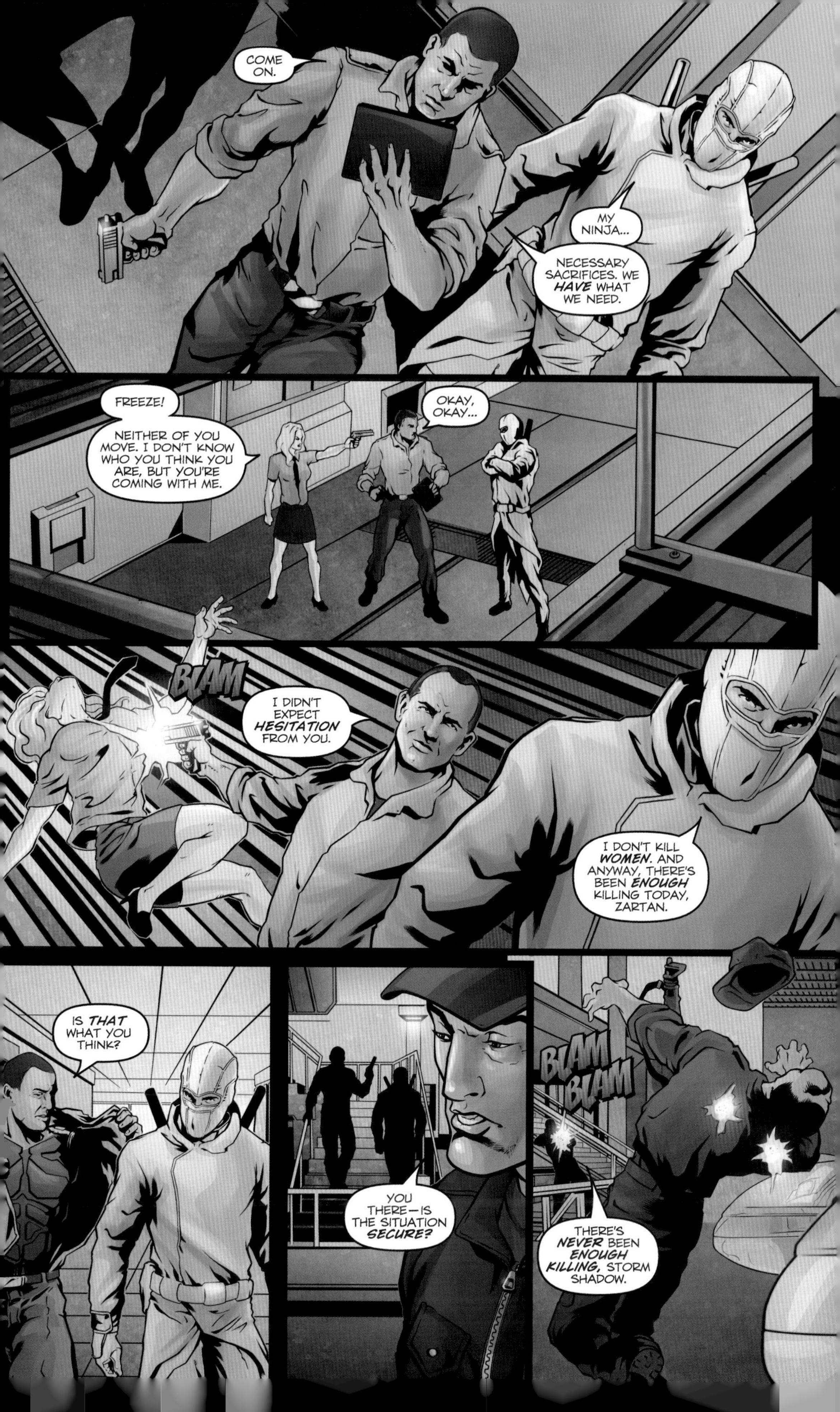
COME ON.
MY NINJA...
NECESSARY SACRIFICES. WE HAVE WHAT WE NEED.
FREEZE!
NEITHER OF YOU MOVE. I DON'T KNOW WHO YOU THINK YOU ARE, BUT YOU'RE COMING WITH ME.
OKAY, OKAY...
BLAM
I DIDN'T EXPECT HESITATION FROM YOU.
I DON'T KILL WOMEN. AND ANYWAY, THERE'S BEEN ENOUGH KILLING TODAY, ZARTAN.
IS THAT WHAT YOU THINK?
YOU THERE—IS THE SITUATION SECURE?
BLAM
BLAM
THERE'S NEVER BEEN ENOUGH KILLING, STORM SHADOW.

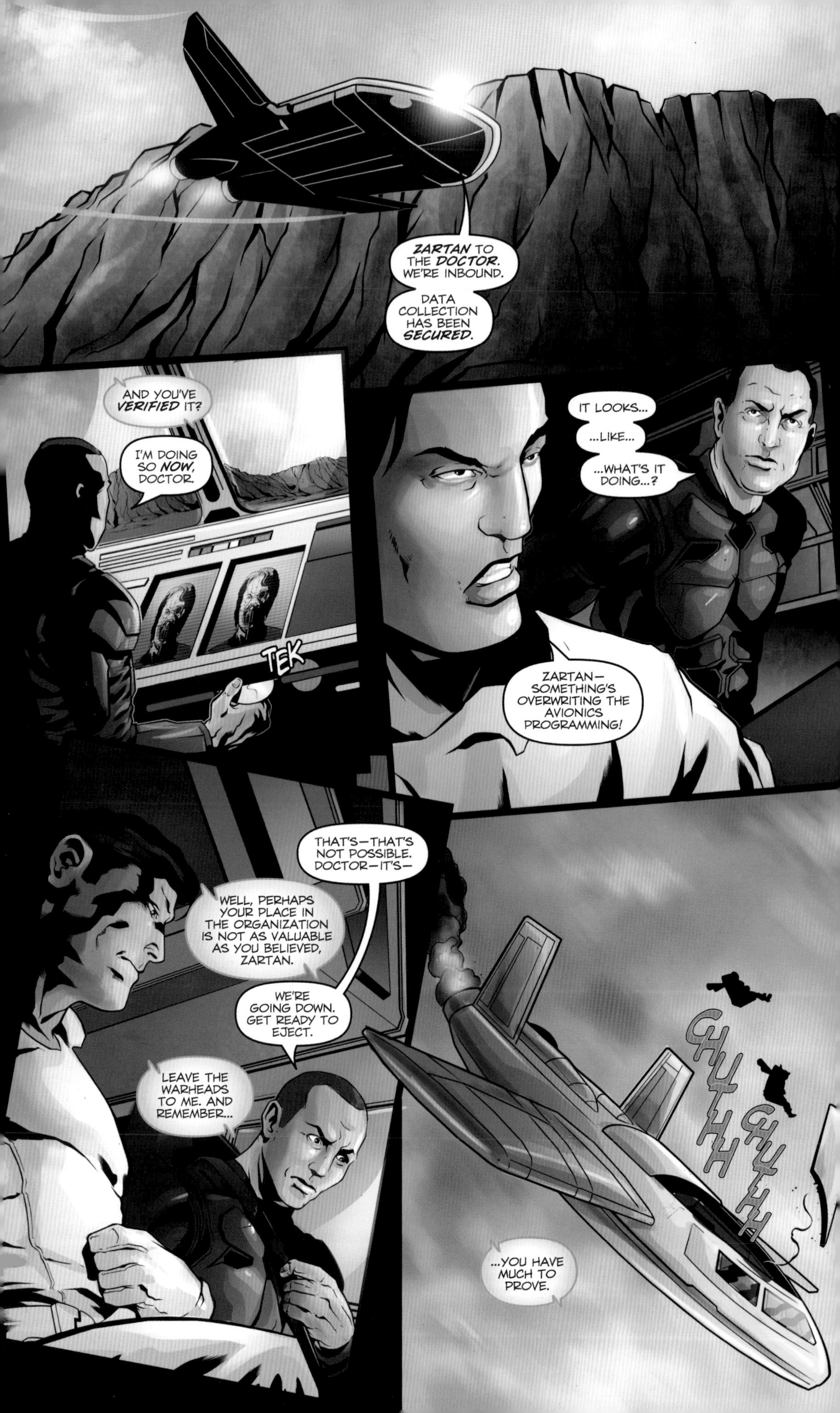
ZARTAN TO THE DOCTOR. WE'RE INBOUND.
DATA COLLECTION HAS BEEN SECURED.
AND YOU'VE VERIFIED IT?
I'M DOING SO NOW, DOCTOR.
TEK
IT LOOKS...
...LIKE...
...WHAT'S IT DOING...?
ZARTAN—SOMETHING'S OVERWRITING THE AVIONICS PROGRAMMING!
THAT'S—THAT'S NOT POSSIBLE. DOCTOR—IT'S—
WELL, PERHAPS YOUR PLACE IN THE ORGANIZATION IS NOT AS VALUABLE AS YOU BELIEVED, ZARTAN.
WE'RE GOING DOWN. GET READY TO EJECT.
LEAVE THE WARHEADS TO ME. AND REMEMBER...
CHUHHH
CHUHHH
...YOU HAVE MUCH TO PROVE.

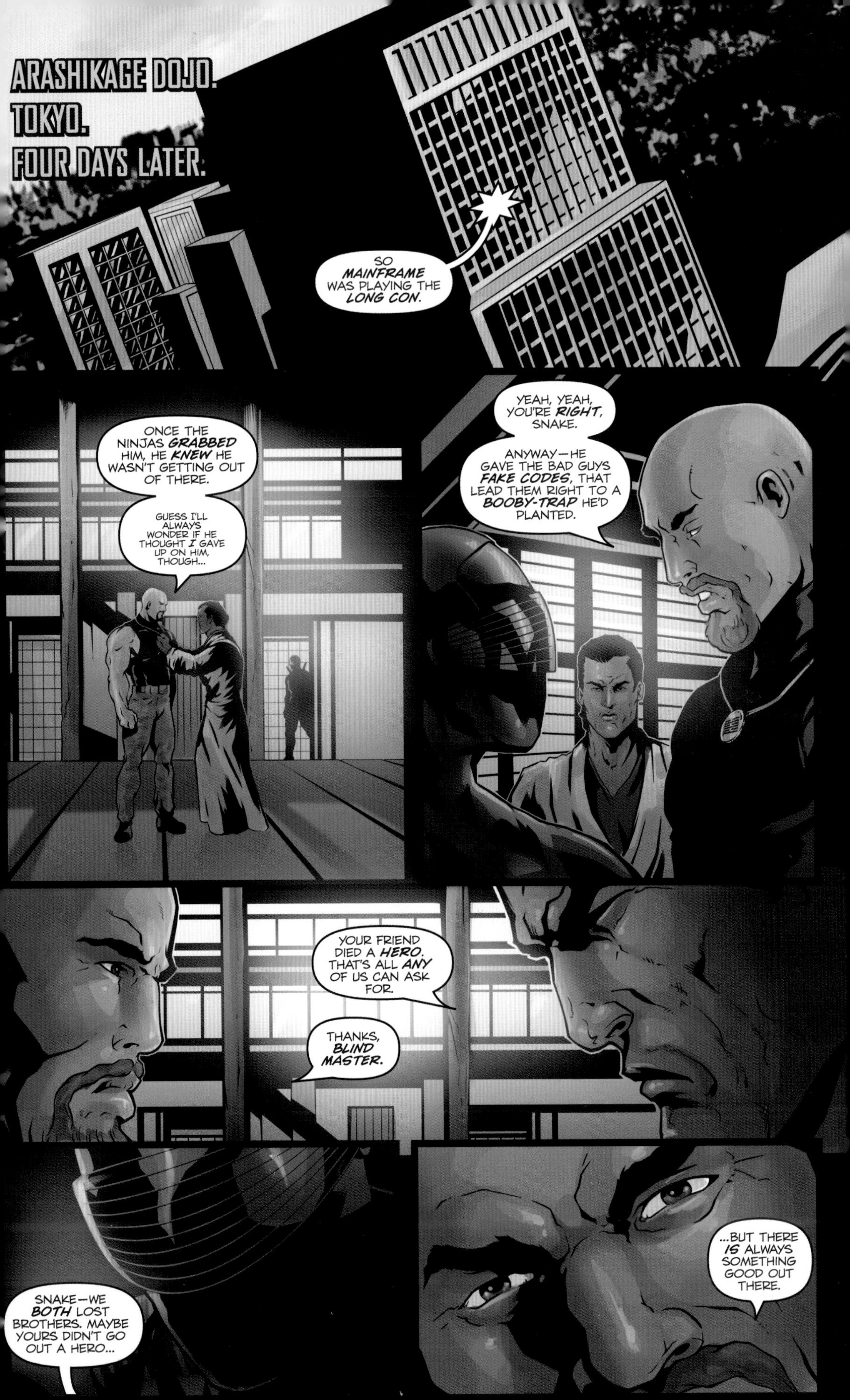
ARASHIKAGE DOJO.
TOKYO.
FOUR DAYS LATER.
SO MAINFRAME WAS PLAYING THE LONG CON.
ONCE THE NINJAS GRABBED HIM, HE KNEW HE WASN'T GETTING OUT OF THERE.
GUESS I'LL ALWAYS WONDER IF HE THOUGHT I GAVE UP ON HIM, THOUGH...
YEAH, YEAH, YOU'RE RIGHT, SNAKE.
ANYWAY—HE GAVE THE BAD GUYS FAKE CODES, THAT LEAD THEM RIGHT TO A BOOBY-TRAP HE'D PLANTED.
YOUR FRIEND DIED A HERO. THAT'S ALL ANY OF US CAN ASK FOR.
THANKS, BLIND MASTER.
SNAKE—WE BOTH LOST BROTHERS. MAYBE YOURS DIDN'T GO OUT A HERO...
...BUT THERE IS ALWAYS SOMETHING GOOD OUT THERE.

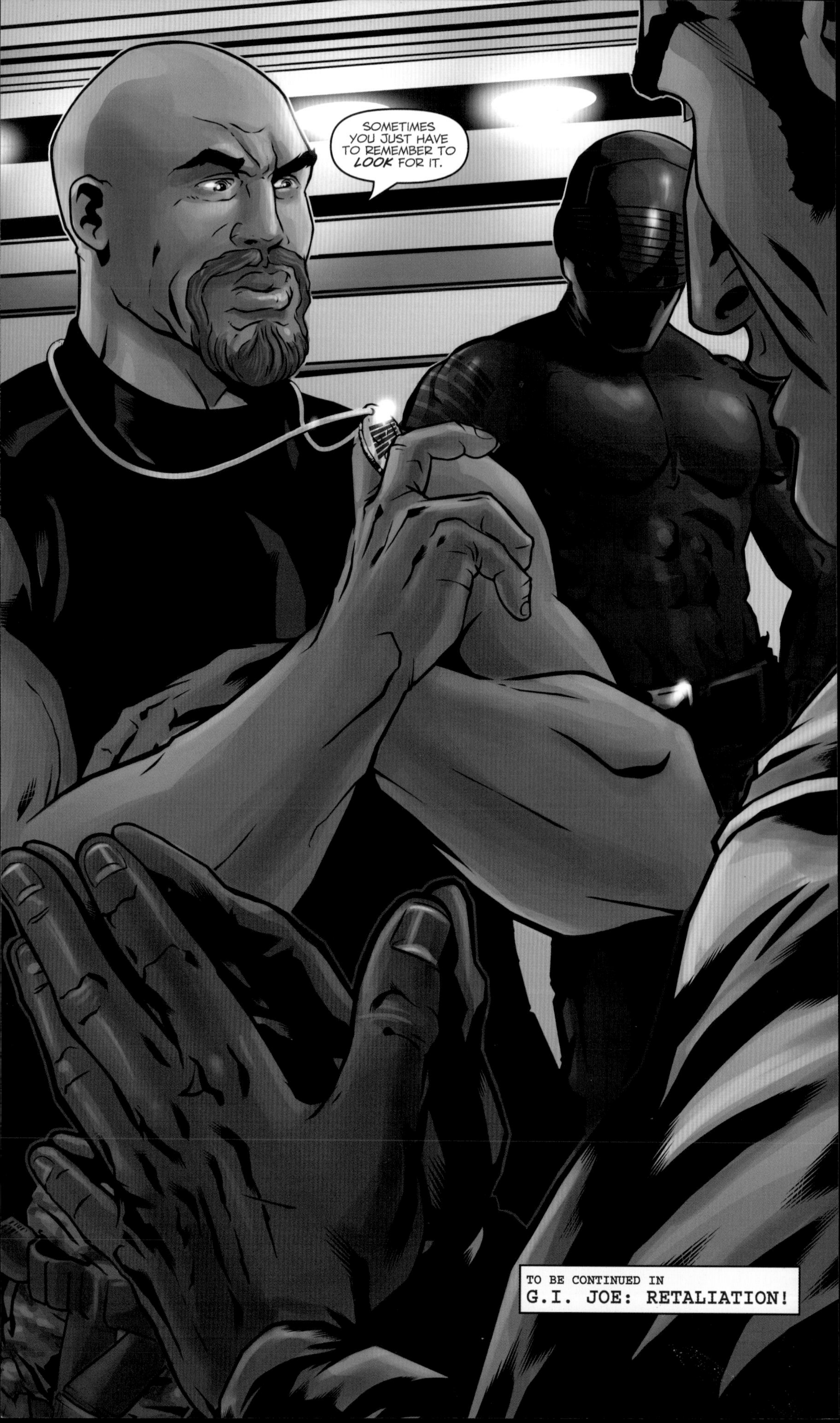
SOMETIMES YOU JUST HAVE TO REMEMBER TO *LOOK* FOR IT.
TO BE CONTINUED IN G.I. JOE: RETALIATION!

ART GALLERY

ART BY SALVADOR NAVARRO

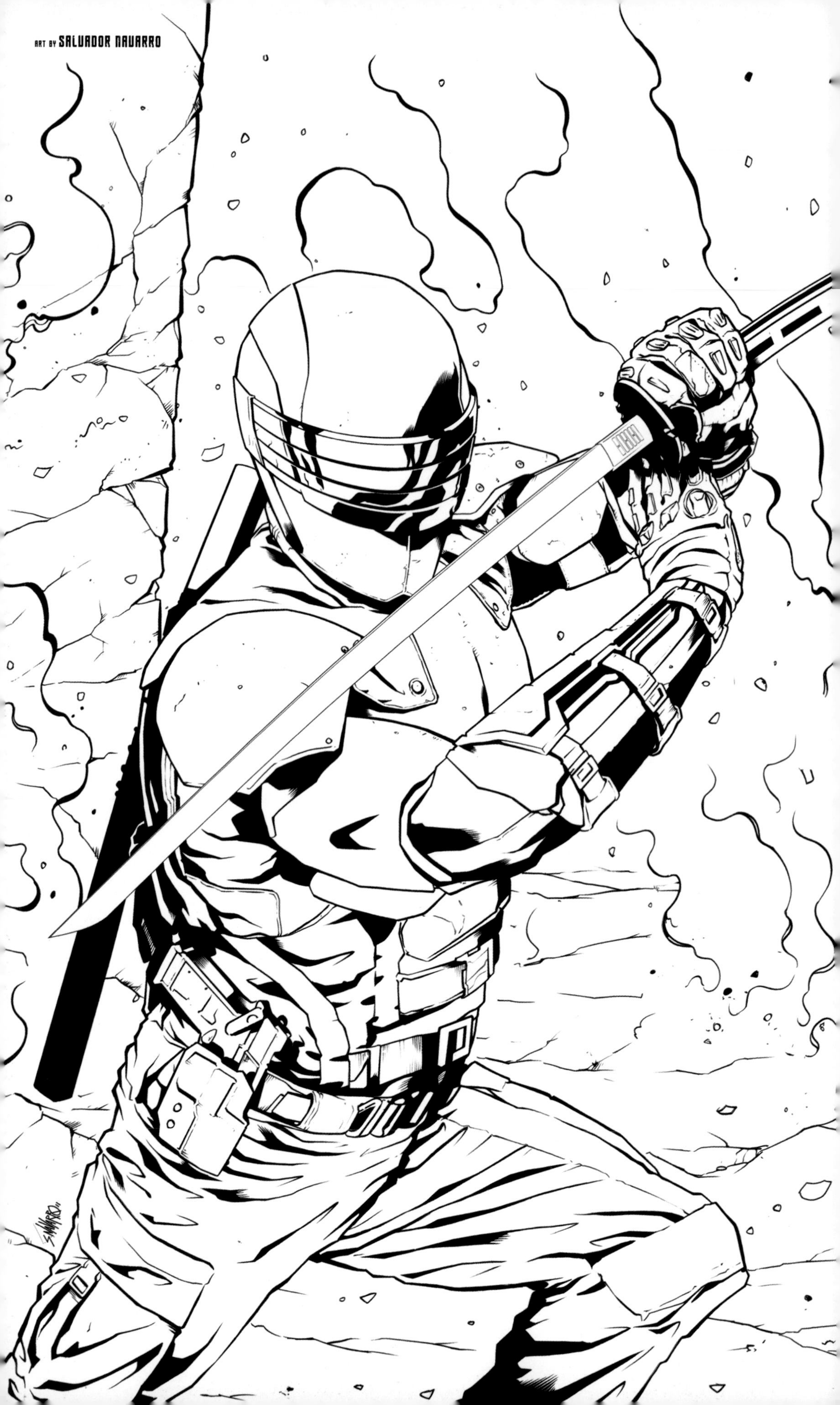

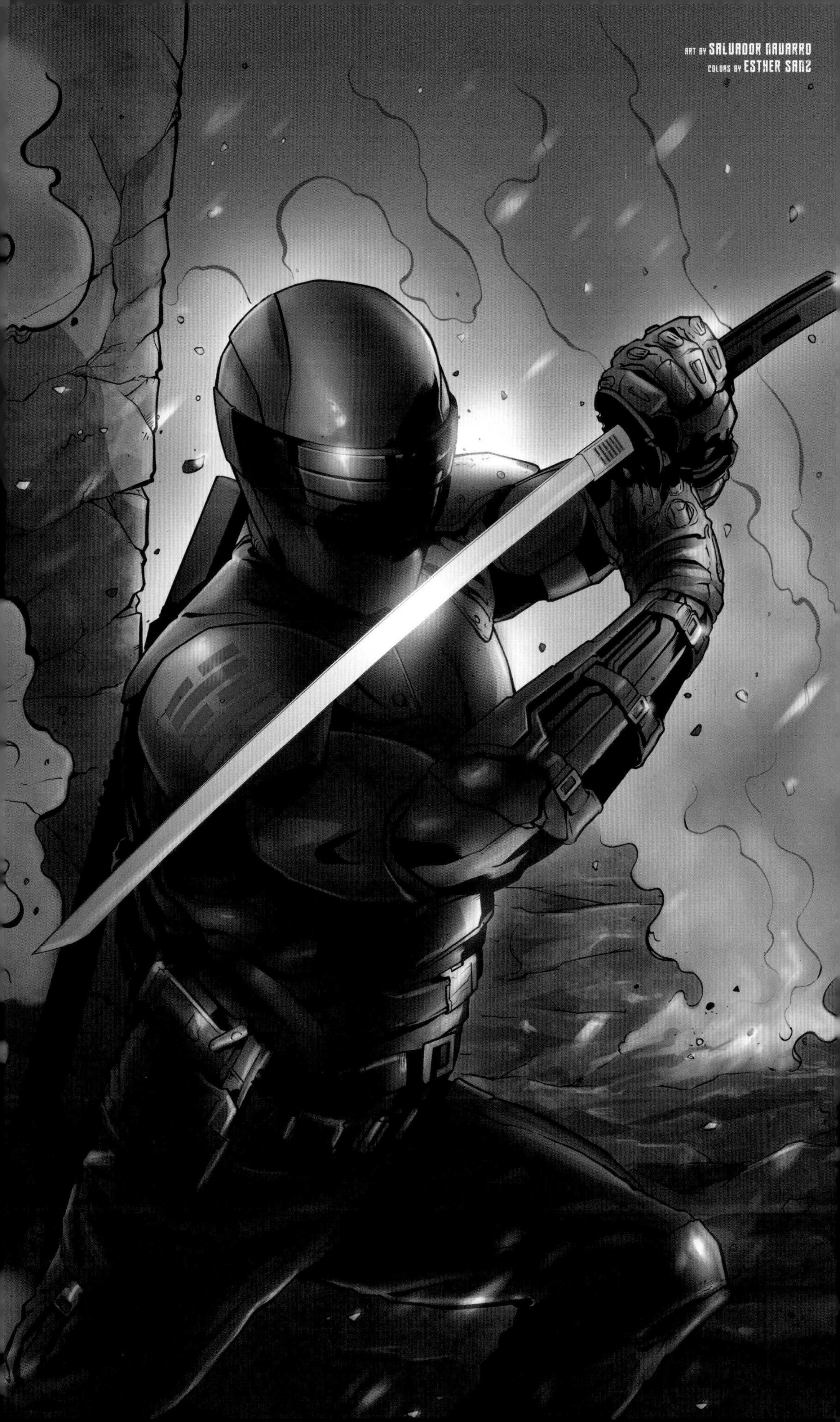
ART BY SALVADOR NAVARRO
COLORS BY ESTHER SANZ

ART BY SALVADOR NAVARR

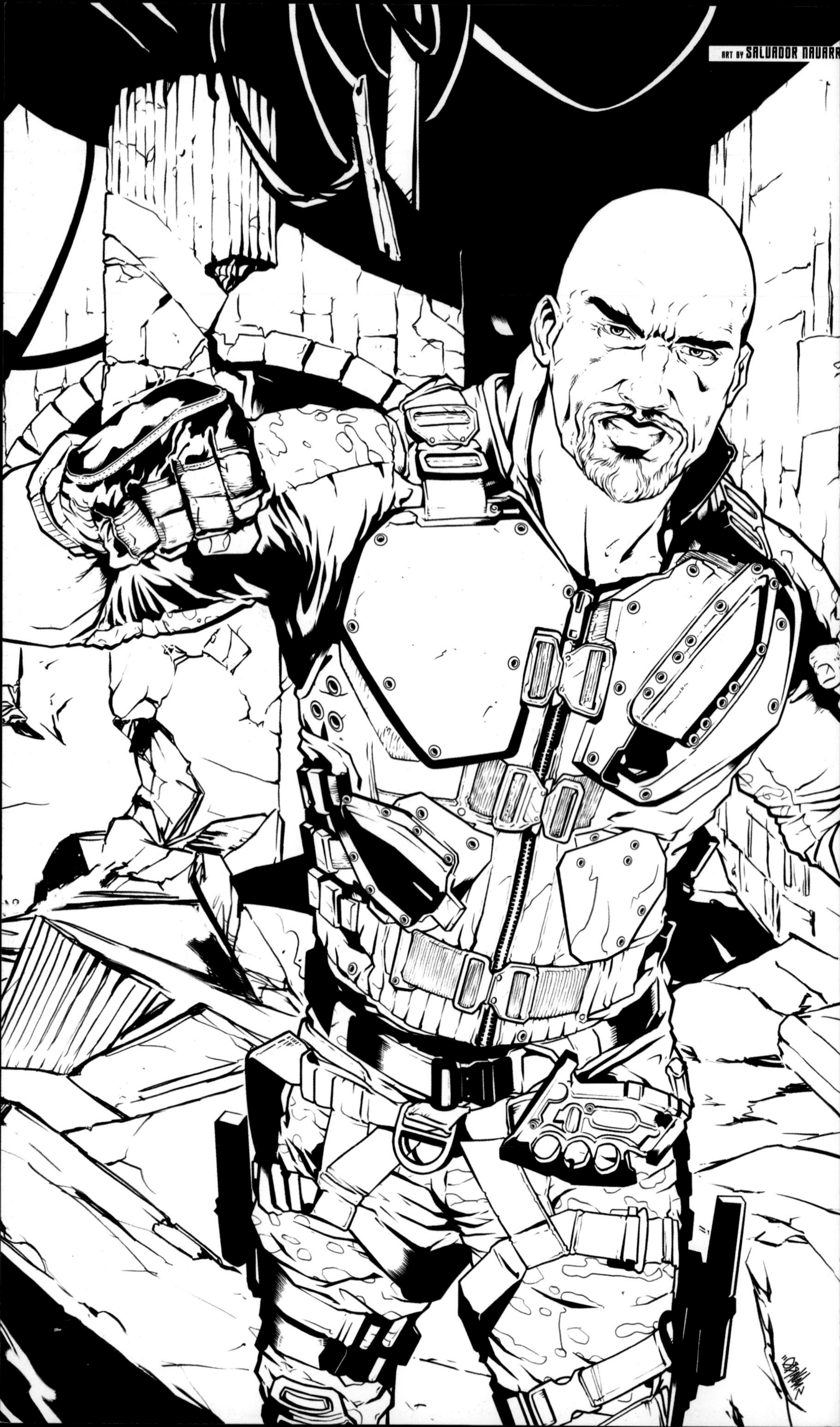

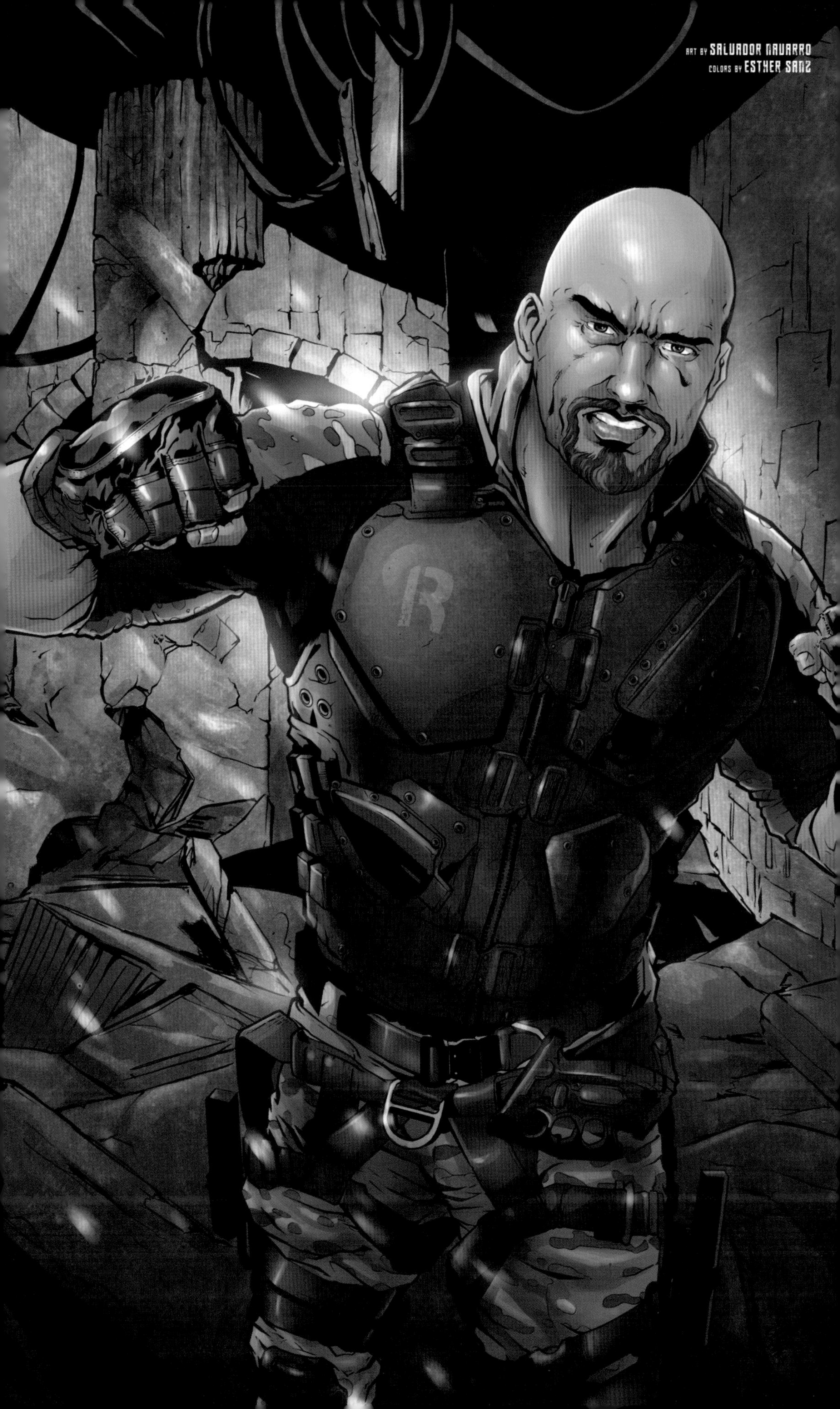
ART BY SALVADOR NAVARRO
COLORS BY ESTHER SANZ

ART BY SALVADOR NAVARRO

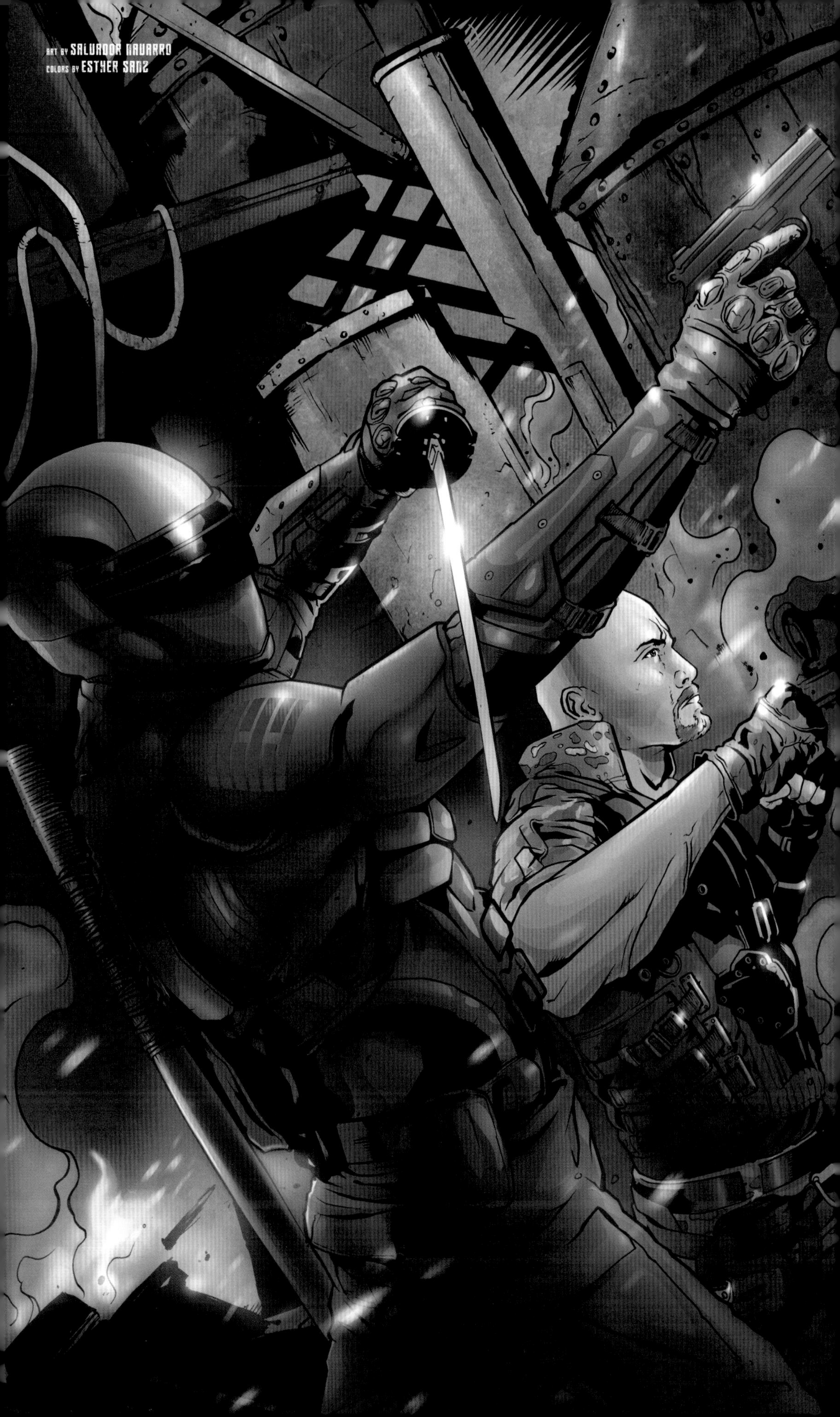
ART BY SALVADOR NAVARRO
COLORS BY ESTHER SANZ

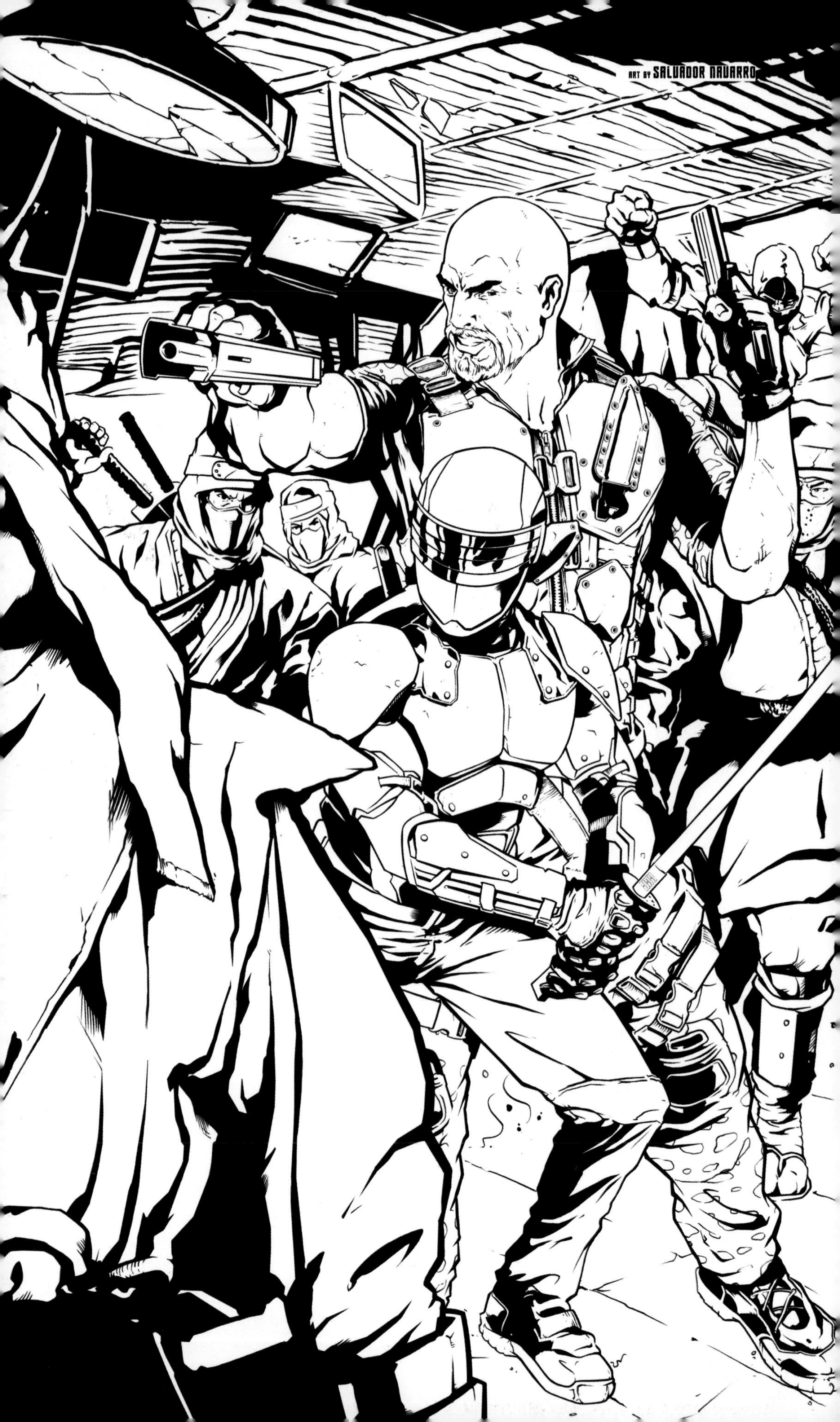
ART BY SALVADOR NAVARRO

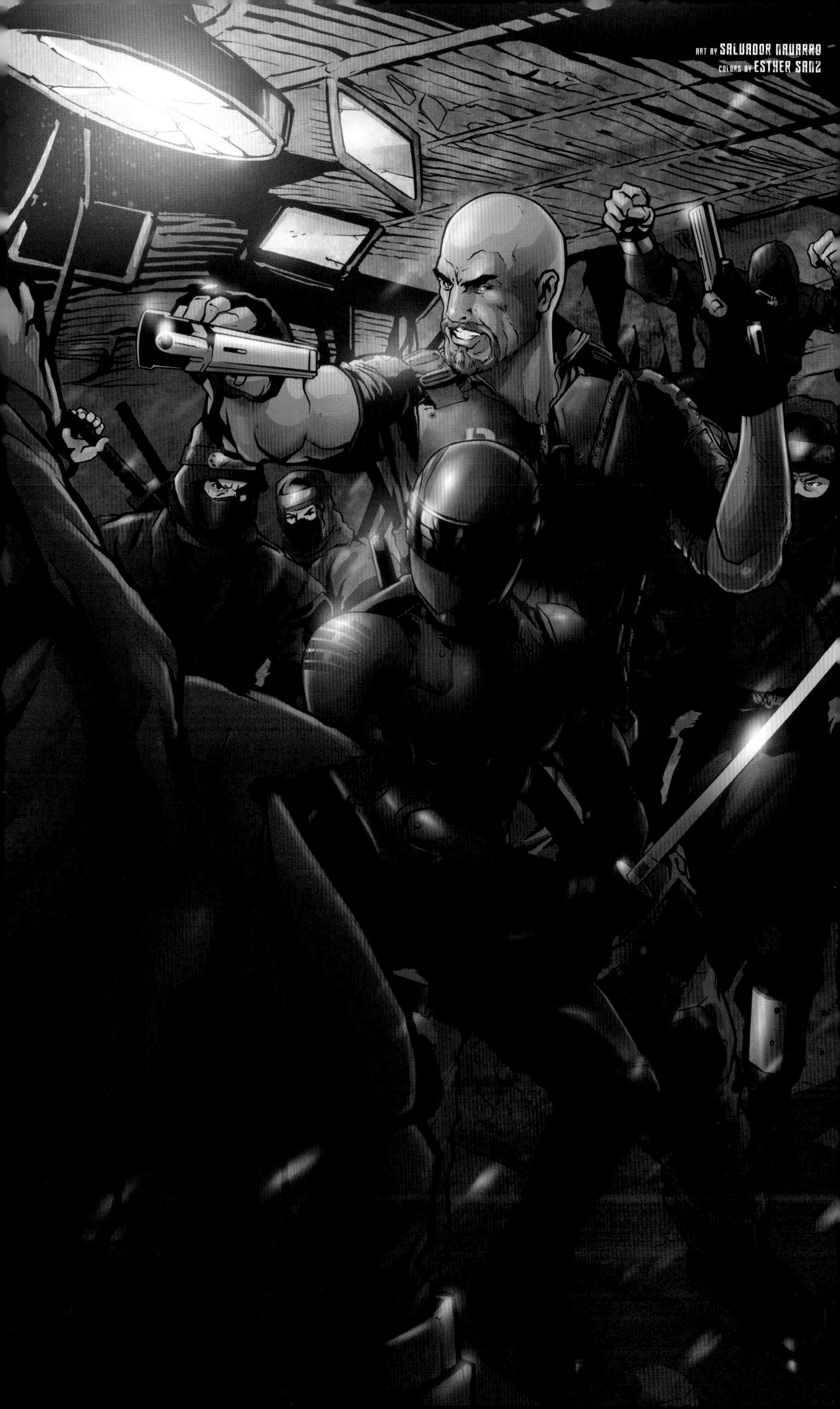
ART BY SALVADOR NAVARRO
COLORS BY ESTHER SANZ

Art by Salvador Navarro

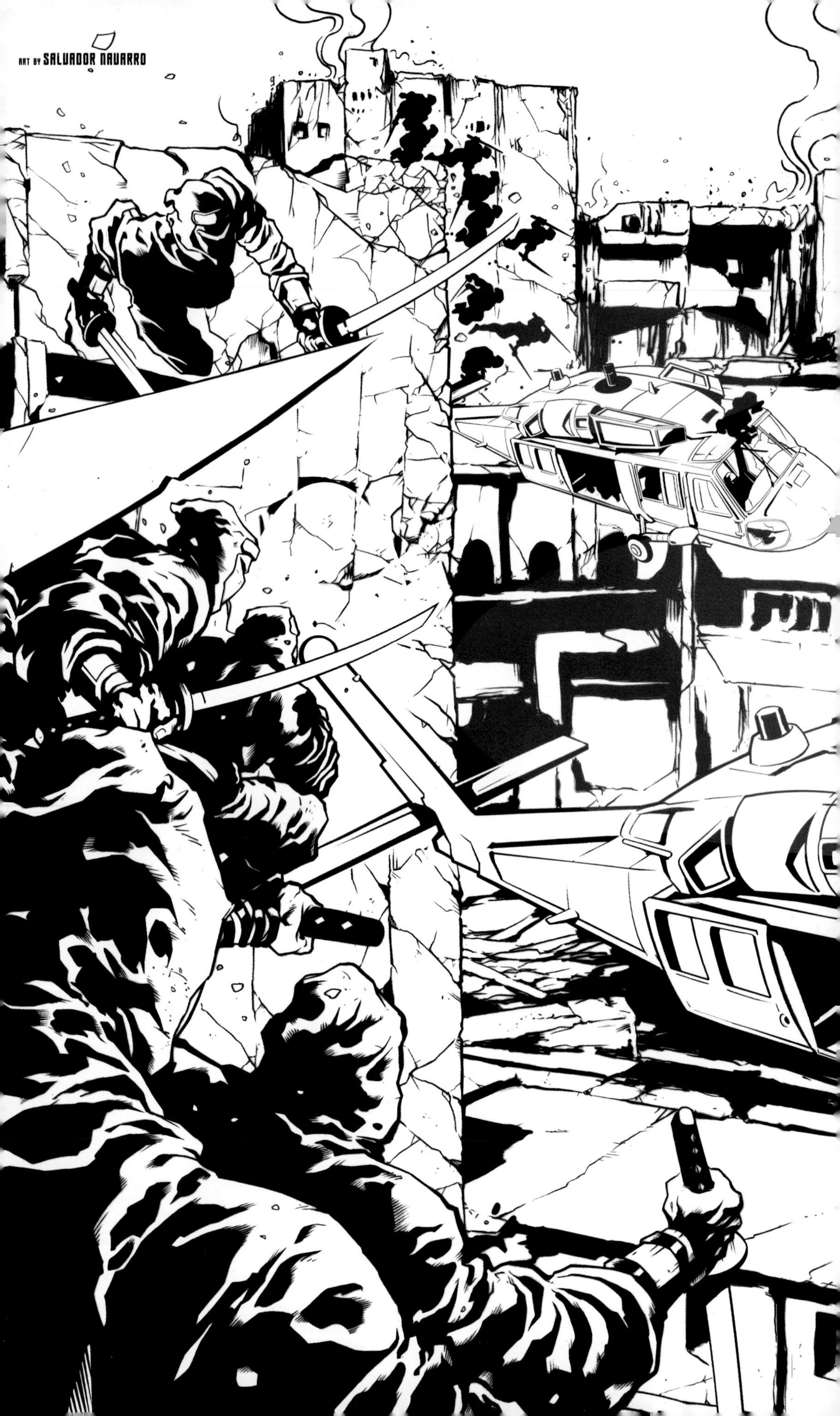

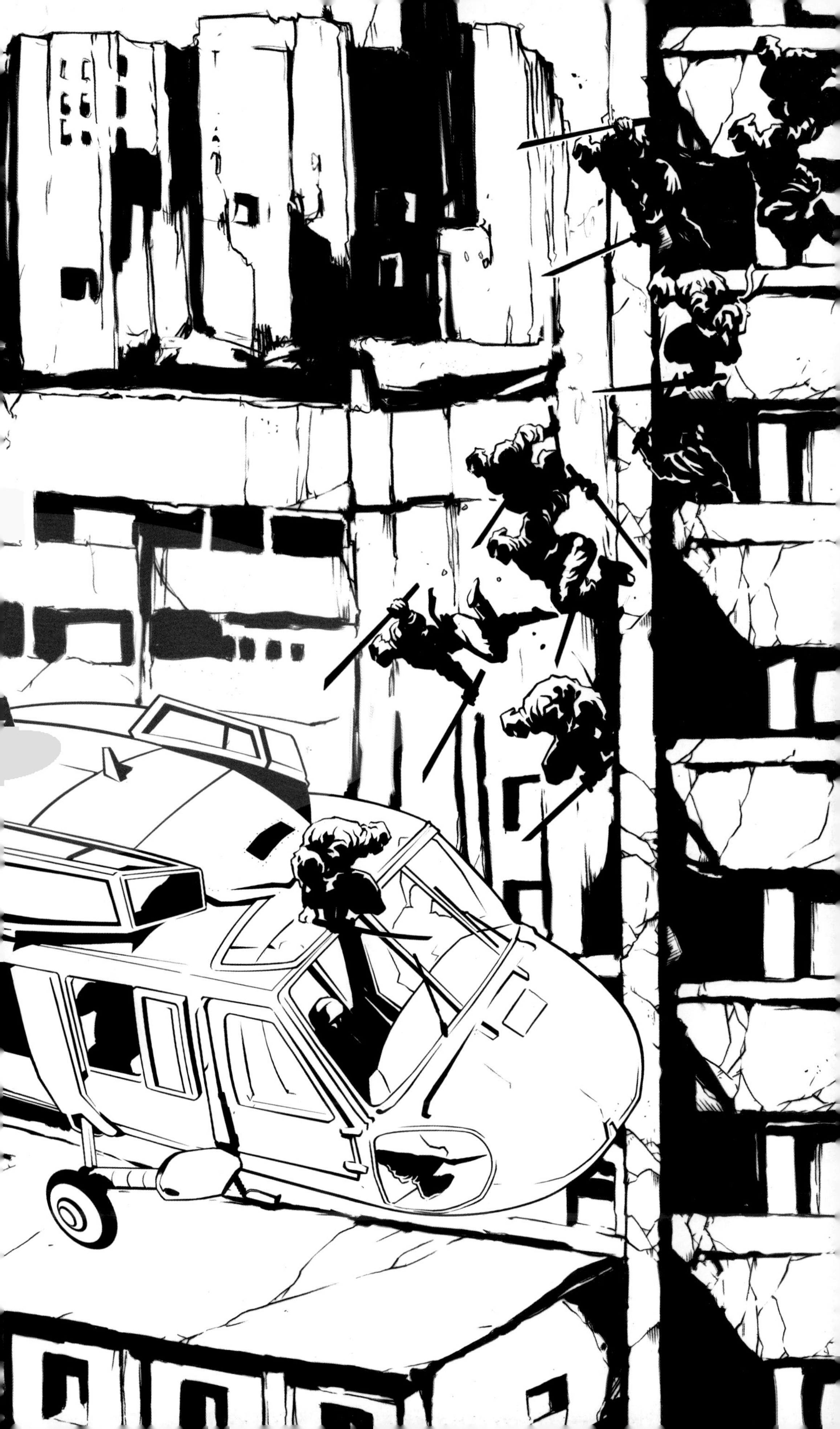

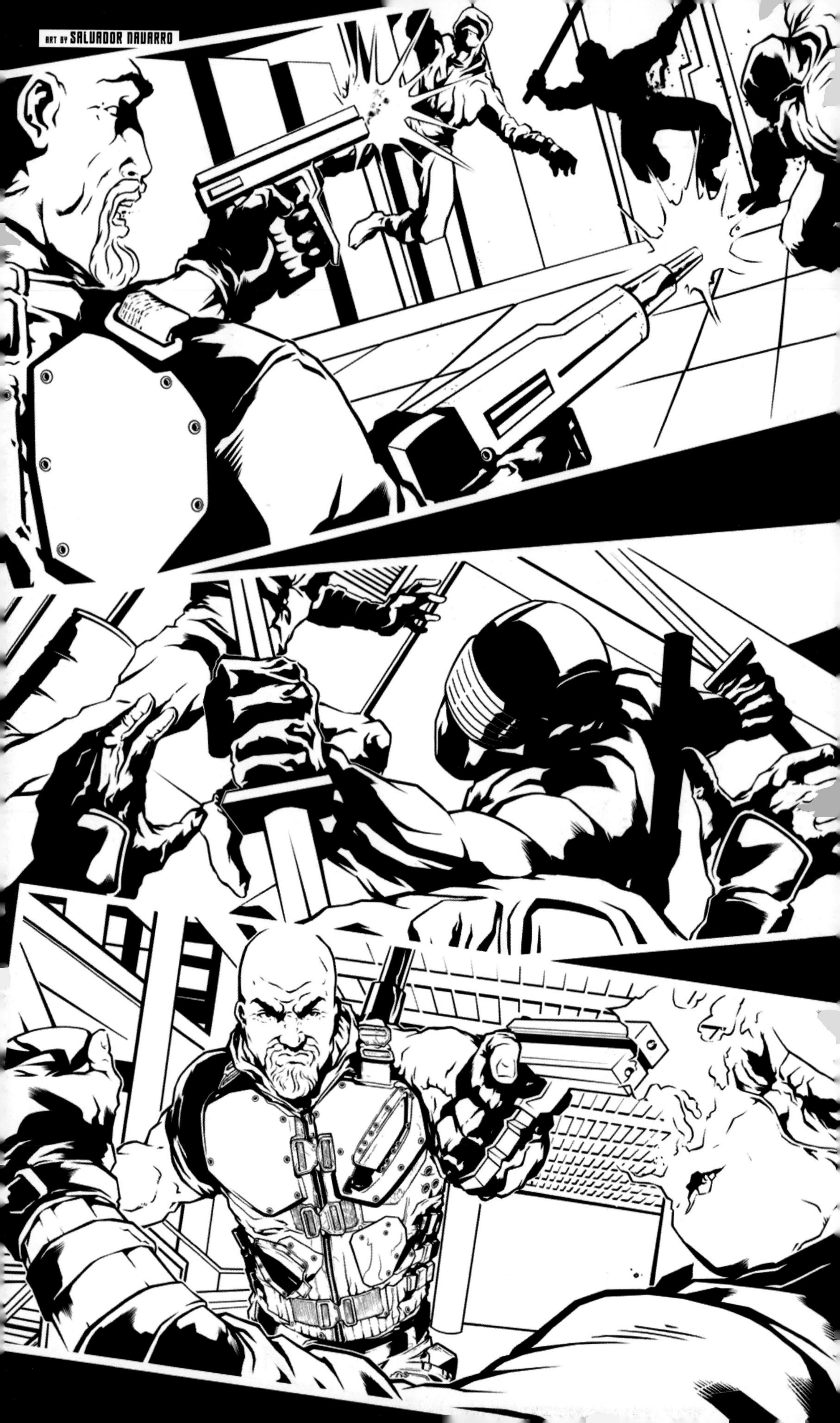
ART BY SALVADOR NAVARRO

ART BY SALVADOR NAVARRO

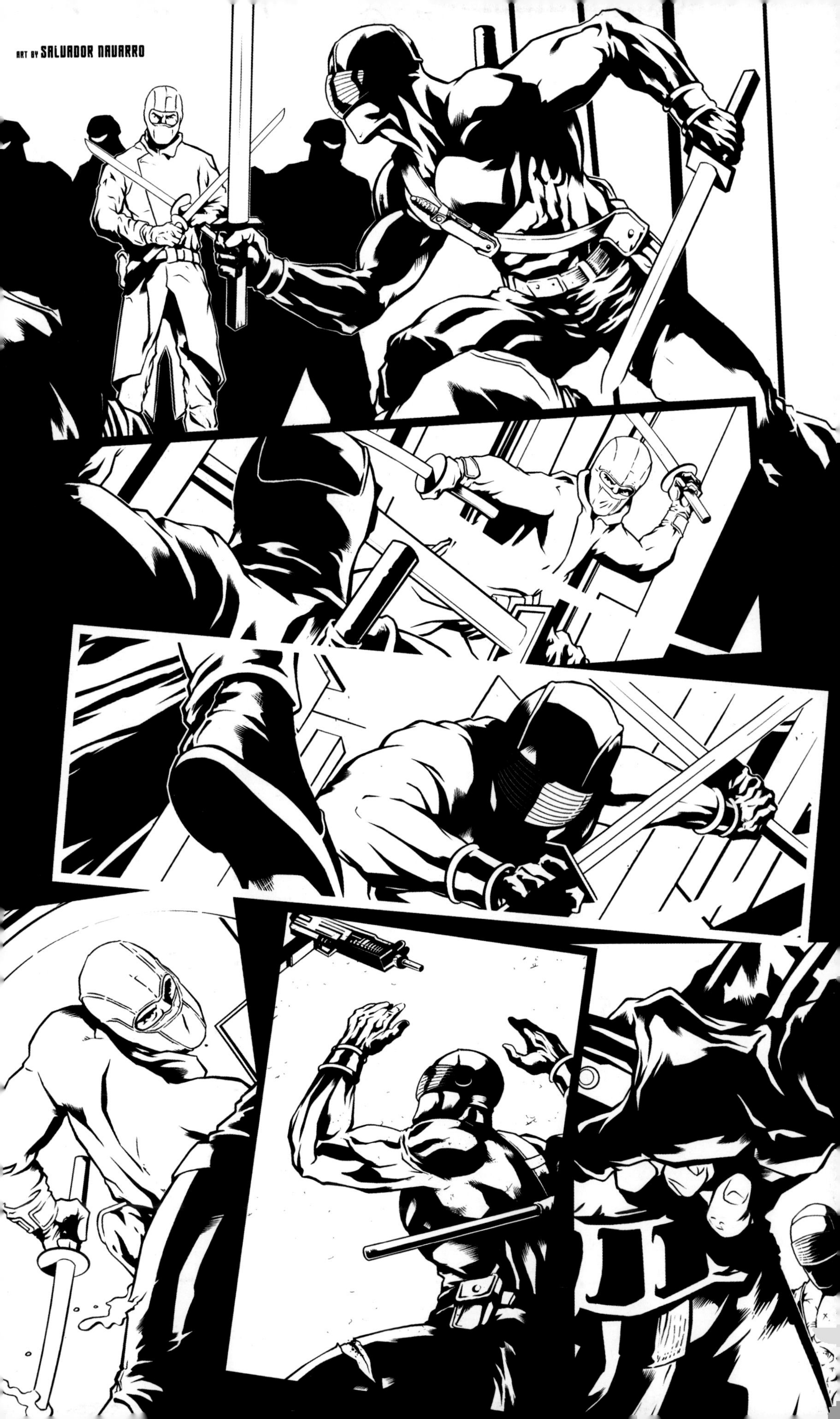

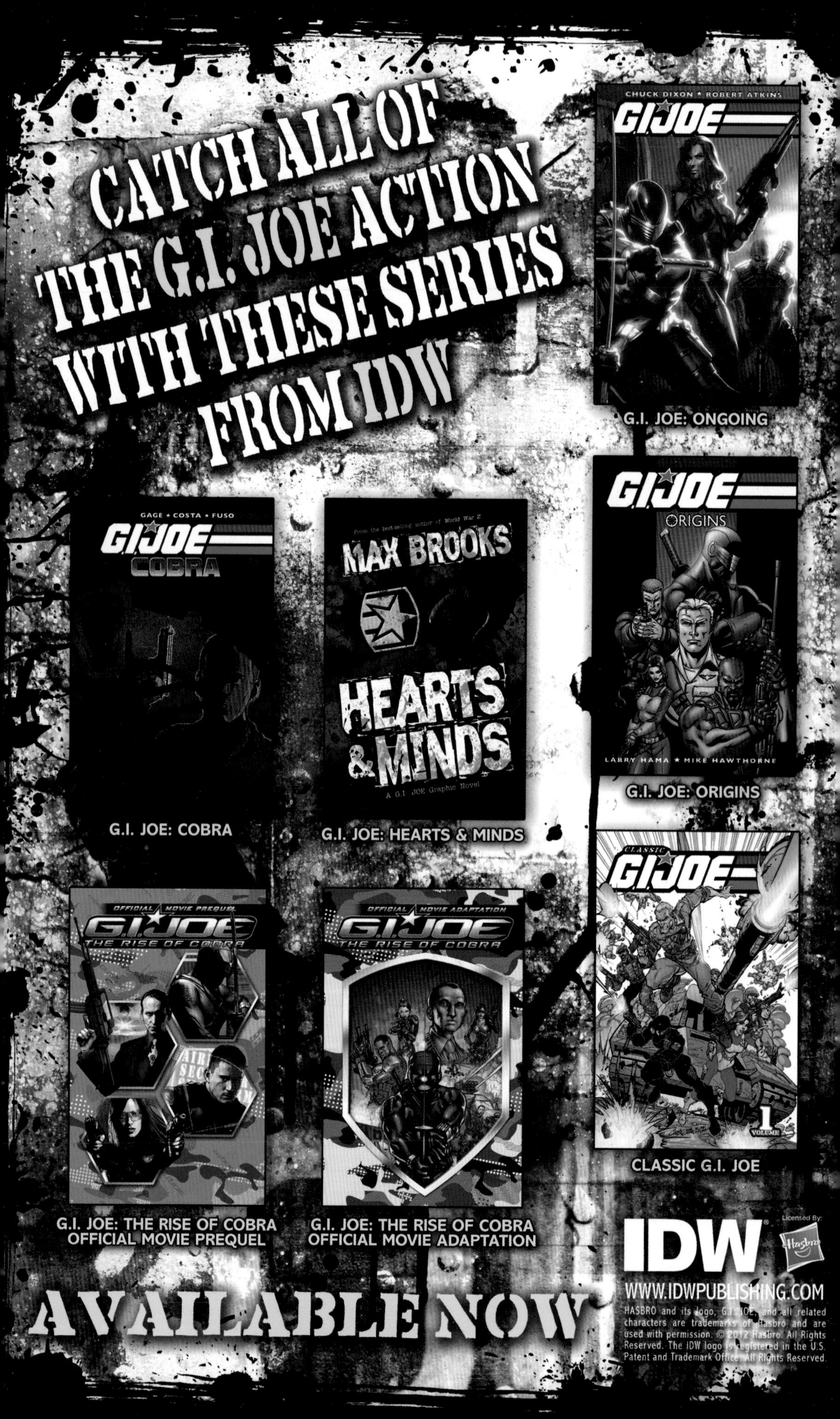
CATCH ALL OF
THE G.I. JOE ACTION
WITH THESE SERIES
FROM IDW
CHUCK DIXON ★ ROBERT ATKINS
G.I. JOE
G.I. JOE: ONGOING
GAGE ★ COSTA ★ FUSO
G.I. JOE
COBRA
G.I. JOE: COBRA
From the best-selling author of World War Z
MAX BROOKS
HEARTS & MINDS
A G.I. JOE Graphic Novel
G.I. JOE: HEARTS & MINDS
G.I. JOE
ORIGINS
LARRY HAMA ★ MIKE HAWTHORNE
G.I. JOE: ORIGINS
OFFICIAL MOVIE PREQUEL
G.I. JOE
THE RISE OF COBRA
G.I. JOE: THE RISE OF COBRA
OFFICIAL MOVIE PREQUEL
OFFICIAL MOVIE ADAPTATION
G.I. JOE
THE RISE OF COBRA
G.I. JOE: THE RISE OF COBRA
OFFICIAL MOVIE ADAPTATION
CLASSIC
G.I. JOE
1
VOLUME
CLASSIC G.I. JOE
AVAILABLE NOW
IDW
Licensed By:
Hasbro
WWW.IDWPUBLISHING.COM
HASBRO and its logo, G.I. JOE, and all related characters are trademarks of Hasbro and are used with permission. © 2012 Hasbro. All Rights Reserved. The IDW logo is registered in the U.S. Patent and Trademark Office. All Rights Reserved.